THE drama and excitement of the Cheltenham Festival has passed and now the Flat season is upon us. After the Lincoln has signalled the beginning of a new season on turf, soon our attention will turn to the first Classics. Is Camelot the wonder horse he hinted at with his impressive Racing Post Trophy success? Then there's Frankel . . . can he pick up where he left off last season and enthral us once again with his performances throughout the summer? There is so much to look forward to.

In this Guide to the Flat we preview a fascinating season with exclusive, invaluable insight from the leading British trainers, while the Racing Post's experts in Britain, Ireland and France pick the horses they believe can set the scene alight.

In addition, we present the 250 horses in this year's Totepool & Racing Post Ten to Follow competition with advice and suggestions to help win you a slice of a fortune.

However you use the information in these 176 pages, I hope you back plenty of winners and enjoy a successful and exciting season.

David Dew,
Editor

Contributors

Colin Boag
Scott Burton
Dave Edwards
Dylan Hill
Brian Morgan
Kevin Morley
Nick Pulford
Nancy Sexton
Simon Turner
Johnny Ward
Nick Watts

Published in 2012 by Racing Post Books
Raceform, High Street, Compton, Newbury,
Berkshire, RG20 6NL

The Racing Post specifies that post-press changes may occur
to any information given in this publication.

A catalogue record for this book is available from the British
Library.

ISBN: 978-1908216281

Edited and designed by **David Dew**
Printed by Buxton Press

Lowdown from the trainers

Totepool & Racing Post Ten to Follow

Statistics

Frankel heads the team but Warren Place is by no means a one-horse yard

WHAT a season and what a horse. It is impossible to overstate the impact Frankel's 2011 season had on Sir Henry Cecil and on the wider racing world, but the master trainer has many more strings to his bow than his wonder horse. Interviewed for this book, Cecil's first words were "Let's start with Twice Over, shall we?" It was only later that he mentioned Frankel.

From the Greenham, where he ran a bit freely but won easily, right through to his imperious win in the Queen Elizabeth II, **Frankel** *(right)* was the horse of the season and the best many people have ever seen. The 2,000 Guineas win was extraordinary as he was ten lengths clear at halfway and never looked in any danger – it was, visually, the most spectacular race you can imagine. He won the St James's Palace despite possibly being a tad below his best, and the Sussex Stakes was a romp. The colt's career record is now nine from nine, and his sporting owner, Prince Khalid Abdullah keeps him in training at four.

"The first thing to say about him is that he has grown. He looks much stronger and physically things have gone right with him," Cecil says. "Mentally he has improved too, settling much better, which will hopefully help him at the end of his races. In the early part of his three-year-old season he was always trying to do too much too soon and taking something out of himself, but he got away with it.

"He's settled enough now that you would be pretty certain that he'd get a mile and a quarter. You can't ever be 100 per cent certain until they've done it, but I'm confident he'll stay. However, I won't start him off at a mile and a quarter. He'll probably have a racecourse gallop and then go for the Lockinge. After that we can make a decision on whether it's the Queen Anne over a mile or the Prince of Wales's Stakes at a mile and a quarter – it will depend on what he's showing me and the likely competition. There's always the option of saving the longer trip until the Eclipse at Sandown.

"Everything is open at this stage. He'll be in all the top mile and mile-and-a-quarter races – he might even have the entry in the King George at a mile and a half. Frankel will tell me what I should be doing with him."

Moving to **Twice Over**, it's great that he stays in training as a seven-year-old. Cecil has got Group 1 victories from him at four, five and six – last season it was the Juddmonte International.

"We decided not to send him to Dubai this year. I thought he had a great chance in last year's Dubai World Cup but he takes a long time to get over the trip. He's a great money earner and he could run in Britain, France and Ireland – even if he didn't win he

could pick up a lot of prize-money. He's almost part of the furniture here and is in very good form at present. If we get a clear run he could start out in the Earl of Sefton at the Craven meeting."

Chachamaidee seemed to thrive for her busy season, winning a Group 3 and being placed in Group 1 and Group 2 company. Her run in the Sun Chariot proved she isn't out of place at the top level.

"She's done really well and is knocking at the door of top level. Seven furlongs or a mile are her trips and I'd rather keep her to fillies' company, but the lack of opportunities might force me to take on the colts."

Cecil knew the time of day with **Timepiece** (*far right*), Passage Of Time's half-sister, right back in her two-year-old days. In the 2010 Guide he said he regarded her as a top prospect as a three-year-old. After disappointing in the Oaks she was

dropped back half a mile in trip and landed the Sandringham Handicap at Royal Ascot off a mark of 105. At the end of the season she won a Listed contest over 1m2f.

Last season was when it all came together for Timepiece. She rewarded her trainer's and owner's patience when winning the Listed Warwickshire Oaks over ten furlongs and then coped brilliantly with the step up to Group 1 company to win the Falmouth Stakes at Newmarket back over a mile under a superb ride from Tom Queally.

There was no disgrace in her subsequent placed efforts behind Goldikova and Announce and the ground was probably a bit quick when she was last of eight in the Group 1 Sun Chariot.

"Timepiece is in very good order and has got stronger. She won a Group 1 and was placed in another over a trip that was too short for her – I think she's a mile-and-a-

quarter filly. If she goes the right way over that trip, then with her speed she could rather interesting."

Vita Nova was probably the season's unluckiest loser when she was second behind Gertrude Bell in the Group 2 Lancashire Oaks at Haydock. She was cruising and looked sure to win when Queally's saddle slipped. After that she ran really well to be second in the Yorkshire Oaks, giving Blue Bunting 10lb, before disappointing in the British Champions Fillies' and Mares' Stakes at Ascot.

"She was working really well before Ascot but I think she might just have been over the top, which would explain her poor run. She's had a really good rest, has come back in good form and will contest the top mile-and-a-half races, mainly against fillies. She might, on occasion, take on the colts. When she's right she's very useful.

"**Air Traffic** ran once, when he was second in the Wood Ditton, and had a little problem after that, although he's fine now. He's a big horse and, while at present he's just a nice maiden, he could make up into a useful colt. He should get a mile and a quarter, and maybe a bit further.

"**Solar Sky** was second in the Queen's Vase at Royal Ascot and could be a decent stayer. He goes on quick ground and if we have a drought this year he could be useful.

"I ran **World Domination** at Newbury last April and when he won they made him favourite for the Derby. After that he worked like a potentially very good horse but then ran into a problem with a little chip that was bothering him. We tried to get away with it but didn't. Anyway, that's been extracted and he's back in training. He has a lot of ability.

"The filly **All Time** was immature last year and had a few minor teething problems. She wants some warm weather and,

Jet Away could be useful, if he can find some consistency

although she still has to prove herself, she could be pretty good.

"**Wild Coco** looked nice and then something went amiss – I don't know what it was. From being very encouraging and winning a Listed race at Newmarket, she didn't progress as I had hoped – maybe it was nature. She's had a good winter, has strengthened up and is going well. I'm hopeful she can improve.

"I hope **Jet Away** has grown up a bit – he has ability but it's a matter of getting the best out of him. He works well and then runs disappointingly but runs well on his next start. He could be useful if he can become a bit more consistent."

Cecil starts the season with more than 50 well-bred three-year-olds, around half of whom didn't race at two. We started by discussing the colts.

"**Ace Of Valhalla** is by Authorised and ran well to finish second at Wolverhampton in November. He could make up into a nice colt.

"**All That Rules** is a light-boned, slightly delicate horse who had one run on the all-weather at Lingfield and finished sixth. They went very slowly, but if they'd gone a decent gallop I think he might have got there. The main thing was that I got a race into him. He was a bit green but he could be all right.

"**Continuum** didn't run last season because he was a backward, babyish sort, but he could be nice.

"I couldn't get a race into **Crystal Monarch**, so I sent him for a racecourse gallop. I think he's got potential. We had to clean up his knees a little bit – he was never lame and is 100 per cent now, but he'll take a little bit more time and won't be out until around May. He should improve as time goes on and he might be one to watch.

"**Dr Yes** started to work well last year but was immature and a bit weak behind. He's much stronger now and if he goes the right way he could be all right.

"**Hologram** is a very big colt but has done well and I'm hopeful he'll progress through the season.

"**King of Dudes** ran nicely to finish

second at Wolverhampton in November. He'll start out as a maiden but I think he can go on from that.

"**Noble Mission** is Frankel's brother, so he has attracted a lot of attention. He started to go nicely and then got sore shins. He took a long time to get over it and the season was coming to an end but I got him back into work, although I hadn't done as much with him as I would have liked. It was very important he got a race on turf and the only one I could find was a maiden at Yarmouth. It poured with rain and he got beaten by a very fit Godolphin horse. He ran on the wrong side of the course, with Tom accepting it when he knew he couldn't win. He's done well, and who knows what he could become.

"**Regency** is a medium-sized Galileo colt. He'd just started to show me something when he put his hind leg down and cracked it. He had to have a screw put in but is 100 per cent now. I'll take my time with him, but he's interesting.

"**Stipulate** won on his debut at Leicester but was then a little bit disappointing. I think it was down to immaturity but he's got stronger now and should be okay.

"**Thomas Chippendale** is a big, strong colt who won at Leicester on his second start and should be better this season.

"**Touch Gold** is a nice colt who ran on horrifically hard ground at Redcar in October – he's quite heavy and it didn't suit him at all. He's a nice maiden.

"**Wrotham Heath** is a big colt who was backward last year but won easily at Nottingham in October. It's hard to know what he beat but he did it nicely by six lengths. Considering that it wasn't D-Day and that he was so backward, it was impressive. He'd be one of my better three-year-old prospects, and hopefully we'll be able to give him some good entries.

"Moving to the three-year-old fillies, I like **Amaraja**. She was a backward sort who was scheduled to run but then couldn't.

"**Aquilla** was fourth at Nottingham right at the backend – she should be all right, as should **Bon Allumage**.

"**Corsetry** could be quite nice. She's by Distorted Humor out of Lingerie and showed promise on both of her starts. Similar comments apply to **Defy The Odds**.

"When I say these fillies could be all right, you have to remember they need to go on improving. Group-class horses are few and far between but hopefully some of these will make it. Time will tell.

"**Epoque** is quite a nice filly. She was third in a Newmarket maiden that has produced a few winners.

"**Fragonard** is by Teofilo and was just beaten in a Newmarket maiden that is working out well. She was light-framed and backward but flew at the end of that debut and almost got there. She cracked a leg after that but is fine now and back in training. Overall, I like what I see of Teofilo's stock and I think he could come good.

"**Isatis** was backward but I got a run into her at Kempton late in the year – I think she was a bit unlucky not to win. She got to the lead inside the final furlong and then got pipped by something that was pretty fit.

"**Popular** is Midday's sister and finished just ahead of Bon Allumage at Kempton. She's a sensible filly who is going to be much better this year.

"Finally, **Tickled Pink** was second on both of her starts and is an athletic sort. I'll be disappointed if she can't win her share of races.

"I think we've got more depth in the yard than we had last year and if everything goes right it could be a good season. However, to be right up there at the top of the trainers' table, you need the good horses. Some of the yards who have much bigger teams could win 50 races around Britain, worth £150k, but if you can win a really good race you can earn much more than that – it's the Group winners that make your season. So the hope is that we've got some that are a bit better than average."

I'm sure there are more than a few of those Group-race winners among the Warren Place ranks and it is far from impossible that Sir Henry Cecil could yet add to his ten trainers' titles. *[Colin Boag]*

CECIL AND THE STATS

Although not the dominant force he was in the 1990s, Cecil has enjoyed a resurgence in recent seasons. In 2005 his seasonal tally dipped to 12 but that figure has gradually risen to around the 60 mark for the last few years. Thanks largely to his principal owner Khalid Abdullah, Cecil is more than competitive again in races at the highest level and in Frankel he has a racehorse to conquer the world.

Frankel was his only three-year-old to be successful at Group level last term, so it was down to the older brigade to keep the scoreboard ticking over in that area. Twice Over, Midday and Timepiece all picked up Group 1 races last term and would have contributed significantly to Cecil's older horses turning a level-stakes profit in Group races. In fact, the Warren Place handler has been profitable to follow in that area for the last three seasons.

July was Cecil's most successful month last term with 15 winners at a 37 per cent strike-rate – and those following him during that period would also have made money for the two previous seasons.

Cecil knows how to place his string at a more modest level as well and it is best taking notice of his runners at certain tracks in this respect. Last year he operated at no lower than 40 per cent at Folkestone, Lingfield (turf), Salisbury and Warwick. It is interesting to note that the strike-rates dip only slightly when looking at his five-year record for those courses.

Stable jockey Tom Queally has a solid strike-rate for the yard with the market reacting accordingly to his mounts for his employer. Following those ridden by Ian Mongan and Eddie Ahern would have incurred a loss last term but they ride their fair share of winners for Cecil and their level-stake returns have reaped rewards in previous seasons.

The biggest disappointment for Cecil last term was the performance of the juveniles. His two-year-olds were profitable to follow in 2009 and 2010, with a good strike-rate of winning debutants, but that was not the case in 2011. He had just six two-year-old winners last year with only one successful at the first time of asking. That suggests he is likely to struggle to make any waves in the 2012 Classics unless he possesses a secret weapon we have yet to see.

Cecil is not one to over-burden his horses, so it is possible he could pick up some decent prize-money in handicaps with the three-year-olds, particularly in races over middle distances. *[Kevin Morley]*

SIR HENRY CECIL

NEWMARKET, SUFFOLK

	No. of Hrs	Races Run	1st	2nd	3rd	Unpl	Per cent	£1 Level Stake
2-y-o	30	56	6	8	5	37	10.7	-30.38
3-y-o	43	155	32	19	17	87	20.6	-45.28
4-y-o+	16	74	17	17	10	30	23.0	+2.39
Totals	**89**	**285**	**55**	**44**	**32**	**154**	**19.3**	**-73.27**
2010	85	298	62	50	35	151	20.8	-3.34
2009	94	324	63	54	47	160	19.4	+2.82

BY MONTH

2-y-o	W-R	Per cent	£1 Level Stake	3-y-o	W-R	Per cent	£1 Level Stake
January	0-0	0.0	0.00	January	0-0	0.0	0.00
February	0-0	0.0	0.00	February	0-0	0.0	0.00
March	0-0	0.0	0.00	March	0-0	0.0	0.00
April	0-0	0.0	0.00	April	6-26	23.1	-10.98
May	0-1	0.0	-1.00	May	6-29	20.7	-15.95
June	0-2	0.0	-2.00	June	4-32	12.5	-15.40
July	0-3	0.0	-3.00	July	9-21	42.9	+8.57
August	2-11	18.2	+2.50	August	2-20	10.0	-11.39
September	1-13	7.7	-9.00	September	3-17	17.6	+3.00
October	2-14	14.3	-7.88	October	2-9	22.2	-2.14
November	0-9	0.0	-9.00	November	0-1	0.0	-1.00
December	0-1	0.0	-1.00	December	0-0	0.0	0.00

4-y-o+	W-R	Per cent	£1 Level Stake	Totals	W-R	Per cent	£1 Level Stake
January	0-0	0.0	0.00	January	0-0	0.0	0.00
February	0-0	0.0	0.00	February	0-0	0.0	0.00
March	0-0	0.0	0.00	March	0-0	0.0	0.00
April	0-4	0.0	-4.00	April	6-30	20.0	-14.98
May	4-16	25.0	-2.40	May	10-46	21.7	-19.35
June	2-12	16.7	-6.88	June	6-46	13.0	-24.28
July	5-15	33.3	+17.50	July	15-41	36.6	+23.07
August	3-9	33.3	+6.25	August	7-40	17.5	-2.64
September	1-9	11.1	-4.00	September	5-39	12.8	-10.00
October	2-8	25.0	-3.08	October	6-31	19.4	-13.10
November	0-1	0.0	-1.00	November	0-1	10.0	-2.00
December	0-0	0.0	0.00	December	0-1	0.0	0.00

DISTANCE

2-y-o	W-R	Per cent	£1 Level Stake	3-y-o	W-R	Per cent	£1 Level Stake
5f-6f	0-7	0.0	-7.00	5f-6f	1-2	50.0	+2.50
7f-8f	6-47	12.8	-21.38	7f-8f	10-36	27.8	-1.85
9f-13f	0-2	0.0	-2.00	9f-13f	20-112	17.9	-46.43
14f+	0-0	0.0	0.00	14f+	1-5	20.0	+0.50

4-y-o	W-R	Per cent	£1 Level Stake	Totals	W-R	Per cent	£1 Level Stake
5f-6f	0-0	0.0	0.00	5f-6f	1-9	11.1	-4.50
7f-8f	4-20	20.0	+11.25	7f-8f	20-103	19.4	-11.98
9f-13f	13-44	29.5	+1.14	9f-13f	33-158	20.9	-47.29
14f+	0-10	0.0	-10.00	14f+	1-15	6.7	-9.50

TYPE OF RACE

Non-Handicaps	W-R	Per cent	£1 Level Stake	Handicaps	W-R	Per cent	£1 Level Stake
2-y-o	6-53	11.3	-27.38	2-y-o	0-3	0.0	-3.00
3-y-o	24-106	22.6	-28.23	3-y-o	8-49	16.3	-17.04
4-y-o+	14-48	29.2	+84.00	4-y-o+	3-26	11.5	-13.25

RACE CLASS

	W-R	Per cent	£1 Level Stake
Class 1	16-67	23.9	-9.28
Class 2	0-15	0.0	-15.00
Class 3	9-35	25.7	-2.75
Class 4	5-48	10.4	-19.04
Class 5	23-111	20.7	-30.55
Class 6	2-9	22.2	+3.36
Class 7	0-0	0.0	0.00

FIRST TIME OUT

	W-R	Per cent	£1 Level Stake
2-y-o	1-30	3.3	-25.00
3-y-o	5-43	11.6	-23.84
4-y-o+	3-16	18.8	-6.15
Totals	9-89	10.1	-54.99

Notes

Beckhampton buzzing as Top Offer heads promising team

L AST season saw Roger Charlton's Beckhampton team collect more than £700,000 in prize-money in Britain, his highest total since 2003, and another £685,000 abroad, giving the trainer his best overall tally to date. At 18 per cent the strike-rate was excellent and for the second year running there was a level-stakes profit from following all of the yard's runners. A particularly significant statistic was 16 juvenile winners – Charlton's best for some years and generally an indication of good things to come in their three-year-old careers. The big buzz in the yard this season is the colt Top Offer, who is prominent in the ante-post 2,000 Guineas market.

Top Offer comes from a good Juddmonte family and won his only start at two when landing a Newbury maiden in impressive style. The form of the race is starting to look solid and Top Offer falls firmly into the 'could be anything' category.

"He's a big, strong, physically imposing colt with a good action and he has always shown me above-average ability," says Charlton.

"He's 16-1 for the Guineas and it seems ridiculous to me that he's so short in the market – I think that says something about the lack of alternatives. Although he won very nicely, you could argue he is a 95-rated horse, as he is only a maiden winner at this stage of his career.

"That said, he's a promising colt and the plan is to go for a trial – probably the Greenham – on the way to the 2,000 Guineas. All is well and he's on course to follow that route."

Talking about his three-year-old **Mince**, Charlton says: "She's very much like her mother, who was laid back and no-one thought she was any good, but then went on to win a Listed race. She shows nothing at home, is very lazy and falls out of the stalls in her races. However, after running on at Newbury on her debut she went back there and won. For whatever reason she got a low handicap rating and bolted up in a Pontefract nursery. As a result we had to run her quickly under a penalty, dropped back to five furlongs, she was beaten a short head at Haydock on ground that was pretty soft, having perhaps not had the best of runs.

"She'll start out in handicaps but could progress as she has that laid-back style. I hope she's going to be fun.

"**Rex Imperator** seemed to find his niche when dropped to five furlongs in the Cornwallis at Ascot on his final start last season. We should probably have put a blindfold on him at the stalls because he wriggled and squirmed once he got in and was all over the place when the gates opened. In the end he ran very well, finishing strongly.

"The problem is that life can be tough for three-year-old sprinters. He lacks a little size. That said, his form looks pretty good.

"**Estrela** showed promise on her debut at Salisbury and then stepped up on that when winning a maiden at Newbury. She made virtually all that day and drew clear in the closing stages. The question with her is quite what her trip will be as her pedigree gives mixed signals – it will be interesting to see whether she stays beyond a mile.

"**Trader Jack** is a big, strong colt who showed promise at Newbury when finishing third on his debut before winning on heavy ground over a mile at Ffos Las. It's hard to know how good the form is, although the second subsequently came out and won a race at Wolverhampton."

Waterclock is intriguing. He won his only start, over a mile at Newbury, at odds of 25-1, apparently being the less fancied of

Charlton's two runners. Was his win a surprise?

"It was a bit of a shock because Captain Cat, my other runner, was more forward and had, I thought, more ability than Waterclock, who was almost the first one off the bridle. However, Waterclock battled away and stayed on in resolute fashion. If you look at his pedigree you would think he has to improve and that he should stay a mile and a half. The worry with him winning first time out is quite what the handicapper will make of it – there are plenty of horses who do that and struggle to win again. However, Waterclock has done well over the winter and we'll be positive and assume he can improve.

"**Captain Cat** is a big colt and, despite being beaten on his sole start, showed promise at Newbury. I hope he'll stay ten furlongs.

"**Newnton Lodge** is a big, strong colt who made a good impression when winning a seven-furlong Sandown maiden on his debut. I ran him in a hood at Leicester on his second start and he disappointed, which was a surprise as he often trains in one at home because the strong wind tends to unsettle him. However, despite that, I hope he'll develop into a nice colt.

"**Moidore** improved with racing last season, winning on his third start, at Nottingham over a mile. He can be a bit nervy but I hope that will settle down as he gets more experience. He has a handicap mark of 78 and should stay a mile and a half.

"**Silver Lime** showed plenty of promise on his debut, over seven furlongs at Sandown. He then went on to win over a mile on soft ground at Ffos Las. He should stay a mile and a quarter, perhaps further.

"**Priceless Jewel** won her second start, staying on really well over the extended six furlongs at Newbury and showing a decent turn of foot. Her pedigree suggests she should stay a mile.

"**Rosslyn Castle** wasn't beaten far when finishing fourth at Sandown on his only start

Priceless Jewel (top) and Waterclock (left, centre) look to be bright prospects

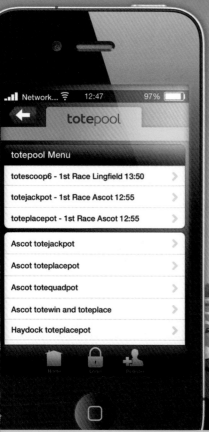

totepool.com

fancy a placepot at the parade ring?

place your favourite **tote**pool bets on the move with our new mobile service!

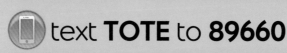 text **TOTE** to **89660**

at two. He showed signs of inexperience that day but stayed on really well up the hill. Unfortunately he got ringworm after that and we couldn't run him again. He should improve and should stay at least ten furlongs, and perhaps a mile and a half."

Moving to the older horses, the star of the show last season was the excellent **Cityscape**, who came close to winning that elusive Group 1 on a couple of occasions. He was second in the Group 2 Bet365 Mile at Sandown on his seasonal debut and won Group 3s at the Curragh and at Saint-Cloud. He was beaten only a short head in an Italian Group 1 and then went down by a neck in the Hong Kong Mile.

"I think he's suited by a flat track or one with an incline. Sandown was the perfect place to start him out and he just got a bit tired in the closing stages. When he ran in Italy we were being assured that the going was soft, so we sent him out there only to find that the ground had changed – in the end they broke the course record, so it had to be pretty fast.

"He's a solid money-earner – he won £520,000 in five different countries last year – but we still hope we can win a big one with him. We're considering running him in Dubai, in the Duty Free, as long as everything goes well between now and then. He's training here and if he runs then I'll send him out a few days before the race – the trip to Hong Kong showed he's a good traveller."

Bated Breath won a conditions race at Haydock and a Listed race at Windsor and then went back to Haydock later in the year for the Betfred Sprint Cup, where he came close to landing the Group 1 contest, beaten only by the tiniest of margins. He then ran another cracker at Woodbine in the Nearctic Stakes, beaten only a neck, before finishing his season when unplaced in the Hong Kong Sprint.

"He's a consistent and commendable colt – the only times he ran less well he had a valid excuse such as Hong Kong, where he was drawn 12 of 14. Like a lot of good sprinters, it's a case of hoping his day will come at the top level – he's certainly up to that grade. He's the highest-rated sprinter I've

trained – he's now got a mark of 118, having been 120 – and the likes of Avonbridge and Patavellian never got above about 115, so he could well get lucky. Mind you, if Black Caviar comes over, and is as good as she looks, then it could be tough!

"**Al Kazeem** is a nice, good-looking colt who deserves to win a Group race or two. I don't think he did much wrong last season and was beaten by horses who were better than him at that stage of his career. He was never going to win the Voltigeur, but there were plenty of good horses behind him and he hadn't run for ages.

"At Newbury he came up against what is probably a Group 1 horse, and then a Group 2 horse, in a pair of Group 3 races. He improved nearly 20lb last year and he's the sort who can keep on progressing. It would be nice to start him out in a Listed race, but there just aren't any, so the Brigadier Gerard or the John Porter might be where you see him first."

Sea Of Heartbreak was a progressive handicapper the season before last, but in 2011 she stepped up to Pattern company, winning a Listed event at Newbury and then the Group 2 Prix de Royallieu at Longchamp on Arc weekend.

"She possibly got a bit lucky as there were only four runners but she showed a really good turn of foot to outsprint the French runners. She's a charming filly in every way and is extremely consistent – she just keeps on trying.

"It's lovely that she stays in training for her owner-breeder and the aim is to be at least Group 1-placed. Her turn of foot will always stand her in good stead.

"I think there's better to come from **Primevere**. She's a big, rangy filly, whose work at home was probably better than her racecourse form, but then she stepped up in trip and won nicely in Listed company at Salisbury in course-record time. She's lightly raced and, if we can prepare her properly and find the right Group race, I think she can win at that level.

"**Cry Fury's** run in the Cambridgeshire is best forgotten as he needs further than that now and he's possibly better in

smaller fields too. He's been gelded and I hope there's more to come from him in heritage handicaps."

Camberley Two *(above, left)* won six handicaps on the bounce last season, starting off rated 53 and finishing up winning off a mark of 79.

"He started off on a low rating because of his two-year-old form. His debut run at Sandown was a total embarrassment – I would never have run him if I'd known he would be beaten 37 lengths. He then was in the maiden won by Carlton House and everything was beaten a long way.

"As a three-year-old he just seemed to improve mentally with every run and with a horse rated that low there are any number of races open to him. Also, when you get on a roll, as he did, people don't want to take you on, so that also makes life easier. It was a revelation and it was fantastic fun.

"I'd like to think he'll stay a mile and a quarter and if he does, although he won't win another six, he might be able to win again. What is annoying is that he won those six races, rose to a mark of 85 and won less than £15,000 – it's a sad system."

Charlton seems to have more strength this season in the older horse ranks and, based on last year's juvenile form, the three-year-olds look to be a better bunch too. It's hard to foresee anything other than a successful season for the Beckhampton team, and if Top Offer comes good then who knows just how good it might be? *[Colin Boag]*

CHARLTON AND THE STATS

Charlton is a patient trainer and it's no surprise that his older horses have returned the best level-stakes profit over the last five seasons. Those aged four and above put followers in the black again last term and he'll no doubt be strong in that department again. Success isn't confined to the older brigade and he has similar strike-rates with both the two- and three-year-olds, although profits are harder to find.

It's only with the older horses that Charlton has achieved Group-race success from 2008 onwards but it is worth noting he hasn't had many two- or three-year-olds running at Pattern level during that period.

Handicaps are where Charlton is best followed and his runners in that category are often a useful weapon for punters. He is renowned as a master trainer of sprinters and contests over the shorter trips should be the focus of attention as he has returned his biggest profits in all races up to a mile. His rare ventures into apprentice handicaps are well worth watching out for, with three of his four runners in such contests over the last five seasons having obliged.

Summer is the best period for the stable and he tends have around a two-month purple patch during the sunny season. July and August are usually the best months for the yard but he can hit form slightly earlier than that on occasions – in 2010 June and July were best with the yard's form dipping in August.

When placing his string at a modest level, Brighton is a track where he does particularly well with more than half of his 13 runners during the last five seasons winning (two from two in 2011), although Newbury is without doubt his favourite racecourse. Charlton's runners were regularly seen in the winner's enclosure at the Berkshire track last term, maintaining a trend that has been strong over the last few seasons.

Newbury is where you're most likely to see his best horses, so it was no surprise when he introduced the potentially high-class Top Offer at the course last season. He looks a serious candidate for Classic glory.

Top Offer was able to oblige on his sole start last term but Charlton's runners nearly always come on significantly for their first run and he doesn't send out many debut winners. However, while that has long held true, some of his juvenile debutants have been overpriced as a consequence in the last two seasons and backing his youngsters first time up returned a profit in 2010 and 2011.

Charlton focuses on quality rather than quantity and, while his figures on the turf are solid in most areas, his record on the all-weather is weaker. He was two from 32 on artificial surfaces last year and his strike-rates at all the sand tracks are modest. *[Kevin Morley]*

ROGER CHARLTON

BECKHAMPTON, WILTS

	No. of Hrs	Races Run	1st	2nd	3rd	Unpl	Per cent	£1 Level Stake
2-y-o	32	84	16	11	4	53	19.0	+13.37
3-y-o	24	89	16	11	9	52	18.0	-3.43
4-y-o	+16	60	11	10	6	33	18.3	+7.92
Totals	**72**	**233**	**43**	**32**	**19**	**138**	**18.5**	**+17.86**
2010	64	239	48	19	21	151	20.1	+28.63
2009	67	240	35	28	43	134	14.6	-1.00

BY MONTH

2-y-o	W-R	Per cent	£1 Level Stake	**3-y-o**	W-R	Per cent	£1 Level Stake
January	0-0	0.0	0.00	January	0-4	0.0	-4.00
February	0-0	0.0	0.00	February	0-1	0.0	-1.00
March	0-0	0.0	0.00	March	0-0	0.0	0.00
April	0-4	0.0	-4.00	April	1-11	9.1	-6.00
May	1-5	20.0	-3.27	May	3-22	13.6	+0.33
June	0-5	0.0	-5.00	June	3-12	25.0	-6.98
July	1-11	9.1	-8.00	July	2-11	18.2	-6.25
August	4-14	28.6	-2.60	August	6-12	50.0	+23.47
September	3-18	16.7	+6.83	September	0-10	0.0	-10.00
October	6-23	26.1	+31.50	October	1-5	20.0	+8.00
November	1-33	3.3	-1.09	November	0-1	0.0	-1.00
December	0-1	0.0	-1.00	December	0-0	0.0	0.00

4-y-o+	W-R	Per cent	£1 Level Stake	**Totals**	W-R	Per cent	£1 Level Stake
January	0-0	0.0	0.00	January	0-4	0.0	-4.00
February	0-0	0.0	0.00	February	0-1	0.0	-1.00
March	0-0	0.0	0.00	March	0-0	0.0	0.00
April	1-6	16.7	+7.00	April	2-21	9.5	-3.00
May	3-12	25.0	+15.13	May	7-39	17.9	+12.19
June	2-13	15.4	+0.50	June	5-30	16.7	-11.48
July	4-11	36.4	+0.05	July	7-33	21.2	-14.20
August	0-4	0.0	-4.00	August	10-30	33.3	+16.87
September	1-7	14.3	-3.75	September	4-35	11.4	-6.92
October	0-5	0.0	-5.00	October	7-33	21.2	+34.50
November	0-1	0.0	-1.00	November	1-52	0.0	-2.00
December	0-1	0.0	-1.00	December	0-2	0.0	-1.00

DISTANCE

2-y-o	W-R	Per cent	£1 Level Stake	**3-y-o**	W-R	Per cent	£1 Level Stake
5f-6f	6-39	15.4	-9.87	5f-6f	1-6	16.7	-4.75
7f-8f	10-43	23.3	+25.24	7f-8f	9-43	20.9	-10.43
9f-13f	0-2	0.0	-2.00	9f-13f	6-39	15.4	+12.75
14f+	0-0	0.0	0.00	14f+	0-1	0.0	-1.00

4-y-o	W-R	Per cent	£1 Level Stake	**Totals**	W-R	Per cent	£1 Level Stake
5f-6f	6-24	25.0	+7.88	5f-6f	13-69	18.8	-6.74
7f-8f	1-15	6.7	+6.00	7f-8f	20-101	19.8	+20.81
9f-13f	2-18	11.1	-7.50	9f-13f	8-59	13.6	+3.25
14f+	2-3	66.7	+1.55	14f+	2-4	50.0	+0.55

TYPE OF RACE

Non-Handicaps	W-R	Per cent	£1 Level Stake	**Handicaps**	W-R	Per cent	£1 Level Stake
2-y-o	13-69	18.8	+6.37	2-y-o	5-25	20.0	+7.00
3-y-o	5-41	12.2	+6.00	3-y-o	11-48	22.9	-9.43
4-y-o+	5-35	14.3	+22.00	4-y-o+	6-25	24.0	+13.80

RACE CLASS

	W-R	Per cent	£1 Level Stake
Class 1	5-42	11.9	-8.63
Class 2	4-20	20.0	-6.20
Class 3	4-14	28.6	+25.75
Class 4	11-49	22.4	-1.37
Class 5	13-82	15.9	+8.04
Class 6	6-26	23.1	+0.27
Class 7	0-0	0.0	0.00

FIRST TIME OUT

	W-R	Per cent	£1 Level Stake
2-y-o	4-32	12.5	+4.00
3-y-o	1-24	4.2	-19.00
4-y-o+	1-16	6.3	-3.00
Totals	6-72	8.3	-18.00

Notes

Huge battalion of talent should ensure another profitable campaign

GODOLPHIN, through their two trainers in Britain – Saeed Bin Suroor and Mahmood Al Zarooni – finished second in last season's owners' table with 139 winners at an 18 per cent strike-rate and almost £2m in prize-money. That's just part of the Godolphin story though, and their excellent website reveals they won 186 races worldwide with total earnings over $18.5m.

Racing manager Simon Crisford ran through their main hopes for the 2012 European season.

"We have around 100 horses here in Dubai but there are also plenty of lightly raced others who have stayed behind in Newmarket. Let's start with the three-year-olds who are out here and are trained by Mahmood.

"**Gamilati** won the Cherry Hinton last season before disappointing on soft ground in the Lowther. She won the trial for the UAE 1,000 Guineas over seven furlongs and went on to win the Listed race itself, run over a mile on the Tapeta track at Meydan.

"She was impressive there but that's very different from what she'll have to face in Europe. She's done nothing but please us but she'll have to step up another 5lb to get into the top bracket when she comes back to Britain. She won't get beyond a mile and is suited by fast ground, so I think Royal Ascot might well suit her better than Newmarket."

Zip Top was second in the Racing Post Trophy, albeit outclassed by Camelot, when trained by Jim Bolger. By Smart Strike, he is bred to get a mile or perhaps a little further.

"He had a slight setback, which has prevented him from racing over here, so he's behind schedule. He should be ready to run around the time of Royal Ascot but we haven't got a plan for him at this stage.

"**Kinglet** won the Group 3 UAE 2,000 Guineas, over a mile on Tapeta, and he's going to run in the UAE Derby before coming back to Britain. He's done very well but he'll need to find another 10lb before he's top-class in Europe. The main thing is that he's pleasing us and going the right way.

"**Falls Of Lora** won the UAE Oaks out here in February but that was a muddling race, so it's hard to know what to make of the form. However, she won it well and is progressing. She's won three of her seven starts and is a nice filly for Europe, although, like the others, she'll need to step up on what she has achieved so far.

"Moving to Mahmood's three-year-olds who are in Newmarket, let's start with **Discourse**, who is the unbeaten winner of the Sweet Solera Stakes. I saw her the other day and she has done very well over the winter. Hopefully she'll be one of our top prospects for the season. I think she'll be a

Guineas filly and she might go for the Nell Gwyn at the Craven meeting beforehand.

"**Lyric Of Light** was unbeaten in three juvenile starts, winning both the May Hill and the Fillies' Mile. She has done well and will be aimed at the Guineas initially. The weather has been kind in Britain, but if it changed and the cold knocked them back a bit, then I wouldn't rule out that she, and some of the others, might run in a trial.

"**Mandaean** won the Group 1 Criterium de Saint-Cloud over ten furlongs when trained by Andre Fabre. He's had a good winter and is going well at present – we're looking forward to seeing him on the track. He could start off in the Dante and he would have to be our most obvious Derby contender at this stage – he'll be suited by a mile and a half.

"**Mighty Ambition** won his maiden nicely at Newbury but didn't run again. We liked him at the time of his win and he'll stay middle distances.

"**Minidress** won her maiden on the July course at Newmarket and was fourth in the Group 3 Oh So Sharp Stakes. Her form was decent last year and she looks as though she has the scope to progress.

"**Swedish Sailor** won well at Yarmouth and he's a promising type. We think he's a decent colt who will improve a lot once he gets to race over a trip.

"**Kunooz** won her maiden at Newmarket and then was second to Falls Of Lora in a conditions event at Ascot. She's a nice filly who has done well over the winter but she has to go through the trials process to see where she fits into the pecking order.

"Saeed's three-year-olds tend to be lightly raced, but **Anjaz** will be a nice filly to follow. She won her maiden and then a decent nursery at Doncaster, where the form has worked out pretty well.

"**Saytara** is a promising filly who won her maiden at Newmarket at the backend of the season on her second start. She should improve.

"**Silent Moment** didn't win, finishing fifth in a maiden at Newmarket on her only start. She looks unexposed.

"**Al Saham** won his maiden quite well,

and then was beaten in a Listed race at Pontefract. He looks okay but, like a lot of these, needs to step up to the next level.

"**Rassam** won his maiden at Kempton and then raced out here. He didn't settle at all in Dubai but he's quite a nice horse. Once he learns to drop the bit he'll be more exciting.

"**Asatir** is rated 89 on the back of winning a Redcar maiden that has produced some winners and then a novices' event at Lingfield – we think he's a bit better than that.

"Among Saeed's older horses that are over here, **Rio De La Plata** (*above, left*) is an old favourite. He's not quite good enough to win the top races in England but he wins his fair share overseas – he was just touched off in an Italian Group 1 last season.

"We're hoping **Prince Bishop** can have a good campaign. He's done very well out here and has improved a lot since he was gelded – we think he's going the right way.

"**Campanologist**, who won a couple of European Group 1 last season, stays in training, as does **Delegator**, winner of last year's Duke of York. He's won over seven

furlongs out here and I suspect we'll campaign him at that trip, and at a mile.

"**Songcraft** won a couple of races when with Andre Fabre but has done well over here, winning handicaps off 105 and 110. He is unbeaten in four races but now has to step up in class. He's going well.

"**Grand Vent** ran in the French Derby for Andre Fabre and will be heading back to Europe. He's smallish and lacks a bit of scope, but he tries hard and can do well in the right class.

"**Pisco Sour** joined us after winning a French Group 2 last summer. He looks as though he could be suited by the French style of racing, so I imagine he might have some targets over there.

"Back in England Saeed has **Hunter's Light**, who won three Listed races last season. We like him. He's had the winter off, and will be ready to go in the spring.

"We also like **Khawlah**, who didn't run in Europe last year but won the 2011 UAE Oaks and the UAE Derby. She had a setback just before Royal Ascot last season but we decided to keep her in training as she'd shown us enough to make us believe she can be all right.

"**Ley Hunter** has also come from Andre Fabre, and he won a Group 3 over 1m7½f at Longchamp. He's one for the staying races and could start off in the Henry II at Sandown.

"**Modeyra** is a solid Listed-class filly who could step up a bit from that grade.

"**Saamidd** hasn't run since last year's 2,000 Guineas. He won the Champagne Stakes as a two-year-old, so he's on a comeback mission.

"**Sajjhaa** won a mile-and-a-quarter Listed race last year – she stays in training and is a nice filly.

"**Colour Vision** was third in the Cesarewitch last season when with Mark Johnston, but the more interesting run was when he was third to Fame And Glory in the Ascot Group 3 on Champions Day. He's another possible for the Cup races.

"Moving to the older horses over here in Mahmood's stable, **Monterosso** has been

MAHMOOD AL ZAROONI
NEWMARKET, SUFFOLK

	No. of Hrs	Races Run	1st	2nd	3rd	Unpl	Per cent	£1 Level Stake
2-y-o	92	217	43	30	31	111	19.8	61.82
3-y-o	65	158	32	20	14	91	20.3	+28.78
4-y-o	+14	34	6	6	3	19	17.6	+29.88
Totals	**171**	**409**	**81**	**56**	**48**	**221**	**19.8**	**+120.48**
2010	103	287	43	44	52	148	15.0	-12.50
2009	0							

BY MONTH

2-y-o	W-R	Per cent	£1 Level Stake	3-y-o	W-R	Per cent	£1 Level Stake
January	0-0	0.0	0.00	January	0-0	0.0	0.00
February	0-0	0.0	0.00	February	0-0	0.0	0.00
March	0-0	0.0	0.00	March	0-0	0.0	0.00
April	0-0	0.0	0.00	April	7-22	31.8	+15.35
May	0-8	0.0	-8.00	May	8-28	28.6	+36.42
June	5-18	27.8	+28.00	June	2-42	4.8	-33.50
July	3-34	8.8	+2.50	July	3-15	20.0	+3.75
August	8-38	21.1	+16.00	August	5-13	38.5	+16.75
September	11-58	19.0	-5.38	September	5-21	23.8	-0.23
October	5-56	26.8	+30.70	October	2-14	14.3	-6.75
November	1-5	20.0	-2.00	November	0-3	0.0	-3.00
December	0-0	0.0	0.00	December	0-0	0.0	0.00

4-y-o+	W-R	Per cent	£1 Level Stake	Totals	W-R	Per cent	£1 Level Stake
January	0-0	0.0	0.00	January	0-0	0.0	0.00
February	0-0	0.0	0.00	February	0-0	0.0	0.00
March	0-0	0.0	0.00	March	0-0	0.0	0.00
April	0-2	0.0	-2.00	April	7-24	29.2	+13.35
May	0-1	0.0	-1.00	May	8-37	21.6	+27.42
June	1-6	16.7	+3.50	June	8-66	12.1	-2.00
July	3-6	50.0	+41.50	July	9-55	16.4	+47.75
August	1-8	12.5	-4.00	August	14-59	23.7	+28.75
September	1-7	14.3	-4.13	September	17-86	19.8	-9.74
October	0-4	0.0	-4.00	October	17-74	23.0	+19.95
November	0-0	0.0	0.00	November	1-8	12.5	-3.00
December	0-0	0.0	0.00	December	0-0	0.0	0.00

DISTANCE

2-y-o	W-R	Per cent	£1 Level Stake	3-y-o	W-R	Per cent	£1 Level Stake
5f-6f	9-38	23.7	+41.33	5f-6f	2-8	25.0	-3.00
7f-8f	31-166	18.7	+24.74	7f-8f	11-59	18.6	+12.92
9f-13f	3-13	23.1	-4.25	9f-13f	18-88	20.5	+11.87
14f+	0-0	0.0	0.00	14f+	1-3	33.3	+7.00

4-y-o	W-R	Per cent	£1 Level Stake	Totals	W-R	Per cent	£1 Level Stake
5f-6f	0-2	0.0	-2.00	5f-6f	11-48	22.9	+36.33
7f-8f	1-8	12.5	+13.00	7f-8f	43-233	18.5	+50.66
9f-13f	3-19	15.8	+14.38	9f-13f	24-120	20.0	+22.00
14f+	2-5	40.0	+4.50	14f+	3-8	37.5	+11.50

TYPE OF RACE

Non-Handicaps	W-R	Per cent	£1 Level Stake	Handicaps	W-R	Per cent	£1 Level Stake
2-y-o	40-200	20.0	+61.74	2-y-o	3-17	17.6	+0.08
3-y-o	23-114	20.2	+19.83	3-y-o	9-44	20.5	+8.95
4-y-o+	4-27	14.8	+21.00	4-y-o+	2-7	28.6	+35.00

RACECLASS / FIRST TIME OUT

	W-R	Per cent	£1 Level Stake		W-R	Per cent	£1 Level Stake
Class 1	16-67	23.9	+43.13	2-y-o	19-92	20.7	+59.00
Class 2	9-31	29.0	+48.50	3-y-o	13-65	20.0	+18.27
Class 3	9-30	30.0	+13.18	4-y-o+	2-14	14.3	+16.50
Class 4	20-92	21.7	+52.97				
Class 5	25-175	14.3	-29.29	Totals	34-171	19.9	+93.77
Class 6	2-14	14.3	-8.00				
Class 7	0-0	0.0	0.00				

off since last year's World Cup and we're aiming him at the race again this year, with a view to him returning to Europe after that.

"**Opinion Poll** will once again be competing in all of the top staying races next season – he was second to Fame And Glory in last year's Ascot Gold Cup and won the Lonsdale and Doncaster Cups.

"**Fox Hunt** joined from Mark Johnston's stable and won a Group 3 for us here over 1m6f. He's another for the good staying races in Europe after he runs in the Sheema Classic on World Cup night.

"**Laajooj** missed the second half of last season but is doing well over here and we're pleased with him. He's officially rated 111 but should do well back in Europe.

"Another who should do well once he returns to the UK is **Biondetti**, who had a short season last year. He has run well over here.

"In Britain Mahmood has **Be Fabulous**, who raced for Andre Fabre last season and won the Group 1 Prix Royal-Oak. She's a staying mare who seemed to have a preference for soft ground when in France,

SAEED BIN SUROOR

NEWMARKET, SUFFOLK

	No. of Hrs	Races Run	1st	2nd	3rd	Unpl	Per cent	£1 Level Stake
2-y-o	46	104	25	15	15	49	24.0	-3.05
3-y-o	37	121	16	29	18	58	13.2	-44.77
4-y-o+	48	150	17	16	13	103	11.3	-52.42
Totals	**131**	**375**	**58**	**60**	**46**	**210**	**15.5**	**-100.24**
2010	132	400	90	62	43	205	22.5	-41.97
2009	182	530	148	83	70	228	27.9	-9.03

BY MONTH

2-y-o	W-R	cent	Per £1 Level Stake	3-y-o	W-R	cent	Per £1 Level Stake
January	0-0	0.0	0.00	January	0-0	0.0	0.00
February	0-0	0.0	0.00	February	0-0	0.0	0.00
March	0-0	0.0	0.00	March	0-0	0.0	0.00
April	0-0	0.0	0.00	April	0-5	0.0	-5.00
May	0-3	0.0	-3.00	May	2-10	20.0	+1.50
June	1-4	25.0	-2.56	June	2-17	11.8	-10.25
July	4-6	66.7	+7.63	July	2-14	14.3	-9.50
August	4-18	22.2	-5.60	August	3-24	12.5	-15.37
September	5-30	16.7	-3.84	September	2-26	7.7	-11.25
October	6-33	18.2	-0.50	October	4-22	18.2	+6.38
November	5-10	50.0	+4.82	November	1-3	33.3	-1.27
December	0-0	0.0	0.00	December	0-0	0.0	0.00

4-y-o+	W-R	cent	Per £1 Level Stake	Totals	W-R	cent	Per £1 Level Stake
January	0-0	0.0	0.00	January	0-0	0.0	0.00
February	0-0	0.0	0.00	February	0-0	0.0	0.00
March	0-0	0.0	0.00	March	0-0	0.0	0.00
April	0-2	0.0	-2.00	April	0-7	0.0	-7.00
May	2-16	12.5	-2.50	May	4-29	13.8	-4.00
June	3-24	12.5	-11.13	June	6-45	13.3	-23.94
July	4-34	11.8	-24.54	July	10-54	18.5	-26.41
August	4-24	16.7	+11.25	August	11-66	16.7	-9.72
September	2-3	16.5	-17.00	September	9-87	10.3	-32.09
October	1-14	7.1	-8.50	October	11-69	15.9	-2.62
November	1-5	20.0	+2.00	November	7-18	38.9	+0.73
December	0-0	0.0	0.00	December	0-0	0.0	0.00

DISTANCE

2-y-o	W-R	Per cent	£1 Level Stake	3-y-o	W-R	Per cent	£1 Level Stake
5f-6f	5-27	18.5	-5.48	5f-6f	0-4	0.0	-4.00
7f-8f	19-72	26.4	+0.92	7f-8f	5-42	11.9	-17.99
9f-13f	1-5	20.0	+1.50	9f-13f	11-72	15.3	-19.77
14f+	0-0	0.0	0.00	14f+	0-3	0.0	-3.00

4-y-o	W-R	Per cent	£1 Level Stake	Totals	W-R	Per cent	£1 Level Stake
5f-6f	1-6	16.7	0.00	5f-6f	6-37	16.2	-9.48
7f-8f	8-62	12.9	-26.63	7f-8f	32-176	18.2	-43.70
9f-13f	8-69	11.6	-12.79	9f-13f	20-146	13.7	-31.06
14f+	0-13	0.0	-13.00	14f+	0-16	0.0	-16.00

TYPE OF RACE

Non-Handicaps	W-R	Per cent	£1 Level Stake	Handicaps	W-R	Per cent	£1 Level Stake
2-y-o	23-90	25.6	+2.95	2-y-o	2-14	14.3	-6.00
3-y-o	11-79	13.9	-36.02	3-y-o	5-42	11.9	-8.75
4-y-o+	13-98	13.3	+17.00	4-y-o+	4-52	7.7	-24.50

RACE CLASS / FIRST TIME OUT

RACE CLASS	W-R	Per cent	£1 Level Stake	FIRST TIME OUT	W-R	Per cent	£1 Level Stake
Class	112-97	12.4	-29.60	2-y-o	12-462	6.1	+10.73
Class	24-69	5.8	-43.50	3-y-o	7-37	18.9	-0.42
Class	37-42	16.7	+0.41	4-y-o+	6-48	12.5	-23.38
Class	48-48	16.7	-6.25				
Class	526-115	22.6	-18.74	Totals	25-131	19.1	-13.07
Class	61-4	25.0	-2.56				
Class	70-0	0.0	0.000				

but she's showing us a fair bit of speed, so all options are open with her. She's very well at present.

"**Sadeek's Song** is an interesting handicapper who came through the ranks last season and should have a rewarding campaign this time. He seems to go well with some cut in the ground.

"**Sandusky** lacks the quality of some of the others but I think he's one to follow. He can be placed to win races and isn't too high in the ratings on what we've seen of him."

Godolphin's website lists more than 200 horses in training excluding their army of juveniles. Little wonder they have added Mickael Barzalona and Silvestre de Sousa to the roster of jockeys alongside Frankie Dettori. The question with Godolphin is not whether they will have a good season but, rather, will it be exceptional? With the wealth of talent they have at their disposal, my money would be on the latter. [*Colin Boag*]

GODOLPHIN AND THE STATS

2010 saw a change in the way Godolphin train, with Sheikh Mohammed employing a second handler in Mahmood Al Zarooni to split the workload with Saeed Bin Suroor. Now that the twin-yard template has been in place for two seasons some patterns are becoming apparent.

It seems the operation can be largely broken down in two ways. Al Zarooni looks to be in charge of more two-year-olds and is given the task of providing the winners in the early part of the season. Bin Suroor has more older horses at his disposal and his runners are geared more towards the latter half of the campaign.

Perhaps everything didn't go according to plan last season as Al Zarooni's string outperformed Bin Suroor's for most of the year. Sure enough, Al Zarooni's squad hit the ground running for the first part of the season but seemed to keep the momentum for almost the remainder of the year. Bin Suroor, as expected, started the season slowly and picked up gradually but the only month where he bettered Al Zarooni was November.

Al Zarooni's runners returned a huge level-stakes profit last term. Money could be made in handicaps, Group races and maidens but he will surely be hard pushed to repeat such figures now his name is as familiar as Bin Suroor, whose runners incurred followers a loss in all areas except juvenile maidens.

Al Zarooni had plenty of big-race victories last term and experienced Classic success with Blue Bunting in the 1,000 Guineas. He was best backed at all the top tracks, returning profits at Ascot, Goodwood, Newmarket (Rowley Mile and July course) and York.

Bin Suroor generally struggled at the top level last term. Punters were best advised to take note of his runners who had their sights lowered as his best figures came on the all-weather at Lingfield and Kempton.

Riding arrangements differed slightly for the trainers. Frankie Dettori received most of the best rides for both but, unsurprisingly, was best followed for Al Zarooni given the better fortune that yard enjoyed. For back-up, Al Zarooni largely had the services of Ahmed Ajtebi and Mickael Barzalona, while Bin Suroor mostly called upon Ted Durcan and William Buick.

Although Ajtebi and Durcan received more mounts, Barzalona and Buick had superior strike-rates and it's probably more significant when these two are called upon. Another rider to watch out for is Kieren Fallon. He rode on a few occasions for both trainers last term, returning an impressive strike-rate and profit for both.

It could be another fine season for Al Zarooni, who has some major talent on his hands as he goes for more Classic glory. Unbeaten fillies Lyric Of Light and Discourse both look strong 1,000 Guineas candidates. *[Kevin Morley]*

Big ambitions for flagbearers Nathaniel and Masked Marvel

Nathaniel could return at Sandown in May

IT WAS another outstanding season for John Gosden with 99 winners on the board at a strike-rate of 18 per cent and prize-money well up at almost £2.5m. Star of the show was Nathaniel, winner of the King George VI and Queen Elizabeth Stakes. His final run of the year was back over ten furlongs in the Champion Stakes, but for whatever reason he couldn't reproduce his best form.

"He had a great season and was undoubtedly helped by the summer rain. Ascot plays to his strengths as it's a galloping track with a stiff finish, and with some cut in the ground conditions were right up his street. He can go on quicker ground – he ran well from a horrible draw on fast going in the Champion.

"It's possible he could start out in the Group 3 Brigadier Gerard Stakes at Sandown towards the end of May, which would suit because we might well consider the Eclipse, and after that there's the King George.

"I'm not worried about taking him back to ten furlongs because I think it was the draw that was the problem in the Champion. That's one of the drawbacks with running the race at Ascot, as if you're drawn six or seven out, which is a high draw nowadays, then it's a huge disadvantage."

Masked Marvel set a new record on the clock when winning the St Leger last season

The St Leger is proving to be a successful race for Gosden and **Masked Marvel** gave him a fourth win in the race and his third in a five-year period when winning the race last September. After that he was supplemented into the Arc but ran moderately, fading from two furlongs out.

"We've had a good run in the St Leger with three decent horses in Lucarno, Arctic Cosmos and this fellow – all of them proper Leger types. Masked Marvel was in great form that day, as he had been when he won his previous race, the Bahrain Trophy. At Doncaster he recorded the fastest-ever time for the St Leger and William Buick had a job to pull him up after the post.

"The Arc probably came a bit too quickly after Doncaster and in any event it might have been a case of one race too many. William twigged that was the case and looked after him.

"He could start out in the Jockey Club Stakes at the Guineas meeting and then perhaps the Grand Prix de Saint-Cloud before the King George. We've resisted the temptation to go to Dubai with him over the winter but that could be something for next year."

The 2010 St Leger winner **Arctic Cosmos** stays in training. He had a short campaign last season, reappearing in October and having just two starts, finishing second in the Cumberland Lodge and then fourth in the Canadian International.

"He cracked a cannon bone after the Leger and had three screws put in it. He's come back well but it takes time to get over that sort of injury. I was very happy with his first run back but he ended up making the running, which wouldn't have suited him.

"In Canada he got distracted by the ponies and then he, and the filly who won the race, were in the starting gate by themselves – having got revved up by the ponies he then got revved up by her and I'm not sure he was that focused in the race. I think the filly

would have won anyway but I'd like to think we should have finished second.

"He's just cantering at present and we're looking towards the John Porter as long as we get a normal spring."

Izzi Top had a good season, winning a Newbury Listed race and a Saint-Cloud Group 3 either side of finishing third in the Oaks.

"She sustained a little injury at Epsom and had to have time off but she came back well to win in France. Her initial target is the Middleton Stakes at York in May, the mile-and-a-quarter Group 2 for older fillies. She's by Pivotal and, although she handles most types of ground, like most of her sire's stock she likes to get her toe in.

"I like **Eshtibaak** but he's delicate and hasn't been the easiest to train. He had to win his final start at Nottingham to avoid being sent to the sales and thankfully he did it well. At this stage he's only the winner of a backend maiden, so we shouldn't get too carried away, but I like him. He's going well and he appreciates give underfoot."

As always there are plenty of fascinating three-year-old prospects in Gosden's team,

none more so than the filly **Elusive Kate**.

After winning a maiden at Kempton she followed up in Listed company at Deauville and completed her hat-trick in a Group 3 at the same track. She then won the Group 1 Prix Marcel Boussac at Longchamp before being sent to Churchill Downs for the Breeders' Cup Juvenile Fillies' Turf, where she finished down the field.

"She's a tough filly who is beautifully bred. She's from a fabulous family – her second dam won the Prix Morny. She won her maiden lazily but she loved travelling to France and really enjoyed racing there. She's a character and strong-willed but has a lot of ability and wound up as joint top-rated juvenile filly in Europe.

"Because she's a Group 1 winner we'll most likely point her at the Fred Darling and if that went well, then the 1,000 Guineas – I'm pretty sure she's a miler.

"**Eastern Sun** won his maiden nicely at Newbury – the form worked out well – and we sent him to the Group 3 Solario Stakes at Sandown. The ground was perfect when we entered him and was perfect right up until about lunchtime and then the heavens

opened. I was at York that day and had I been at the track he probably wouldn't have run, but he took his chance and I don't think he liked it at all. We put him away afterwards and I'm hoping to run him in the Greenham and take it from there."

Fallen For You won her maiden at Newbury and was then second in the Group 2 May Hill before finishing fifth in the Fillies' Mile.

"Ideally I prefer to have a stepping stone in between races, so I think she was probably caught out a bit by lack of experience when runner-up at Doncaster. The winner leaned on her a bit in the May Hill, but that's racing. She still ran a blinder.

"I take the blame for the Fillies' Mile defeat. When it's fast ground on the Rowley Mile horses ridden prominently can quicken down into the Dip and can be hard to peg back, so I encouraged William Buick to be handy on her and I don't think she likes to be ridden that way. If we'd ridden her differently she would have run better.

"She's in good form and her main target is the Prix de Diane. She's in the French Guineas, but also the Prix Saint-Alary over ten furlongs."

Fencing won a Newmarket maiden and followed up in the Listed Washington Singer Stakes at Newbury before rounding off his season with third place in the Racing Post Trophy.

"The Newbury race is a restricted Listed one, so I always like to have a look at it in case it's vulnerable – it was really more of a nice allowance race the way things turned out. However, he's a Listed winner, which is great because he's the first foal of a mare who won the Prix de Diane.

"He was a bit babyish at Doncaster and with a bit more experience he might have been second to the exceptional winner – he was the best two-year-old I saw last season.

"Fencing's in great form and we'll look at races like the Free Handicap or the Craven, and he'll have entries in the 2,000 Guineas and the French Derby. I put a tongue-tie on him at Doncaster and I might do so again as he was playing with his tongue.

"**The Fugue** is a classy filly – tall, leggy and light-framed and I took my time with her. She came to me very late with the express purpose of running in that maiden where the owner's Dar Re Mi had finished second in 2007.

"She'd trained beautifully beforehand and won it well and I hold her in some esteem. I wouldn't be afraid to run her over the same trip and track in the Nell Gwyn and she'll have a 1,000 Guineas entry. However, her mother won a Ribblesdale and The Fugue will have no trouble staying ten furlongs, so it may be that's more her style and we'll also enter her in the Oaks."

Starscope won her only start last season, in the other division of the Newmarket maiden won by The Fugue. The time was slower but the manner of her victory was even more impressive, with her quickening nicely and bolting clear.

"She's in nice form right now and like The Fugue is one we could run in a race like the Nell Gwyn. I see her as more of a mile to ten furlongs filly.

"**Starboard** works nicely at home but when he went to Ascot for his debut run he got stage fright, fretting about everything going on around him and trying to hold his breath – that can happen with a two-year-old first time out.

"In the race he was going well but just stopped. I knew he was better than that, so we took him home, settled him down and got him working nicely again.

"I hadn't been to Redcar for two years because the prize-money is so poor, but fortunately there was a race that was above tariff, so we took him up there. He won comfortably but he was still babyish, rearing up as he entered the winner's enclosure, which is unusual. So, he's still got that immature mentality to some extent but he has a nice win under his belt and I like him. We'll let him tell us when he's ready but I wouldn't be afraid to run him in a trial if he's going well.

"**Gathering** is a sweet filly. First time out she ran fourth on the July course and after that I freshened her up and gave her some time. Robert Havlin rode her beautifully when she won on the Rowley Mile.

"She's a leggy, long-striding filly who is having a good winter. She's in the French and

English Guineas and we'll have a look at how she's doing nearer the time.

"**Jungle Beat** won his maiden in July but ran into a minor hiccup after that, which was a shame as I wanted to run him in the Royal Lodge. He's training nicely at the moment and has some decent entries – if all goes well, he'll run in a trial and hopefully take up one of those entries. He has the speed to compete at a mile and will stay a mile and a quarter – beyond that, you never know."

Thought Worthy is a brother to Lucarno and won over a mile at Newcastle on his only juvenile start. Would his trainer have the Leger in the back of his mind even at this early stage?

"When a horse has a certain kind of frame and build you train them knowing that the Leger is a possibility, and Thought Worthy falls into that category. He's a lovely horse who fills the eye, he has a long stride and a good mind, so yes, I have thought about him as a Leger type.

"Lucarno was fourth in the Derby and Masked Marvel ran in the race too, so I'm not afraid to go down that route – some horses come to their peak towards the backend of their three-year-old season.

"**Shantaram** was green when he was beaten a whisker at Sandown and is a lovely, big colt. I like him and he'll stay well.

"**Qaadira** was third in a Yarmouth maiden and is a nice sort – a bit highly strung but she has above-average ability. **The Nile** was third at Newbury and there's more to come from him. **Hepworth** stayed on well to be second at Doncaster but the bird had flown. She's going to be a mid-season filly and will need a mile and a quarter – I like her, though. **Gregorian** won well at Doncaster and is progressive – again, I like him and I'll give him some smart entries."

Gosden starts the season with a formidable team. His older horses look particularly smart and there is great strength among the 80 or so three-year-olds, with more than 35 well-bred sorts still to see the racecourse. Another excellent season looks assured. *[Colin Boag]*

JOHN GOSDEN
NEWMARKET, SUFFOLK

	No. of Hrs	Races Run	1st	2nd	3rd	Unpl	Per cent	£1 Level Stake
2-y-o	68	161	26	17	20	96	16.1	-6.78
3-y-o	78	309	58	48	49	153	18.8	-63.41
4-y-o	+24	83	15	9	14	45	18.1	+57.38
Totals	**170**	**553**	**99**	**74**	**83**	**294**	**17.9**	**-12.81**
2010	159	518	105	76	70	267	20.3	+15.03
2009	159	516	88	79	65	284	17.1	+16.50

BY MONTH

2-y-o	W-R	Per cent	£1 Level Stake	**3-y-o**	W-R	Per cent	£1 Level Stake
January	0-0	0.0	0.00	January	2-4	50.0	+14.25
February	0-0	0.0	0.00	February	2-21	00.0	+2.48
March	0-0	0.0	0.00	March	1-6	16.7	-3.38
April	0-4	0.0	-4.00	April	11-53	20.8	-13.76
May	0-4	0.0	-4.00	May	9-48	18.8	-6.05
June	6-19	31.6	+29.16	June	10-56	17.9	-23.68
July	3-15	20.0	-6.25	July	8-37	21.6	-8.93
August	2-29	6.9	-22.75	August	5-30	16.7	+0.50
September	7-36	19.4	-10.82	September	6-35	17.1	-1.17
October	6-33	18.2	+22.38	October	1-23	4.3	-21.00
November	1-15	6.7	-13.50	November	2-12	16.7	-4.00
December	1-61	6.7	+3.00	December	1-33	3.3	+1.33

4-y-o+	W-R	Per cent	£1 Level Stake	**Totals**	W-R	Per cent	£1 Level Stake
January	0-0	0.0	0.00	January	2-4	50.0	+14.25
February	0-0	0.0	0.00	February	2-21	00.0	+2.48
March	0-0	0.0	0.00	March	1-6	16.7	-3.38
April	2-11	18.2	+10.50	April	13-68	19.1	-7.26
May	3-12	25.0	-3.13	May	12-64	18.8	-13.18
June	2-17	11.8	-0.50	June	18-92	19.6	+4.98
July	3-14	21.4	+29.50	July	14-66	21.2	+14.32
August	2-13	15.4	+5.50	August	9-72	12.5	-16.75
September	2-11	18.2	+11.50	September	15-82	18.3	-0.49
October	0-4	0.0	-4.00	October	7-60	11.7	-2.62
November	1-11	00.0	+8.00	November	4-28	14.3	+4.00
December	0-0	0.0	0.00	December	2-9	22.2	+1.33

DISTANCE

2-y-o	W-R	Per cent	£1 Level Stake	**3-y-o**	W-R	Per cent	£1 Level Stake
5f-6f	5-44	11.4	-2.51	5f-6f	0-11	0.0	-11.00
7f-8f	20-11	317.7	-2.52	7f-8f	14-98	14.3	-41.80
9f-13f	1-4	25.0	-1.75	9f-13f	40-185	21.6	-27.60
14f+	0-0	0.0	0.00	14f+	4-15	26.7	+17.00

4-y-o	W-R	Per cent	£1 Level Stake	**Totals**	W-R	Per cent	£1 Level Stake
5f-6f	0-0	0.0	0.00	5f-6f	5-55	9.1	-13.51
7f-8f	2-14	14.3	+6.50	7f-8f	36-225	16.0	-37.82
9f-13f	10-51	19.6	+45.25	9f-13f	51-240	21.3	+15.90
14f+	3-18	16.7	+5.63	14f+	7-33	21.2	+22.63

TYPE OF RACE

Non-Handicaps	W-R	Per cent	£1 Level Stake	**Handicaps**	W-R	Per cent	£1 Level Stake
2-y-o	23-142	16.2	-4.78	2-y-o	3-19	15.8	-2.00
3-y-o	42-193	21.8	-24.99	3-y-o	16-116	13.8	-38.42
4-y-o+	4-30	13.3	+6.00	4-y-o+	11-53	20.8	+70.13

RACE CLASS | FIRST TIME OUT

	W-R	Per cent	£1 Level Stake		W-R	Per cent	£1 Level Stake
Class 1	13-102	12.7	-25.25	2-y-o	10-68	14.7	+34.75
Class 2	10-59	16.9	+51.00	3-y-o	16-78	20.5	+1.87
Class 3	4-45	8.9	-22.63	4-y-o+	3-24	12.5	+1.25
Class 4	25-123	20.3	+19.46				
Class 5	43-213	20.2	-35.90	Totals	29-170	17.1	+37.87
Class 6	4-11	36.4	+1.51				
Class 7	0-0	0.0	0.00				

Notes

GOSDEN AND THE STATS

Gosden may have failed to break the century barrier by the narrowest of margins last season but a tally of 99 winners was an excellent return. The Newmarket trainer enjoyed plenty of big-race success in 2011, chiefly with the three-year-olds Nathaniel and Masked Marvel, who landed the King George and St Leger respectively. Expect any progressive three-year-old at Clarehaven stables to be earmarked for the Doncaster Classic as Gosden has now landed three of the last five renewals.

It should come as no surprise that it is in the staying events Gosden has achieved most at the highest level – the figures show his strike-rate and level-stake profits increase in races beyond a mile. The numbers posted last year mirrored those achieved over the last five seasons, so always watch out when his horses are upped in distance. That's not to say Gosden does not know how to train sprinters, as his excellent handling of Oasis Dream in 2002 and 2003 proved – it just doesn't pay to follow his runners over the short distances on a consistent basis.

Gosden had a solid amount of juvenile winners last term, ensuring he goes into 2012 with reasonable hope that his three-year-olds earn their fair share of prize-money. His two-year-olds were profitable to follow first time up last season but that isn't usually the case as his youngsters normally come on significantly for their debut.

William Buick doesn't incur his supporters as big a loss as other stable jockeys riding for big yards but a level stake would still leave you in the red. Robert Havlin's mounts returned a profits as did Nicky Mackay's rides, but it is the latter who is more likely to do punters a favour as he has been profitable to follow for Gosden over the last five seasons.

Although Gosden regularly makes an impact at Group level, it is his runners in handicaps who have returned healthy level-stakes profits for three of the last four seasons.

Gosden is also recognised as a trainer to follow in the latter part of the season, although his figures in 2011 seemed to buck that trend as his most fruitful periods came in June and July. That was a break from the norm and when looking at his stable it is best to work on the assumption that his string will peak in the autumn.

Given that he started his training career in America, it is no surprise Gosden has a fantatstic strike-rate on the all-weather tracks, having returned a level-stakes profit over the last five years. Wolverhampton is the only sand track where he shows a loss, with Kempton the venue you are most likely to see one of his runners in the winner's enclosure. *[Kevin Morley]*

High achiever out to work his magic with unexposed string

F ROM his humble beginnings with a few horses at a small yard near Louth in Lincolnshire, Mark Johnston is now firmly established in the upper branches of the training tree, yet the past few seasons have seen a dramatic change in the way he operates. A look through the list of his horses in training shows how important the Maktoum family is to his business, but it is not as simple as just training for their Darley operation as he has a more complex role within the team.

"For slightly more than fifty per cent of my string, I'm a feeder yard for Godolphin," the trainer says. "It works both ways as horses come back to me from Darley and Godolphin – I've got 52 three-year-olds who fit into that bracket. These include some beautifully bred horses and if they do well with me they may well go back to Godolphin, as the likes of Fox Hunt and Colour Vision did at the end of last season."

When Johnston trains juveniles for Darley he does so knowing the better ones will more than likely move to Godolphin at the end of their two-year-old season. Similarly, many of the unexposed or more modestly rated Godolphin juveniles will move to Johnston's yard to further their careers.

Starting with the three-year-olds, Johnston says: "It's slightly unusual this season as we have two three-year-olds rated over 100 who haven't gone to Godolphin and that's presumably because they're quite well-exposed sprinters who will be difficult to place early in the year.

"**Vocational** *(opposite, red cap)* is a lovely filly whose form has been a little in and out but on her day she's very good. She's rated 104 and will be difficult to place early in the season, as is the case with most three-year-old sprinters.

"**Bannock** is rated 110 and it's unusual he hasn't gone but again he is exposed. He was placed twice in Group 2 company and won a Listed race at York in October.

"**Cravat** is another exposed horse but he's a Dubai Destination colt out of a Sadler's Wells mare and he won first time up over five furlongs. Although he was seventh of eight on his final start, in a Listed race at Pontefract, that was over a mile and I'm sure he'll stay further. He had 12 runs as a two-year-old but they took nothing out of him and I'm sure he'll be better as he steps up in trip.

"**Leqqaa** has frustrated me no end. He won first time up and then was always the bridesmaid, being placed in Listed company and finishing second in the Houghton on his final start. I just hope he improves with age. He's bred to stay ten furlongs but he can be a bit keen in his races.

"**Rafeej** is a nice horse who has done nothing wrong, being unbeaten in two starts. He's rated 87, so I won't be throwing him in a Guineas trial or anything like that and he'll work his way through the handicap route.

"**Assizes** would have been one of those I was most excited about for this season, but he's had a problem and won't be out until the middle of the year. He showed fantastic promise when he won his only start, at Newbury, and his absence until the middle of the year is a huge blow as I might well have run him in a trial.

"**Sir Graham Wade** is still a maiden and that's where we'll start him out. He's a nice horse with the potential to improve. He was backward last season and when he was second in that ten-furlong maiden at Pontefract the commentators went on about how he was the one to take out of the race. He'll stay at least a mile and a half.

"I'm jam-packed with well-bred, middle-of-the-road three-year-olds who are relatively

low-rated and hopefully there are some good ones among them, but at this stage I can't say which ones they might be because their form, particularly on the all-weather, is so hard to weigh up.

"The big issue is whether they can go on and win anything else after their all-weather successes – we've had 30 winners on the all-weather over the winter and have won not much more than £90,000. The worry is how much that will affect the rest of the season – it certainly does with some horses.

"I really like **Galician** but she's a 78-rated handicapper and will work her way through.

"We put **Kingloch Castle** away after he won at Southwell in November as we'd decided not to campaign him over the winter. He's rated 82 based on an all-weather win, so we need to get him back on the turf and see whether he can live up to that mark.

"**El Lail** was second on her debut and then won really well at York – I can't wait to get going with her. She's rated 83 and will start out in handicaps.

"**Switzerland** has been slightly disappointing, especially on his latest start on the Polytrack at Lingfield, and he's another highly rated all-weather handicapper.

"We've been really pleased with **Prussian**, with him finishing second at Lingfield and then winning at Kempton, but the form is suspect, so we don't really know much about him or where we should go with him.

"When I say it's hard to know exactly how good the horses are that got their rating on the all-weather, **Red Orator** is a prime example. He has run just once and won what was probably a poor three-runner maiden at Kempton. There has been quite a lot of talk about him but I just wouldn't have a clue how good he is.

"It's the same story with **Rosby Waves** and I've got plenty more in the same boat. To be fair, that's how the handicapper sees it too as she has a rating of only 72. She won a five-runner Wolverhampton maiden and she did it nicely, but who knows?"

Rainbow Gold is seriously unexposed, having run once, at Goodwood in August, when she finished nearer last than first in a maiden after missing the break.

"She's bred to be a stayer and you'd think she's sure to win races – she's from the same family as Lady Jane Digby, who won a Group 1 in Germany."

Jukebox Jury (*above*) dead-heated with Duncan in the Irish St Leger last season. His final start was in the Melbourne Cup, where he finished lame and was found to have sustained a serious injury.

"He's back in training and we're looking at a middle-to-late-May return to the track. He ran right up to his best last season and was more consistent than he had ever been. The plan was a Cup campaign but the injury might scupper it a bit as everything has to go perfectly between now and then. If it does the Ascot Gold Cup might still be possible but another trip to the Melbourne Cup is the target."

One of the oldest cliches in racing when discussing a three-year-old's career is the line that the horse should be even better at four, but that notion gets short shrift from Johnston: "They're all better at four!" Better to say that on occasions there are reasons to believe a horse might do better than most as it matures in the winter after its three-year-old season, and **Gulf Of Naples** falls into that category.

He won his maiden at Catterick over 1m4f and then won a handicap over 1m6f before rounding off his season by winning off a mark of 87 over two miles at Newmarket. What gives hope for above-average improvement is that his half-brother Dream Eater improved at five and also that he's a stayer, so he's likely to improve further as he reaches his physical peak.

"He's a progressive handicapper who was going in the right direction at the end of last season and hopefully will improve more as he matures. Although he won over two miles, I think he can be effective at a bit shorter than that. He has a way to go before he steps up beyond handicap company and I'm a firm believer in moving one step at a time, so we'll see.

"**Fascinating** won his last three starts, two at Wolverhampton and then at Kempton, and was clearly progressing well, albeit from a modest starting point. Hopefully he can go on to better things and I think he'll stay beyond a mile and a half."

Queen Of Denmark is a beautifully-bred filly, being a half-sister to the Sheema Classic winner, Vengeance Of Rain, as well as others with decent form in Australia. She didn't appear until she was four and has two wins and a second on the all-weather to her name.

"I can get quite annoyed about her. The media spent a long time talking about her pedigree before she appeared but as she didn't race until she was four I thought they went over the top on that. Then, after one of her wins, the handicapper went to talk to Joe Fanning about her and could do nothing other than go on about her breeding – well, frankly, handicappers rate on performance,

not pedigree. So here we have a filly who has won £7,000 and is rated 87. I'm continually having the argument with the handicappers that we're getting horses coming off the all-weather with unrealistic ratings after winning small races – it throws those horses rapidly into the deep end.

"Life will be harder for her from now on as she's moving into a tough grade but she is well bred, stays well, and we have to be hopeful the handicapper is right.

"**Hurricane Higgins** has had a few problems and he's obviously temperamental, but he's a gelding now, so we're hoping that will make a big difference. He has got ability, as he showed when second in the Lingfield Derby Trial.

"**Eternal Heart** *(above, left)* won three races early in his three-year-old career and, even though he has now run 11 times, there's every hope he'll get better with time and as he steps up in trip. He's from that Yavana's Pace family and they seem to improve as they mature. He'd be one of my big hopes for the season.

"**Tmaam** is nice. Although he's four, he has run only four times – he went to the races on two other occasions but didn't run as he has tender feet. He's lightly raced and is off 90 – he's a good horse.

"We wouldn't have kept **Jeu De Vivre** in training unless we thought she could improve some more. She has had 19 starts and has progressed steadily from a rating of 62 to 81 and I think she'll be nicer as she matures.

"**Smart Step** is rated only 67 but has managed to win three races and I think there's more to come from her. Like Jeu De Vivre, she's a soft-ground filly – that seems to be the key to them."

The way Johnston's training operation now works means there is more potential than exposed form among his string, particularly with the three-year-olds, and spotting the stars is difficult. However, there will be plenty of winners coming from his Middleham yard this year and his runners in the staying division will warrant the usual utmost respect.
[Colin Boag]

MARK JOHNSTON

MIDDLEHAM MOOR, N YORKS

	No. of Hrs	Races Run	1st	2nd	3rd	Unpl	Per cent	£1 Level Stake
2-y-o	83	331	37	42	37	215	11.2	-162.32
3-y-o	111	634	107	83	75	369	16.9	-31.23
4-y-o	+44	346	35	32	31	248	10.1	-72.88
Totals	**238**	**1311**	**179**	**157**	**143**	**832**	**13.7**	**-266.43**
2010	262	1458	211	166	167	911	14.5	-86.04
2009	250	1227	216	161	138	707	17.6	-32.01

BY MONTH

2-y-o	W-R	Per cent	£1 Level Stake	3-y-o	W-R	Per cent	£1 Level Stake
January	0-0	0.0	0.00	January	14-22	63.6	+13.19
February	0-0	0.0	0.00	February	4-31	12.9	-16.17
March	0-0	0.0	0.00	March	9-33	27.3	+0.44
April	0-8	0.0	-8.00	April	9-83	10.8	-42.00
May	8-35	22.9	+5.02	May	14-72	19.4	+12.00
June	5-40	12.5	-21.38	June	10-99	10.1	-19.23
July	6-50	12.0	-34.58	July	16-87	18.4	+5.67
August	4-47	8.5	-29.25	August	5-63	7.9	-11.70
September	2-54	3.7	-46.00	September	12-76	15.8	+8.75
October	9-72	12.5	-10.00	October	12-47	25.5	+33.70
November	3-19	15.8	-12.14	November	0-12	0.0	-12.00
December	0-6	0.0	-6.00	December	2-9	22.2	-3.88

4-y-o	W-R	Per cent	£1 Level Stake	Totals	W-R	Per cent	£1 Level Stake
January	2-10	20.0	-4.38	January	16-32	50.0	+8.81
February	3-11	27.3	+4.00	February	7-42	16.7	-12.17
March	0-9	0.0	-9.00	March	9-42	21.4	-8.56
April	1-38	2.6	-34.00	April	10-129	7.8	-84.00
May	5-58	8.6	+6.25	May	27-165	16.4	+23.27
June	4-54	7.4	-17.00	June	19-193	9.8	-57.61
July	4-60	6.7	-38.13	July	26-197	13.2	-67.04
August	4-45	8.9	-8.00	August	13-155	8.4	-48.95
September	8-39	20.5	+20.53	September	22-169	13.0	-16.72
October	4-21	19.0	+7.83	October	25-140	17.9	+31.53
November	0-0	0.0	0.00	November	3-31	9.7	-12.00
December	0-1	0.0	-1.00	December	2-16	12.5	-4.88

DISTANCE

2-y-o	W-R	Per cent	£1 Level Stake	3-y-o	W-R	Per cent	£1 Level Stake
5f-6f	17-134	12.7	-68.57	5f-6f	6-31	19.4	-16.55
7f-8f	20-187	10.7	-83.75	7f-8f	31-209	14.8	-39.06
9f-13f	0-10	0.0	-10.00	9f-13f	63-356	17.7	+19.13
14f+	0-0	0.0	0.00	14f+	7-38	18.4	+5.25

4-y-o	W-R	Per cent	£1 Level Stake	Totals	W-R	Per cent	£1 Level Stake
5f-6f	0-2	0.0	-2.00	5f-6f	11-48	22.9	+36.33
7f-8f	1-8	12.5	+13.00	7f-8f	43-233	18.5	+50.66
9f-13f	3-19	15.8	+14.38	9f-13f	24-120	20.0	+22.00
14f+	2-5	40.0	+4.50	14f+	3-8	37.5	+11.50

TYPE OF RACE

Non-Handicaps	W-R	Per cent	£1 Level Stake	Handicaps	W-R	Per cent	£1 Level Stake
2-y-o	31-245	12.7	-109.32	2-y-o	6-86	7.0	-53.00
3-y-o	39-204	19.1	+1.70	3-y-o	68-430	15.8	-32.93
4-y-o+	5-28	17.9	+17.00	4-y-o+	30-318	9.4	-64.75

RACE CLASS / FIRST TIME OUT

Race Class	W-R	Per cent	£1 Level Stake	First time out	W-R	Per cent	£1 Level Stake
Class 1	7-65	10.8	-23.00	2-y-o	9-83	10.8	-26.42
Class 2	13-207	6.3	-96.84	3-y-o	20-111	18.0	-31.43
Class 3	17-144	11.8	+6.38	4-y-o+	6-44	13.6	-13.88
Class 4	36-309	11.7	-73.47				
Class 5	70-443	15.8	-79.79	Totals	35-238	14.7	-71.73
Class 6	36-143	25.2	+15.04				
Class 7	0-0	0.0	0.00				

Notes

JOHNSTON AND THE STATS

Johnston is never going to be the ideal trainer to follow blindly. Given the amount of runners he has, he is always going to return a level-stakes loss in most ways you break down his string. But that doesn't mean it's impossible to find profitable angles.

The most obvious place to start with Johnston is his three-year-olds. The Classic generation accounts for nearly 60 per cent of his winners and money can be made when stamina comes to the fore. Last season, his three-year-olds racing over 1m3f-plus returned healthy profits with a solid strike-rate. The older horses also delivered over the longer trips to a smaller scale in 2011 but from a long-term perspective it's the three-year-olds who deliver in this area on a consistent basis. The Middleham trainer believes that the weight-for-age allowance is generous to the younger horses, particularly from the summer onwards, so watch out for when he pitches in his three-year-olds against their elders.

His strike-rate is neither outstanding nor poor in Group races but he has returned a small profit over the seasons. Where Johnston has disappointed is his haul in of Group 1 wins in Britain with just two victories in the highest grade from 2007 onwards – he has had more Group 1 success abroad during this period. Johnston hasn't really threatened to win a Classic since Attraction landed the British and Irish 1,000 Guineas double in 2004 and it will take one of last year's juveniles to improve significantly to step up to that level.

Beverley is the turf track where you are most likely to see one of his come home in front as he sent out more winners there than anywhere else last term – and that has been the case since 2007. A level-stakes profit is usually made at the Yorkshire venue and you will also be quids in if following his runners in Sussex. Ventures to Brighton are often successful but his favourite course on the south coast, perhaps anywhere in Britain, is Goodwood. Johnston returned poor figures at the course in 2011 but that was an aberration and there are often big-priced winners from his yard to be found at the track, particularly at the Glorious meeting in the height of summer.

Also take note when Johnston drops those aged three and over into sellers or claimers. It's not something he does with regularity but his runners always pay their way in this grade. The best track to watch out for a Johnston two-year-old is Leicester. His youngsters normally need a run but if they make a winning debut it's most likely to be there.

Given the amount of horses he has, Johnston calls upon the services of several jockeys. Joe Fanning is likely to have the majority of rides, though, while Franny Norton was an interesting booking for the yard last term and returned a big level-stakes profit from nine winners. *[Kevin Morley]*

'York Glory is stronger and there's every reason to expect more this year'

R YAN had a year of personal bests in 2011, finishing ninth in the trainers' table with 133 winners, record prize-money of more than £1.3m and a strike-rate of 17 per cent. Making his first appearance in this guide, the Yorkshire-based trainer shared his thoughts on the prospects for the Hambleton Lodge team.

Ryan has established a big reputation for his handling of sprinters and it was with some of the older horses in this category that we started.

Masamah *(above, right)* won a five-furlong York handicap off a mark of 100 and a Listed race over the same course and distance, but the six-year-old's biggest day came when he landed the Group 2 King George Stakes at Glorious Goodwood. Jamie Spencer grabbed the stands rail and scooted clear, winning pretty well as he liked. Masamah was a bit below his best in the Nunthorpe and the Betfred Sprint Cup but ran a blinder under his Group 2 penalty in the Dubai International World Trophy at Newbury, before finishing down the field in the Prix de l'Abbaye.

"He was very consistent last season and rarely disappointed – on the few occasions he did, there was a good reason," Ryan says.

"He was in great form going into the Abbaye, but got a bit upset in the stalls, but still ran really well after missing the break. He's wintered well and I'm looking forward to this season. His owner [Dr Marwan Koukash] likes to have runners at Chester, so I'm hoping there's something for him there, and Goodwood will be on the agenda again. Although his best form was at five furlongs, I'm convinced six won't be a problem for him."

Our Jonathan's win in the Ayr Gold Cup and his Great St Wilfrid Stakes success ensured it was a great season for Ryan's four-year-old. Now five, what are the plans for the horse?

"He's another who was very consistent and the Ayr Gold Cup had been his target for a while. That day he got the soft ground he wants and was an impressive winner. He'll have to step up from handicap company now and all being well he'll have an entry in the Duke of York Stakes. I'm not convinced he truly gets seven furlongs in good company, but he's a year older now and I wouldn't rule out trying that trip again."

Tiddliwinks won a conditions race at Nottingham in August and earlier in the season had been placed in Group 2 and 3 company, being beaten just a length in the Duke of York Stakes.

"He ran really well at York and he's a smart sprinter on his day. He's come in looking really well and could start out in the Cammidge at Doncaster. He could well run in Ireland at the Curragh – there are five good

sprint handicaps there, races like the Greenland and I'd imagine he'd run in one or two of those.

"**York Glory** did well last season, winning a classified race at Pontefract and handicaps at Thirsk and York, finishing up by running well in the Portland. He's a year older, much stronger, and is still improving. I think there's every reason to expect more from him as a four-year-old.

"**Louis The Pious** never missed a beat all through the season, even at Doncaster and Ascot at the backend. He's another who is now four and he should be up to contesting the better seven-furlong handicaps. We'll see whether he can go on from there.

"**Lightning Cloud** is similar to Louis The Pious and unfortunately he could end up running in the same seven-furlong races as him. I hope he'll show plenty of improvement from three to four.

"We got **Lexi's Hero** ready early last season as we wanted him to run at Chester, where he won. He then landed a decent handicap at York and was a good second at Newmarket in a heritage handicap. After that his form tailed off a bit, but he was only a

three-year-old and he'd been on the go for a while – he'd done more in the first half of the season than many horses do in the whole year. He's grown and strengthened over the winter and we'll start out in handicaps – as to whether he will progress beyond that, he'll point us in the right direction.

"Although **Dickie's Lad** is only a maiden winner, he was just nailed on the line in his last two runs, at Lingfield and then at Dundalk. He was a big, raw colt who was always going to take a bit of time to mature and we've always thought he wouldn't be at his best until he was four. He shows lots of speed and he's the kind who could compete in the big six-furlong handicaps.

"**Shoshoni Wind** is a decent filly on her day and is another we have hopes for now she's a four-year-old. She was progressive last season and I hope she can continue that and improve a bit more. Her best runs were at five furlongs last year and that's probably where we'll start her out but I wouldn't rule out trying her again over six."

Murura joined Ryan in mid-season having previously been with James Hartnett

Murura (leading) is in his first full season with Ryan, who is looking forward to testing out the sprinter

in Ireland, and before that with James Given. Ryan got immediate improvement from the five-year-old gelding, who won a Newmarket handicap over six furlongs and was second in a valuable event at the Curragh.

"He looked set to win in Ireland but didn't quite get home on very soft ground. We've had a lot more time with him now and know him a bit better – he's one I'm really looking forward to."

Activate and Capaill Liath have joined Ryan from Michael Bell's yard.

"**Activate** was second favourite for the Northumberland Plate last season and then was brought down at Goodwood. I think he might have lost his confidence a bit after that. He's had a nice break and we're feeling our way with him. We have it in mind that he could be one for the Chester Cup, but he's off a mark of 92 and would probably have to win before then to get into the race.

"**Capaill Liath** is a big colt who has done really well over the winter and is a half-brother to Masamah. He's been running at between seven and nine furlongs but I'm not sure what his best trip is – we might try him back sprinting."

Ryan starts the year with some nice three-year-old prospects, including **Bapak Chinta**, winner of the Norfolk Stakes at Royal Ascot. After that he was being prepared for the Nunthorpe but sustained a cut on the inside of his hock and had to miss the engagement. He then went for the Middle Park but didn't run up to his best.

"He's only small but he has grown a bit and has filled out. We tested him thoroughly after Newmarket but couldn't find anything wrong, so I think maybe he was simply growing and needed a break. He's come back looking well and will be contesting the big five-furlong races – the King's Stand at Royal Ascot will be his main objective in the first half of the season.

"**Bogart** has always shown me he has plenty of talent. He was a weak horse last season, so it's to his great credit that he could achieve as much as he did, winning the sales race at York and then the Totepool Two-Year-Old Trophy at Redcar. The only two occasions he let us down were at Goodwood, where he didn't handle the track, and when he went to France for the Group 2 Criterium de Maisons-Laffitte and the ground was desperate.

"He has matured well and there should be plenty of improvement in him. I shouldn't think we'll go beyond six furlongs with him.

"**Nagham** hasn't been easy to train but has had some treatment over the winter and, if we get a clear run with her, I think she's at least up to Listed class. It was a decent performance to finish third in the Weatherbys Super Sprint at Newbury.

"**Inetrobil** ran really well when second in the Albany and then fourth in the Cherry Hinton. I'd ignore her final start, at Salisbury, as there were signs she'd had enough for the season. She went back to Highclere after that and has returned to us looking marvellous. She's a big, scopey filly who will make a lovely broodmare, so the main aim is to get some black type with her. Six furlongs, and maybe seven, looks to be her trip.

"**Pea Shooter** was impressive at York when winning his maiden. He's a big colt, with loads of scope and we've always thought highly of him. He has a mark of 87.

"**Dam Beautiful** won on her debut and was placed in Listed company. She had a foot problem after that and, although we could have got her back, we decided to give her the remainder of the season off. She's always shown us plenty at home and has come back looking really well. She's very forward in her work and I'll be disappointed if she doesn't progress quite a lot.

"**Desert Philosopher** was due to run at Ayr's Western meeting but didn't have a great scope beforehand, so we were patient with him. He's a nice, laid-back colt who won his maiden well at Wolverhampton and I'm hopeful he'll improve from two to three.

"**Discression** was a big, backward type who ran twice at York and showed he has plenty of ability. We decided to leave him alone and let him mature, but he's back and looks a picture. We've always thought highly of him and there's no reason why he can't go forward. I see him as more than likely being a seven-furlong horse."

Ryan starts the season with a strong team of older horses and some lovely three-year-old prospects, so there's every reason to expect the stable's progressive form of the last few seasons to continue. Another century of winners looks to be on the cards. [Colin Boag]

RYAN AND THE STATS

Ryan enjoyed his best season last term since taking out a licence back in 1998. Not only did the Hambleton trainer send out a personal best of 133 winners, he amassed more than £1.3 million in prize-money and his strike-rate of 17 per cent was the highest it's been over the course of a season. Ryan's level-stakes column was also at an all-time high with profits fairly split across all age groups.

His biggest-priced winners came in all-weather races but being able to back Ryan blind and make money is a rarity. In most seasons he will return a substantial loss, which is hardly surprising given the amount of runners he has. For some reason, his achievements last season seemed to catch out the layers. Perhaps it was the quality of his juveniles last year, which were of a higher standard than usual, with several obliging at decent prices first time up.

That doesn't explain the profits returned on the three-year-olds and older horses, however. It could be that bookies and punters didn't pay close attention to the stable's riding arrangements. In past seasons, the majority of Ryan's horses were ridden by Neil Callan, Paul Hanagan and Jamie Spencer. However, last term it was Phillip Makin who assumed the role of stable jockey and he was ably assisted by Ryan's daughter Amy and Julie Burke.

Makin rode most winners but those ridden by the two female apprentices reaped greater rewards for punters. Jamie Spencer is still a significant booking for the yard and he has a higher strike-rate than any other rider for the stable and is the one Ryan often turns to for big races.

Ryan likes to crack on as early as possible with his runners. Sometimes they hold their form until the end of the summer but it's unusual for the stable to have high strike-rates in the latter months of the season.

He doesn't win often on his raids to the south and he tends to keep the majority of his success closer to home. Winners at tracks like Ascot, Goodwood, Newmarket and Ascot are hard to come by and big-race victories are most likely to come at York. His two-year-olds are often seen in the winners' enclosure at Catterick and Ripon but the two best courses at which to back him are further north. Carlisle and Hamilton are where he consistently returns the biggest level-stake profits with winners in all age groups.

Handicaps were a profitable area last term, although that was a break from the norm. Two-year-old maidens, where he also returned good figures in 2011, might be a better bet this year, particularly if he has another talented batch of juveniles. *[Kevin Morley]*

KEVIN RYAN
HAMBLETON, N YORKS

	No. of Hrs	Races Run	1st	2nd	3rd	Unpl	Per cent	£1 Level Stake
2-y-o	61	237	32	26	27	152	13.5	+7.53
3-y-o	36	231	54	35	21	121	23.4	+11.31
4-y-o	+41	329	47	39	30	213	14.3	+15.22
Totals	**138**	**797**	**133**	**100**	**78**	**486**	**16.7**	**+34.06**
2010	127	813	107	90	89	525	13.2	-158.18
2009	142	867	96	120	79	571	11.1	-98.55

BY MONTH

2-y-o	W-R	cent	Per £1 Level Stake	3-y-o	W-R	cent	Per £1 Level Stake
January	0-0	0.0	0.00	January	2-8	25.0	-3.90
February	0-0	0.0	0.00	February	4-13	30.8	+2.13
March	0-1	0.0	-1.00	March	4-14	28.6	+0.99
April	1-11	9.1	-6.00	April	2-21	9.5	-18.07
May	9-24	37.5	+20.94	May	12-34	35.3	+18.04
June	5-32	15.6	+28.88	June	8-31	25.8	+22.79
July	5-40	12.5	-23.59	July	10-34	29.4	+19.80
August	3-39	7.7	+0.50	August	5-20	25.0	-1.25
September	4-45	8.9	+4.00	September	3-23	13.0	-7.38
October	4-33	12.1	-13.20	October	1-15	6.7	-13.00
November	1-61	6.7	+3.00	November	1-71	4.3	-3.75
December	0-6	0.0	-6.00	December	2-11	18.2	-5.09

4-y-o+	W-R	cent	Per £1 Level Stake	Totals	W-R	cent	Per £1 Level Stake
January	7-24	29.2	+3.88	January	9-32	28.1	-0.02
February	5-22	22.7	+1.70	February	9-35	25.7	+3.83
March	4-15	26.7	+15.75	March	8-30	26.7	+15.74
April	4-34	11.8	-2.25	April	7-66	10.6	-26.32
May	7-46	15.2	-1.46	May	28-104	26.9	+37.52
June	4-41	9.8	+6.00	June	17-104	16.3	+57.67
July	6-37	16.2	+20.50	July	21-111	18.9	+16.71
August	2-28	7.1	-20.27	August	10-87	11.5	-21.02
September	4-38	10.5	8.00	September	11-106	10.4	-11.38
October	1-17	5.9	-8.00	October	6-65	9.2	-34.20
November	2-18	11.1	+14.00	November	4-31	12.9	+10.25
December	1-9	11.1	-6.63	December	3-26	11.5	-11.723

DISTANCE

2-y-o	W-R	cent	Per £1 Level Stake	3-y-o	W-R	cent	Per £1 Level Stake
5f-6f	26-180	14.4	-13.97	5f-6f	31-130	23.8	+11.75
7f-8f	6-56	10.7	+22.50	7f-8f	14-68	20.6	-8.52
9f-13f	0-1	0.0	-1.00	9f-13f	9-33	27.3	+8.08
14f+	0-0	0.0	0.00	14f+	0-0	0.0	0.00

4-y-o	W-R	cent	Per £1 Level Stake	Totals	W-R	cent	Per £1 Level Stake
5f-6f	24-201	11.9	-37.52	5f-6f	81-511	15.9	-39.74
7f-8f	16-82	19.5	+45.66	7f-8f	36-206	17.5	+59.64
9f-13f	4-28	14.3	+7.58	9f-13f	13-62	21.0	+14.66
14f+	3-18	16.7	-0.50	14f+	3-18	16.7	-0.50

TYPE OF RACE

	Non-Handicaps			Handicaps		
	W-R	cent	Per £1 Level Stake	W-R	cent	Per £1 Level Stake
2-y-o	28-187	15.0	+9.03	4-50	8.0	-1.50
3-y-o	15-58	25.9	+6.98	39-173	22.5	+4.33
4-y-o+	8-56	14.3	+13.00	39-273	14.3	+35.62

RACECLASS / FIRST TIME OUT

	W-R	cent	Per £1 Level Stake		W-R	cent	Per £1 Level Stake
Class 1	4-45	8.9	-21.00	2-y-o	14-61	23.0	+12.55
Class 2	11-128	8.6	-36.17	3-y-o	8-36	22.2	-13.47
Class 3	13-88	14.8	-1.36	4-y-o+	5-41	12.2	-18.38
Class 4	27-142	19.0	+71.68				
Class 5	49-247	19.8	+28.96	Totals	27-138	19.6	-19.30
Class 6	29-147	19.7	-7.05				
Class 7	0-0	0.0	0.00				

Notes

Plenty of firepower to help bounce back from disappointing season

FORM is temporary, class is permanent. The old adage has never been more appropriate than when discussing Sir Michael Stoute's 2011 season. The ten-times champion trainer had his own 'annus horribilis', with fewer winners trained than in any season for more than 25 years. Seventh place in the trainers' list is not where you expect Stoute to be and, although more than £1.5m in prize-money would please many trainers, it was his lowest tally since 1999. All in all it was a season Stoute is unlikely to look back on with any great affection – but he has more than enough firepower to bounce back this term.

Carlton House *(right)* remains in training and is sure to be one of the yard's main hopes for 2012. Owned by the Queen, he made his seasonal debut last year in the Dante, winning, as Raceform described it, 'in the style of a proper horse'. On the back of that he was made favourite for the Derby. In the

run-up to Epsom there was an injury scare when Carlton House knocked a near-fore joint but he was allowed to take his chance.

The 2011 Derby isn't a race that will hold good memories for Ryan Moore, as the favourite had a desperate passage through the race. He started slowly and then found no-hopers getting in his way as they fell back through the field. Forced wide, he then had to use valuable energy to quicken into position at the head of the straight, and was one-paced from a furlong out.

After that it was the Irish Derby, where he ran disappointingly, seeming to be perfectly placed but finding little when asked the question and looking as though he didn't stay the mile and a half on a galloping track.

"It's great that he stays in training. He has ability and we'll start him out at a mile and a quarter this season," says Stoute.

"He's had a few niggles and we'll have to get him right and going again. He came back sore from the Curragh and we can't be sure the trip was the problem, but we feel it's worth taking him back to the Dante distance as he was so impressive there."

At this time last season **Sea Moon** was being widely talked of as a Derby horse but he wasn't forward enough to be trained for Epsom, so he made his seasonal debut in a York handicap off 92. That was over ten furlongs and he won in workmanlike fashion, looking as though he would be suited by a step up in trip. That came in the Great Voltigeur, where he bolted up and was immediately made favourite for the St Leger.

At Doncaster he finished third, beaten more than three lengths by Masked Marvel, having had a troubled passage and being hampered on two occasions. He probably wouldn't have won but he should certainly have been second. He rounded off his season with a fine second to St Nicholas Abbey in the Breeders' Cup Turf.

"He was very impressive in the Voltigeur, didn't have the best of luck in the Leger, but then came back and ran a huge race at Churchill Downs. He's a big, scopey horse with a good attitude and he should improve again – he still has a bit of furnishing to do.

"The Breeders' Cup was only his sixth start and I'm hoping there's more to come from

Fiorente pulled a muscle on his final start last season and is held is high regard by his trainer

him. We know he gets a mile and three-quarters and he's very effective at a mile and a half, so he could start out in a race like the Ormonde at Chester or the John Porter at Newbury."

Fiorente won his maiden at Newbury over ten furlongs, looking as though he would stay further. He got his chance to prove that in the King Edward VII Stakes but he never really took a hand in the race owing to the combination of a slow start and the decision to race under the trees on the far side on account of the rain-softened ground. He stayed on from off the pace to finish second, five lengths behind Nathaniel.

The final start of his three-year-old campaign came in the Gordon Stakes at Goodwood, where he lost out by a neck to the tough Mark Johnston-trained Namibian.

"He's another nice, scopey horse and we were disappointed when he got beaten at Goodwood but he pulled a muscle and came back lame, so we couldn't run him again. I still hold him in high regard."

After the King Edward VII, Stoute was asked about Fiorente's prospects for the Leger but he hinted that he saw the horse as being able to handle the better mile-and-a-half contests.

Labarinto was a progressive juvenile who broke his duck on his third start. On the basis of that he had a mark of 87 with which to start his three-year-old career. When he finished second in the London Gold Cup at Newbury that mark went up to 92 and he went up another pound after finishing third in a valuable Newmarket event. He went on to land a decent Goodwood race but was then off for two months before disappointing on his final start.

"He's a top-class handicapper but at some stage we'll have to dabble in Listed or Group 3 company. The ground is important as he doesn't want it too quick, and he seems well suited by ten furlongs."

Moving to the three-year-olds, the first thing to note is how many from the stable are unraced. By my reckoning Stoute starts with around 45 well-bred colts and fillies who, for whatever reason, didn't see the track as juveniles.

Looking at the yard's statistics for last

season, the strike-rate for September was nine per cent and ten per cent in October, most untypical for the Stoute team. It's hard to escape the conclusion that the horses weren't fully on song during those months, which is when many of the better juveniles would be expected to appear. As a result, on public form, Stoute starts this season with fewer obvious three-year-old prospects than is normally the case. Have no fear, the winners are there – it's just a bit tougher to spot them.

"We have a lot of unraced three-year-olds this time around. We never got the two-year-olds sorted out, so we're in the dark about a lot of them – we've got some work to do.

"**Zumbi** won an Ascot maiden and then I thought he had the Acomb won but I don't know what happened – I'm not certain he got home over the seven furlongs at York because there's plenty of speed in his family. After the Acomb we gave him some nice entries but then he had a few little niggles and we put him away. I would imagine he'll have the Guineas entry, but the question is whether he'll stay a mile – he certainly won't get further than that.

Tales Of Grimm ran only once as a juvenile, winning a Newbury maiden, the form of which didn't work out too badly.

"That was a useful performance. We wanted to run him in the Horris Hill but he had a mucky scope. He's a colt I like and he'll have a Guineas entry but having had just the one run he'd need to take in a trial first."

Gospel Choir was a promising third in a Newmarket maiden that has produced several winners. That was over a mile and he finished in good style, going into plenty of notebooks.

"He picked up an injury in that race and hasn't been back very long, so we haven't cantered him yet. He's a nice sort."

Gospel Choir is out of Chorist, who was a top-class filly at ten furlongs, and is by Galileo, whose stock stay well. It will be interesting to see what route Stoute pursues with the colt.

"**Revered Citizen** isn't back yet and won't be out for a while. He threw a splint after his second at Newmarket in August, a race that has worked out pretty well."

Russelliana won her maiden over six furlongs at Leicester and then ran well to finish second in the Group 2 Cherry Hinton at Newmarket's July meeting. She ran less well in the Princess Margaret, not looking comfortable in the final stages.

"She was lame in a hind leg after the Ascot race and when she was taking a while to come right we pulled stumps and sent her back to her owner's farm for the winter. So her career to date is two good runs and mitigating circumstances for the failure.

"With her, and a lot of the others, they're so lightly raced we still have to sort them out in terms of trip, ability and so on, but she has already got some black type and we'll have to go for stakes races. I wouldn't give her a 1,000 Guineas entry as she was late back and I won't be rushing to get her ready early."

Dank finished second on her only start at two, racing quite freely, and at one stage looked as though she would bustle up the winner before being outpaced inside the final furlong. It was, however, an encouraging debut.

"She showed a lot of promise that day. She's an unfurnished filly who hasn't been back with us for very long, so we'll try to win a maiden and then map out a programme."

Ultrasonic won over six furlongs at Yarmouth on her debut and then improved, although perhaps not as much as might have been hoped for after she was fourth in the Listed Radley Stakes.

"She was a bit impetuous and was rather keen when we ran her at Newbury, so she'll be going sprinting."

Ladyship didn't manage to break her duck in two starts, finishing third in a Newmarket maiden and then second when odds-on at Windsor. Both races have produced a number of winners.

"She disappointed me a bit at Windsor, so we sent her home for the winter after that. I think it was just that she was growing – some mornings we were happy with her and on other occasions we weren't. I certainly wouldn't be writing her off but equally I can't be confident at this stage that she's a high-class filly. I do, however, like her.

Zumbi (left): maiden winner is not expected to stay beyond a mile

"We like **Shada** too. The form of her race worked out well, with the winner going on to land the May Hill and then the Fillies' Mile. We threatened to run her again but she had a few slight muscle problems caused by immaturity, so we put her away. She's a nice, big, scopey Galileo filly who gives me the impression she'll stay a mile and a quarter, and possibly a bit further.

"**Yanabeeaa** was second in a little race at Kempton and should win races, although I don't think she's a star. It's impossible to tell at this stage whether she's up to getting any black type."

Finally, a couple of three-year-olds who look sure to be decent handicappers, and possibly even a bit better than that.

Debating Society was placed in both of his starts at two, showing promise on each occasion. On his form he can't be rated too highly and he's one to look out for at a mile or a bit further.

Duke Of Firenze won over six furlongs at Carlisle in August, having previously finished third at Windsor. Bred to be suited by a mile, he too is one to look out for and, being by Pivotal, it may well be that soft ground would help his cause.

It is going to be fascinating to watch the progress of the Stoute horses this season. The suspicion is that the three-year-olds who raced at two will show themselves to be better than the bare form suggests and it is worth keeping a close eye on the yard's three-year-old handicappers. Among the unraced ones, it's a pound to a penny that a star or three will emerge. As for the older horses, such is the differential between the top-class races and the rest that their success will be the key factor in deciding just how good a year Stoute's team enjoys. Carlton House and Sea Moon are fancied to fly the flag with distinction at ten and 12 furlongs and after last season's blip it should be very much business as usual at Freemason Lodge. *[Colin Boag]*

STOUTE AND THE STATS

Much was made of Stoute's poor season in 2011 but signs during the previous term hinted that a dip was possible. After sending out 99 winners in 2009, the tally dropped to 73 the next year before last term's low of 53. The exploits of Workforce (Derby and Arc) and Harbinger (King George) covered up the stable's shortcomings in 2010 and the lack of emerging talent was cruelly exposed last year.

Having said that, the likes of Carlton House and Sea Moon didn't enjoy the best of luck in the Derby and St Leger and perhaps the yard's misfortunes would not have been highlighted as much had fortune favoured them – it would certainly have added significantly to Stoute's prize-money total.

Stoute is recognised as an expert handler of older horses and this is where his strike-rate is usually highest. But he has long been near the top of the British training tree and the bookmakers rarely take chances when it comes to his runners. Losses are usually made whether you're blindly backing juveniles, three-year-olds or the older horses. You have to find the best angles to make profit from Stoute's string and there are a few regarding all-age groups.

The Classic generation provide the majority of the Newmarket trainer's winners but the layers are all too aware of this and there aren't many profitable trends regarding his three-year-olds. He has vastly more three-year-old runners and winners at Sandown than at any other course and has an impressive level-stakes return.

Given Stoute's patient approach to training, he rarely overruns his juveniles and money can be made when he gives his youngsters the green light to run in Group company. His two-year-olds are seldom seen in the first half of the season and the period between August and October is most likely to reveal Classic potential for the following season.

The opposite is true of his older horses who are often ready to show their best in the early part of the campaign. April and May is often a good time to be following this age group as the strike-rates and level-stakes profits are decent. However, the elders struggled to make an impact in this period last term, which contributed to Stoute's below-par seasonal tally.

Fewer winners for Stoute has also harmed Ryan Moore's quest for another jockeys' championship, meaning this trainer-jockey combo hasn't been a great weapon for punters recently. Although Frankie Dettori didn't ride for the yard last term he is often successful when he is in the saddle for Stoute. Tom Eaves is another to look out for when riding Stoute's runners in the north, especially as he has high strike-rates at Redcar, Beverley and Carlisle – all his runners won at the latter two courses in 2011.

Stoute didn't appear to be bursting at the seams with young talent last term. so it may be at least another year before he is back to nearing the century mark for the season. *[Kevin Morley]*

seven in the Free Handicap as everything went wrong there."

Alainmaar is a six-year-old who has only run six times in his career but has shown he possesses loads of ability. Last season, having come back from a hairline fracture of a pastern, he ran only once, winning an Ascot Listed event in May and doing it in effortless style.

"He's very talented but also very delicate. He's back with us now and at this stage is moving exceptionally well. Although he's six, he has no miles on the clock and we're hopeful he retains his ability. Who knows, he might even progress with racing as that's something he's never had the chance to do. For the past two years we've tried to get him to the Hardwicke Stakes without succeeding and once again that's the target for the first half of the season. I'd like to run him before that in something like the John Porter or the Jockey Club at the Guineas meeting. He wants a mile and a half and as a Listed winner we need to aim at Group races."

"**Mijhaar** is back, having missed the second half of last season. I wanted to train him for the Cambridgeshire but I couldn't get him back to the same form at home that he was in earlier in the season – in the end it was quick ground at Newmarket and I'd have been in two minds about running him anyway. He's definitely one who doesn't want firm ground – he handles good and good to soft, but he doesn't want 'firm' anywhere in the going report.

"He's a nice horse who didn't get the mile and a half in the King Edward VII, but he ran a huge race to come out of the pack and chase Nathaniel home. It was another fine effort when he was second to Fulgur in a three-year-old handicap at Newmarket, the pair of them finishing well clear of the third. He's exciting and, off a mark of 102, is probably one we'll start out in a handicap and hopefully progress from there."

"The filly **Dark Promise** stays in training for her sporting owners. She's a late-maturing, big filly who improved steadily through her four-year-old career and it was a good performance when she won the Listed race at Newmarket. I think she'd only need to improve four or five pounds to be able to win a Group race. A mile is probably her trip, although she won over ten furlongs as a three-year-old, and we could start her off in

STOUTE AND THE STATS

Much was made of Stoute's poor season in 2011 but signs during the previous term hinted that a dip was possible. After sending out 99 winners in 2009, the tally dropped to 73 the next year before last term's low of 53. The exploits of Workforce (Derby and Arc) and Harbinger (King George) covered up the stable's shortcomings in 2010 and the lack of emerging talent was cruelly exposed last year.

Having said that, the likes of Carlton House and Sea Moon didn't enjoy the best of luck in the Derby and St Leger and perhaps the yard's misfortunes would not have been highlighted as much had fortune favoured them – it would certainly have added significantly to Stoute's prize-money total.

Stoute is recognised as an expert handler of older horses and this is where his strike-rate is usually highest. But he has long been near the top of the British training tree and the bookmakers rarely take chances when it comes to his runners. Losses are usually made whether you're blindly backing juveniles, three-year-olds or the older horses. You have to find the best angles to make profit from Stoute's string and there are a few regarding all-age groups.

The Classic generation provide the majority of the Newmarket trainer's winners but the layers are all too aware of this and there aren't many profitable trends regarding his three-year-olds. He has vastly more three-year-old runners and winners at Sandown than at any other course and has an impressive level-stakes return.

Given Stoute's patient approach to training, he rarely overruns his juveniles and money can be made when he gives his youngsters the green light to run in Group company. His two-year-olds are seldom seen in the first half of the season and the period between August and October is most likely to reveal Classic potential for the following season.

The opposite is true of his older horses who are often ready to show their best in the early part of the campaign. April and May is often a good time to be following this age group as the strike-rates and level-stakes profits are decent. However, the elders struggled to make an impact in this period last term, which contributed to Stoute's below-par seasonal tally.

Fewer winners for Stoute has also harmed Ryan Moore's quest for another jockeys' championship, meaning this trainer-jockey combo hasn't been a great weapon for punters recently. Although Frankie Dettori didn't ride for the yard last term he is often successful when he is in the saddle for Stoute. Tom Eaves is another to look out for when riding Stoute's runners in the north, especially as he has high strike-rates at Redcar, Beverley and Carlisle – all his runners won at the latter two courses in 2011.

Stoute didn't appear to be bursting at the seams with young talent last term. so it may be at least another year before he is back to nearing the century mark for the season.
[Kevin Morley]

SIR MICHAEL STOUTE
NEWMARKET, SUFFOLK

	No. of Hrs	Races Run	1st	2nd	3rd	Unpl	Per cent	£1 Level Stake
2-y-o	57	100	11	17	13	59	11.0	-47.72
3-y-o	53	178	29	34	34	80	16.3	-56.19
4-y-o+	23	88	13	12	3	60	14.8	-26.43
Totals	**133**	**366**	**53**	**63**	**50**	**199**	**14.5**	**-130.34**
2010	148	465	73	82	62	247	15.7	-25.66
2009	133	429	99	81	56	191	23.1	+1.99

BY MONTH

2-y-o	W-R	Per cent	£1 Level Stake	3-y-o	W-R	Per cent	£1 Level Stake
January	0-0	0.0	0.00	January	0-0	0.0	0.00
February	0-0	0.0	0.00	February	0-0	0.0	0.00
March	0-0	0.0	0.00	March	0-0	0.0	0.00
April	0-0	0.0	0.00	April	2-161	2.5	-8.75
May	0-0	0.0	0.00	May	9-332	7.3	-6.58
June	1-3	33.3	+1.50	June	2-34	5.9	-23.33
July	2-141	4.3	-6.64	July	9-332	7.3	+10.00
August	4-192	1.1	+0.92	August	3-31	9.7	-20.86
September	2-36	5.6-	27.50	September	3-231	3.0	-3.67
October	2-26	7.7	-14.00	October	1-7	14.3	-2.00
November	0-2	0.0	-2.00	November	0-1	0.0	-1.00
December	0-0	0.0	0.00	December	0-0	0.0	0.00

4-y-o+	W-R	Per cent	£1 Level Stake	Totals	W-R	Per cent	£1 Level Stake
January	0-0	0.0	0.00	January	0-0	0.0	0.00
February	0-0	0.0	0.00	February	0-0	0.0	0.00
March	0-0	0.0	0.00	March	0-0	0.0	0.00
April	2-8	25.0	-1.97	April	4-24	16.7	-10.72
May	1-16	6.3	-14.00	May	10-49	20.4	-20.58
June	2-121	6.7	+2.50	June	5-49	10.2	-19.33
July	3-28	10.7	-14.80	July	14-75	18.7	-11.44
August	3-112	7.3	+0.83	August	10-61	16.4	-19.11
September	1-81	2.5	-5.00	September	6-67	9.0	-36.17
October	1-4	25.0	+7.00	October	4-37	10.8	-9.00
November	0-1	0.0	-1.00	November	0-4	0.0	-2.00
December	0-0	0.0	0.00	December	0-0	0.0	0.00

DISTANCE

2-y-o	W-R	Per cent	£1 Level Stake	3-y-o	W-R	Per cent	£1 Level Stake
5f-6f	4-17	23.5	-0.33	5f-6f	1-6	16.7	-3.00
7f-8f	7-82	8.5	-46.39	7f-8f	11-69	15.9	-24.47
9f-13f	0-1	0.0	-1.00	9f-13f	17-98	17.3	-23.73
14f+	0-0	0.0	0.00	14f+	0-5	0.0	-5.00

4-y-o	W-R	Per cent	£1 Level Stake	Totals	W-R	Per cent	£1 Level Stake
5f-6f	2-13	15.4	-5.97	5f-6f	7-36	19.4	-9.30
7f-8f	3-17	17.6	-1.47	7f-8f	21-168	12.5	-72.33
9f-13f	8-50	16.0	-11.00	9f-13f	25-149	16.8	-35.73
14f+	0-8	0.0	-8.00	14f+	0-13	0.0	-13.00

TYPE OF RACE

	Non-Handicaps			Handicaps		
	W-R	Per cent	£1 Level Stake	W-R	Per cent	£1 Level Stake
2-y-o	11-9	711.3	-44.72	0-3	0.0	-3.00
3-y-o	18-103	17.	-27.86	11-7	514.7	-28.33
4-y-o+	7-42	16.7	-7.00	6-4	613.0	-9.47

RACE CLASS

	W-R	Per cent	£1 Level Stake
Class	19-67	13.4	-28.25
Class	26-44	13.6	-14.83
Class	34-36	11.1	-18.97
Class	47-81	8.6	-37.77
Class 5	26-13	419.4	-33.02
Class 6	1-4	25.0	+2.50
Class 7	0-0	0.0	0.00

FIRST TIME OUT

	W-R	Per cent	£1 Level Stake
2-y-o	4-57	7.0	-30.00
3-y-o	10-5	318.9	-18.71
4-y-o+	05-2	321.7	-2.47
Totals	19-13	314.3	-51.18

Notes

Talented team can help build on tremendous first season at the helm

LAST September, British racing lost one of its greats when Michael Jarvis died. He had retired from training the previous February after an illustrious 43-year career and handed the reins to his long-term assistant Roger Varian. The transition gave every appearance of being a seamless one and the new trainer's first Group 1 winner was landed just two days after Michael Jarvis's funeral.

Nahrain, appropriately owned by Sheikh Ahmed Al Maktoum, whose patronage had resurrected Jarvis's career when it had hit a tough spot in the 1990s, won the Prix de l'Opera at Longchamp's Arc meeting. That was the filly's fourth straight win of a career that had started only in mid-May and it came after a nerve-racking stewards' inquiry. After that, Varian sent her to the Filly & Mare Turf at the Breeders' Cup, where she ran a blinder, seemingly not quite getting home over the 1m3f trip and finishing a close second to Perfect Shirl.

"We were delighted with her run in the US," says Varian. "I think it was the eleventh furlong that beat her as she looked like the winner at ten furlongs, and at ten and a half. She won her first three races at a mile and

only stepped up to a mile and a quarter in the Opera. I wouldn't worry about dropping her back to a mile as she has lots of speed. We might start her there and then step up in the second half of the season when there are valuable races for her at ten furlongs.

"It's a long way away but ultimately the Filly & Mare could be the target again. We'd be looking to get her there fresh and well having just missed out last season."

Elzaam started out over seven furlongs in the Free Handicap but was then switched back to six furlongs for a sprinting campaign. He won a Listed race at Newbury in fine style and finished fourth in the Group 1 Golden Jubilee at Ascot. He didn't quite match that form in either the July Cup or the Betfred Sprint Cup and rounded off his season with fourth in an Ascot Group 3.

"He ran a cracker in the Golden Jubilee and I agree he didn't quite manage to repeat that form in the second half of the season. He was ready for a break come the end of the season and has had a good two months away at one of the Shadwell farms – he hasn't been back with me for very long but he's moving nicely at present.

"His run in the Golden Jubilee showed us that he isn't out of place in the Group 1 sprints but it's tough for three-year-old sprinters against the older horses, so I'm hoping he might just come into his own this year.

"If you watch replays of his races he was finishing strongly over six furlongs and I wouldn't rule out stepping him up to seven and riding him with restraint. I'd simply put a line through his previous attempt at

seven in the Free Handicap as everything went wrong there."

Alainmaar is a six-year-old who has only run six times in his career but has shown he possesses loads of ability. Last season, having come back from a hairline fracture of a pastern, he ran only once, winning an Ascot Listed event in May and doing it in effortless style.

"He's very talented but also very delicate. He's back with us now and at this stage is moving exceptionally well. Although he's six, he has no miles on the clock and we're hopeful he retains his ability. Who knows, he might even progress with racing as that's something he's never had the chance to do. For the past two years we've tried to get him to the Hardwicke Stakes without succeeding and once again that's the target for the first half of the season. I'd like to run him before that in something like the John Porter or the Jockey Club at the Guineas meeting. He wants a mile and a half and as a Listed winner we need to aim at Group races."

"**Mijhaar** is back, having missed the second half of last season. I wanted to train him for the Cambridgeshire but I couldn't get

him back to the same form at home that he was in earlier in the season – in the end it was quick ground at Newmarket and I'd have been in two minds about running him anyway. He's definitely one who doesn't want firm ground – he handles good and good to soft, but he doesn't want 'firm' anywhere in the going report.

"He's a nice horse who didn't get the mile and a half in the King Edward VII, but he ran a huge race to come out of the pack and chase Nathaniel home. It was another fine effort when he was second to Fulgur in a three-year-old handicap at Newmarket, the pair of them finishing well clear of the third. He's exciting and, off a mark of 102, is probably one we'll start out in a handicap and hopefully progress from there."

"The filly **Dark Promise** stays in training for her sporting owners. She's a late-maturing, big filly who improved steadily through her four-year-old career and it was a good performance when she won the Listed race at Newmarket. I think she'd only need to improve four or five pounds to be able to win a Group race. A mile is probably her trip, although she won over ten furlongs as a three-year-old, and we could start her off in

a race like the Darley Stakes, a nine-furlong fillies' race at the Guineas meeting.

"**Beyond Desire** *(above)* is back and she's a decent sprinting mare. I tried her over six furlongs last season but we're clear now that five furlongs is her trip. She's a Listed winner and has been placed in Group 2 and Group 3 company, so I'd dearly like to win at that level with her."

Among the three-year-olds, **Farraaj** did well as a juvenile, winning twice and finishing second in the Group 3 Somerville Tattersall, then third in the Grade 1 Breeders' Cup Juvenile Turf.

"He had a great year and ran a big race in America – I was especially pleased he handled the journey there like a mature horse. Before that I thought he ran a bit flat in the Somerville Tattersall and he's better than the bare form suggests. However, on the balance of his form so far, you'd have to say he's perhaps a few pounds below Classic grade over here, but as he took his trip to the States so well, we might think about something like the Italian Guineas. I'm confident he gets a mile."

Ektihaam won his maiden at Newbury and followed up in a decent conditions event at Doncaster, looking to be a really smart prospect. Connections obviously thought the same because his final start was in the Dewhurst. That didn't go to plan, however, and he ran disappointingly with things just not going his way.

"I can think of several reasons why he ran poorly: he'd won his previous races very easily, so was perhaps not man enough for the Dewhurst at that stage of his career, and the fast ground made it more of a test for him. When the ground is quick in those good Newmarket backend two-year-old races then a horse needs to be battle-hardened to cope with it. He got himself into the race at halfway but then running downhill he got tightened up, and once his winning chance had gone Richard Hills was kind to him. With the benefit of hindsight I probably threw him in at the deep end.

"I think he's quite a good horse, both on what he has showed in his races and on what he does at home, and he has done well over the winter. We still have high hopes for him and I believe he needs a mile now and might even get ten furlongs. He'll have a 2,000 Guineas entry and if he was training well then we'd head for a trial.

"**Firdaws** is a nice filly who ran a good race in the Fillies' Mile, finishing third – that was particularly pleasing as she was relatively inexperienced. She's moving very well at present and she's one we're quite excited about. My immediate reaction after Newmarket was that she wasn't a Guineas filly – her dam and grand-dam were both Oaks winners – but we'll see how she's going in her fast work nearer the time. If she's going well, then who knows. The alternative would be to start her out in an Oaks trial over ten furlongs. She'll certainly be in all the big races."

Aljamaaheer is one of those hard-to-weigh-up backend maiden winners. He won over six furlongs at Yarmouth and the second subsequently won twice on the all-weather.

"I didn't think it was a great race at the time but he won exceptionally well having shown us a fair bit at home beforehand. The problem is that when a horse wins a maiden like that you don't quite know where you are with him. He's rated 88 and we'll see how he's working as we get nearer to the start of the turf season. We could go for a handicap or, if he's going well, maybe for a trial. I like him.

"**Oojooba** won really well on bad ground at Haydock – she has a high knee action and will always want some give underfoot. When she ran next, in the Listed Montrose Stakes at Newmarket, the ground was a bit quick and she'd started to go in her coat, so I'm inclined to disregard that run. She's a filly we like and she's only off a mark of 82, so I think she'll probably start off down the handicap route. She seems sure to get ten furlongs and I wouldn't know whether she'd get a mile and a half, but we'll always be looking for some cut in the ground.

"**Mazeydd** won on the same Haydock card as Oojooba and like her will always want cut in the ground – he's a half-brother to Mijhaar and like him he tends to hit the ground pretty hard. Unfortunately, he's had a little bit of a setback and won't be out until the summer.

"**Cameron Highland** showed definite promise at Nottingham, travelling well through the race and just getting tired towards the end. He was a little bit weak all of last season, but he's done well physically over the winter and is moving well. He's a maiden we really like but it's hard to know how far he'll progress.

"**Shaleek** ran well on both of her starts, finishing a close second on each occasion. I thought she ran a huge race on her debut, coming from mid field and being ahead a stride after the line. She wasn't quite as good on her second outing, again at Yarmouth, but there was a gale blowing across the track, and as two-year-old fillies they were getting blown about a bit. I would hope she can break her maiden, probably over seven furlongs, and we'll take it from there.

"**Frasers Hill** is a lovely colt but he had surgery to fix a bout of colic, so he's out for the first half of the season. It's frustrating because I like him, but we're going to have to be patient. He's a horse with potential.

"**Henry Allingham** showed promise on his only start, finishing fourth over six furlongs in a Doncaster backend maiden. He'll possibly start out over seven furlongs and I hope he'll give his syndicate owners plenty of fun. He should win races.

"**Go Dutch** was a late foal and he had a rough spring as he wasn't the healthiest horse in the yard, so we were able to give him only three starts. He won nicely at Brighton and we considered going for a nursery off 83 but in the end opted to put him away. He's not a big colt but he has strengthened over the winter and is owned by a syndicate who had horses with Michael for a long time. He'll hopefully give them some fun over the summer, probably in three-year-old handicaps at around a mile."

Varian made a great start to his training career last season and, with continued patronage from Michael Jarvis's established owners, he starts the new season with a solid team of older horses and some promising three-year-old talent. It's hard to imagine that 2012 will be anything other than another progressive year from the Kremlin House team. *[Colin Boag]*

ROGER VARIAN
NEWMARKET, SUFFOLK

	No. of Hrs	Races Run	1st	2nd	3rd	Unpl	Per cent	£1 Level Stake
2-y-o	34	67	13	11	6	37	19.4	+2.71
3-y-o	43	160	34	20	11	95	21.3	+62.36
4-y-o+	15	45	6	4	8	27	13.3	-8.13
Totals	92	272	53	35	25	159	19.5	+56.94
2010	0+							
2009	0							

BY MONTH

2-y-o	W-R	Per cent	£1 Level Stake	3-y-o	W-R	Per cent	£1 Level Stake
January	0-0	0.0	0.00	January	0-0	0.0	0.00
February	0-0	0.0	0.00	February	0-0	0.0	0.00
March	0-0	0.0	0.00	March	0-0	0.0	0.00
April	0-0	0.0	0.00	April	3-13	23.1	+40.95
May	0-1	0.0	-1.00	May	7-29	24.1	+7.38
June	0-0	0.0	0.00	June	9-28	32.1	+20.63
July	2-6	33.3	+9.00	July	5-27	18.5	-7.83
August	2-10	20.0	-3.63	August	3-22	13.6	-15.69
September	7-15	46.7	+22.08	September	3-23	13.0	-11.42
October	1-26	3.8	-23.75	October	4-16	25.0	+30.33
November	1-9	11.1	0.00	November	0-1	0.0	-1.00
December	0-0	0.0	0.00	December	0-1	0.0	-1.00

4-y-o+	W-R	Per cent	£1 Level Stake	Totals	W-R	Per cent	£1 Level Stake
January	0-0	0.0	0.00	January	0-0	0.0	0.00
February	0-0	0.0	0.00	February	0-0	0.0	0.00
March	0-0	0.0	0.00	March	0-0	0.0	0.00
April	1-3	33.3	+8.00	April	4-16	25.0	+48.95
May	3-8	37.5	+6.88	May	10-38	26.3	+13.26
June	1-6	16.7	0.00	June	10-34	29.4	+20.63
July	0-9	0.0	-9.00	July	7-42	16.7	-7.83
August	0-4	0.0	-4.00	August	5-36	13.9	-23.32
September	1-9	11.1	-4.00	September	11-47	23.4	-6.66
October	0-3	0.0	-3.00	October	5-45	11.1	+3.58
November	0-3	0.0	-3.00	November	1-1	37.7	-4.00
December	0-0	0.0	0.00	December	0-1	0.0	-1.00

DISTANCE

2-y-o	W-R	Per cent	£1 Level Stake	3-y-o	W-R	Per cent	£1 Level Stake
5f-6f	4-20	20.0	-11.20	5f-6f	5-24	20.8	+28.56
7f-8f	9-47	19.1	+13.91	7f-8f	13-54	24.1	+40.64
9f-13f	0-0	0.0	0.00	9f-13f	15-74	20.3	-0.75
14f+	0-0	0.0	0.00	14f+	1-8	12.5	-6.09

4-y-o	W-R	Per cent	£1 Level Stake	Totals	W-R	Per cent	£1 Level Stake
5f-6f	0-6	0.0	-6.00	5f-6f	9-50	18.0	+11.36
7f-8f	3-11	27.3	+11.00	7f-8f	25-112	22.3	+65.55
9f-13f	3-28	10.7	-13.13	9f-13f	18-102	17.6	-13.88
14f+	0-0	0.0	0.00	14f+	1-8	12.5	-6.09

TYPE OF RACE

Non-Handicaps	W-R	Per cent	£1 Level Stake	Handicaps	W-R	Per cent	£1 Level Stake
2-y-o	12-63	19.0	+2.96	2-y-o	1-4	25.0	-0.25
3-y-o	18-78	23.1	+37.08	3-y-o	16-82	19.5	+25.28
4-y-o+	3-31	9.7	-9.00	4-y-o+	3-14	21.4	+10.50

RACE CLASS / FIRST TIME OUT

RACE CLASS	W-R	Per cent	£1 Level Stake	FIRST TIME OUT	W-R	Per cent	£1 Level Stake
Class 1	5-46	10.9	-27.63	2-y-o	4-34	11.8	-7.25
Class 2	5-31	16.1	+22.03	3-y-o	8-43	18.6	+28.35
Class 3	6-27	22.2	-2.73	4-y-o+	5-15	33.3	+16.88
Class 4	11-56	19.6	+60.25				
Class 5	22-104	21.2	-6.88	Totals	17-92	18.5	+37.98
Class 6	4-8	50.0	+11.90				
Class 7	0-0	0.0	0.00				

Notes

VARIAN AND THE STATS

2011 was the year Varian became a trainer in his own right. In most cases it is difficult to draw conclusions on the evidence of just one season with regards to any trends that may be useful to punters but it might prove difference in this instance. Varian took over from the late Michael Jarvis as the main man at Kremlin House after serving as his assistant and many of the patterns formed by Jarvis have been maintained by his successor.

For example, between 2008 and 2010, it was Jarvis's three-year-olds who provided the biggest benefit for backers. The Classic generation provided more than 60 per cent of his winners during this three-year period, striking at an impressive 24 per cent while returning a level-stake profit of 51.48pt. These figures bear a striking resemblance to those posted by Varian last season and it's likely we'll see something similar this term.

Jarvis's runners seemed to be massively underrated in three-year-old maidens, proven by the big profits posted in this area, and that trend carried over into Varian's tenure. The difference between them with this particular age group came in handicaps – Jarvis was given massive respect in handicaps by the layers, hence the level-stakes loss, whereas Varian posted a big profit. This could be a case of first-season syndrome where the bookies have not guarded themselves sufficiently and it will be interesting to see how they approach Varian's unexposed three-year-old handicappers this time.

Similarly to Jarvis, Varian had his string forward for the season's early exchanges in 2011. The figures posted in the period of April to June were his most impressive, while September was also a good month for Varian – another period which was usually fruitful for Jarvis.

Haydock was a track where Jarvis was best followed and, sure enough, Varian followed suit last season with eight winners from 23 runners at the Lancashire venue for a level-stakes profit of 22.71pt.

The biggest difference between the two trainers is the distance over which it proved most profitable to follow their runners. Under Jarvis the horses were best backed in races beyond 1m up to 1m4f while in Varian's debut season it was in races over any trip up to 1m2f.

Neil Callan assumed the role of stable jockey at Kremlin House last term, replacing the excellent Philip Robinson, who enjoyed a superb partnership with Jarvis. Callan's mounts provided a level-stake profit, although much of that was down to a 50-1 winning debutant in April and he may be hard pushed to repeat the trend given the number of rides he will have. The promising Andrea Atzeni was a useful weapon for the yard last term and the booking of William Buick should be noted, with his four rides for Varian providing three winners.

The one thing missing from Varian's achievements last term was a Group winner in Britain. He should have a good chance of accomplishing that in 2012, especially if he has a good team of juveniles as he looks reasonably strong in the three-year-old and older-horse departments. *[Kevin Morley]*

Straight from the trainers – ten to keep on your side throughout the season

Following his interviews with the leading British trainers, **Colin Boag** picks his standout ten to follow

Cravat Mark Johnston

At first glance Cravat is an exposed three-year-old, having run 12 times at two. However, he won three times and is expected to improve as he is stepped up in trip. As he apparently loves his racing he'll have every chance to show his best.

Dam Beautiful Kevin Ryan

Life can be tough for three-year-old sprinters, but Ryan is a master with them. Dam Beautiful missed the second half of last season with a minor problem but that isn't always a disadvantage. The trainer rates her highly and she is expected to come on a ton from three to four.

Estrela (right) Roger Charlton

An archetypal 'could be anything' three-year-old. She won her maiden on her last of two starts, a maiden fillies' event at Newbury. Hardly anything has run from that race, so it's impossible to weigh up the form. However, she won it as she liked, her trainer rates her and she's a half-sister to six winners.

Fallen For You John Gosden

Has high-class two-year-old form but is thought to be better than she showed last season. That's good enough for me and I expect Fallen For You to do well in the top French races.

Fiorente Sir Michael Stoute

Things didn't go Fiorente's way last season, as they didn't in general for the Stoute stable. However, the master trainer hasn't lost confidence in this four-year-old colt and I expect him to do well in decent contests over a mile and a half this season.

Mijhaar Roger Varian

Starts this season from a mark of 103 and I'd expect him to land a decent handicap before going on to better things, probably at a mile and a quarter. It wouldn't be the biggest surprise if he showed dramatic improvement as a four-year-old.

Noble Mission Sir Henry Cecil

With no prizes for including Frankel in my list, here's his brother instead. Don't worry about the fact that he got beaten at Yarmouth – if you have read Cecil's comments on the earlier pages you will have noted that the trainer isn't overly-concerned about that defeat. Godolphin rate the winner of that contest and I reckon that little race, worth less than three grand, was red-hot.

Sadeek's Song Mahmood Al Zarooni

In among the depths of Godolphin talent,

Sadeek's Song is a four-year-old who is thought capable of doing better than we've seen so far – quite possibly a lot better. He won a conditions race at Leicester on his final start and the runner-up went on to win in Listed company in France. Interesting.

Sandusky Mahmood Al Zarooni

In a yard stacked full of Pattern-race performers, Sandusky is a handicapper who won his latest start off a modest mark of 81. However, it is clear that he's thought appreciably better than that. He's sure to be placed well this season.

Shantaram John Gosden

Another in the 'could be anything' category. Just beaten at Sandown on his only start, he looks sure to be competitive in decent conditions races at around a mile and a half. He'd even get further if his connections wanted him to.

Camelot has what it takes to deliver another Derby success for Ireland

Johnny Ward on what we can expect from the Irish scene in the coming months

HOPES are strong in Ireland that we can recapture the Epsom Derby crown in 2012, at which point a superstar might have fully emerged.

Sea The Stars' rampant performance in the 2009 edition and New Approach's win the previous year apart, no Irish-trained Derby winner has been celebrated since 2002. It would thus be timely were the Coolmore-Ballydoyle team to get back into the winners' circle at Epsom exactly a decade since High Chaparral beat stablemate Hawk Wing.

A year earlier, Galileo had won the great mile-and-a-half challenge for Aidan O'Brien. Given the yard's access to such stallions as his father Sadler's Wells and, of course, Galileo himself and Montjeu, it is unusual that ten years is on the verge of going by without an O'Brien-trained victor.

They have had bad luck with Horatio Nelson and, of course, the long-time favourite St Nicholas Abbey, who never made it to Epsom at three. Quite a few colts have been placed in the race for Ballydoyle at longish odds down the years and they are due a winning turn.

The death of Sadler's Wells in 2011 was something to be celebrated rather than mourned: he had lived to a huge age and his legacy in racing is incredible. Only five times in the 23 years in which Sadler's Wells has had three-year-olds has one of his descendants failed to finish first or second in the Derby.

In **Camelot**, who is a grandson of Sadler's Wells, O'Brien may have the artillery to strike again. Joseph O'Brien, who rode the Montjeu-bred in the Racing Post Trophy in the manner of a piece of work, has spoken of how the colt has come on since then and wintered well. Camelot, the teenager says, has everything: a lot of speed and a huge amount of class. What is tantalising is that it is impossible to say just how good he is – and at what point his limitations will become apparent.

Although he did it tidily, the maiden he won at Leopardstown was ordinary and you could pick holes in the bare detail of his Doncaster success: runner-up Zip Top had been beaten further again in a Newmarket Group 3 before the Racing Post Trophy.

It is all about the manner of victory that sees Camelot trade at around 3-1 for the 2,000 Guineas and generally shorter for the Derby. He has arguably achieved less than St Nicholas Abbey had at this stage of his career. When St Nick was sent off evens for the Guineas, he lacked the speed needed and one wonders whether things will happen too quickly for Camelot, whose sire is far more capable of getting middle-distance horses.

Concrete plans for Camelot have not been publicly revealed but the markets suggest both the Newmarket Guineas and Epsom are on his itinerary. Certainly his dominance of both ante-post lists owes much to a general paucity of two-year-olds who even threatened to set the world alight in 2011.

Indeed, O'Brien also trains the Guineas second favourite **Nephrite**, third favourite **Power** and a total of 11 Guineas entries. A remarkably consistent sort who ran six times

between May and October last year, Power has rather escaped the public imagination as he has never been other than workmanlike in victory and was beaten in what looked a rather average Dewhurst.

The Dewhurst winner Parish Hall was crediting Jim Bolger with an incredible fourth win in that Group 1 since 2006. But, being out of a Montjeu mare, the prospects of him having the pace for the Guineas seem remote.

That brings us to the Killavullan, which in general has not had a major Classic bearing, although Footstepsinthesand won it en route to Newmarket glory in 2005. Nephrite's ready success last autumn over **Born To Sea** must be treated with caution as the runner-up tore a muscle in his hindquarters.

The three-parts brother to Sea The Stars, generally around the same price as Power, had shown immense precociousness previously to win a Curragh Group 3 on his debut. Oxx is loath to ask much in the early stages of a horse's career and, given his pedigree, looks and raw speed, Born To Sea definitely remains in the Guineas picture.

Another Oxx colt, **Akeed Mofeed**,

disappointed slightly in his final 2011 race but also had excuses with the ground. The Currabeg trainer has some exciting three-year-old prospects this season and another one to remember is **Takar**, who may have escaped the attention of many, although he is not entered in the Guineas.

Takar prompted Oxx to declare a tongue-strap on just his second start, which would indicate he is not straightforward. Even so, the manner of his eight-length win in a Leopardstown maiden was impressive and this strong traveller looks primed to represent Oratorio with distinction in 2012.

Many of the horses at the top of the bookies' Guineas lists are there for the Derby too, reflecting a smudged picture. Although it would be a surprise if Camelot were not favourite come Derby day, his stablemate **Imperial Monarch** is another worthy of note. The Galileo colt was a tidy winner of a 19-runner Curragh maiden on his debut. From a really smart family, Imperial Monarch's three-parts-brother (by Sadler's Wells) The Great Gatsby was worn down only near the wire in the 2003 Derby.

The form has taken a knock or two since

but Imperial Monarch is bred to thrive at three and is an interesting type. He will presumably go the Galileo (Ballysax-Derrinstown) Leopardstown route to Epsom.

Much of the talk between now and the Classics will be about distances. Will such-and-such a horse be better over a mile or a mile and a half? The same debate reigns regarding Ireland's precicious juvenile fillies of 2011, principally Maybe and Wading, and the challenge for Aidan O'Brien is to ascertain which races best suit his high-class pair and of course what their 2012 schedule entails from spring to autumn.

Maybe, general 7-2 favourite for the 1,000 Guineas, was impossible not to like in 2011. Another daughter of Galileo, she nevertheless had the speed to win a high-class six-furlong maiden on fast ground on her debut by four and a half lengths. A Galileo winning over that trip so impressively is most unusual and she duly won her next four starts (all over seven furlongs), culminating in a deceptively easy Moyglare victory in August.

Maybe's speed owes much to her mother Sumora, a Danehill filly who was a Pattern-class sprinter and progressed from two to three. Maybe could still get the Oaks trip, yet it seems more likely that she will be best over a mile to a mile and a quarter. It is quite possible that she has been doing just enough in her races in general, and she was unquestionably the outstanding juvenile filly of 2011.

It is because of the headlines Maybe generated that **Wading** did not get hyped as much. Yet consider this: Wading, who had made her debut less than a month previously, achieved a higher RPR when running away with the Rockfel Stakes in October at Newmarket than Maybe did in any of her five outings.

Wading had previously won a Dundalk maiden and there is no telling how far she can go. Her mother Cherry Hinton never won in five starts but was Group 3- and Listed-placed. It is also noteworthy that Cherry Hinton was out of Urban Sea, so Wading certainly has credentials for the Oaks as well.

What was most impressive was the way she picked up for a squeeze at Newmarket and put the race beyond doubt in a few strides. She seems straighforward for a

Montjeu and it is understandable that she is ahead of Maybe in the Oaks betting.

And what of the gorgeously bred **Up**? Dutch Art's half-sister (by Galileo – who else?) looked classy in winning her maiden and was unlucky not to be placed in the Juvenile Fillies' Turf at Churchill Downs. She has any amount of improving to do.

Ireland ought to be more than adequately represented by older horses in 2012, with O'Brien particularly dominant. **So You Think** is to return to Ballydoyle after the Dubai World Cup with a view to subsequently retiring to Coolmore Stud in Australia.

Clearly no superstar, he nevertheless has been a model of reliability at around ten furlongs to a mile and a half and will have plenty of the usual targets this year. **St Nicholas Abbey** showed at Churchill Downs by winning the Breeders' Cup Turf what he can achieve and will provide considerable back-up.

Ballydoyle is likely to have a strong team of older horses this year, including **Await The Dawn**, **Treasure Beach** and **Memphis Tennessee**. The last-named could yet develop into a useful stayer, a bracket in which the Irish are in good shape. **Fame And Glory's** smooth Ascot Gold Cup win last year and his reassuring success back at the track in October mark him out as the stayer to beat this term, yet there is a younger foe lurking. **Saddler's Rock** *(above, left)* produced a high-class performance to win the Doncaster Cup on his final start last season and the way he made light of Opinion Poll suggests he could be a major challenger to Fame And Glory in the Gold Cup. With **Rite Of Passage** due to return too, the signs suggest this cup will be returning to Ireland.

'Wading, who had made her debut less than a month previously, achieved a higher RPR when running away with the Rockfel Stakes in October at Newmarket than Maybe did in any of her five outings'

O'Brien's squadron packed with a quality impossible to ignore

Johnny Ward with ten Irish-trained horses who look potential big players in this year's competition

Camelot Aidan O'Brien

Strong favourite for both the Guineas and Derby, the son of Montjeu will be on nearly every Ten to Follow list. We should not get carried away with the bare form of the two races he has won but the vibes from the yard have always been strong about Camelot and the fact that some good juveniles have been unable to get him off the bridle suggests he ought to have a Classic in him in 2012. He is expected to start off in the Guineas and, if that is the case, Ballydoyle look certain to ensure the gallop to be much stronger than the one St Nicholas Abbey struggled behind in 2010.

Imperial Monarch Aidan O'Brien

Like Camelot, Imperial Monarch may be more about potential than bare achievement. The Curragh maiden he won in September could have been expected to work out better, but the ease with which the debutant sauntered through the race, particularly given that he is bred to improve as a three-year-old, was eyecatching. Imperial Monarch couold take in the Derrinstown and possibly the Ballysax en route to Epsom, just like his three-parts-brother The Great Gatsby in 2003. If he does not quite step up to that level, there will be plenty of alternatives in order for him to clock up points in the competition.

Power Aidan O'Brien

This colt was a revelation in 2011, running six times and winning four of those starts. When he was beaten (narrowly), there were excuses and the son of Oasis Dream also proved his ability to go on different types of terrain. It was fast ground when he won the Marble Hill, good at Royal Ascot and yielding to soft at the Curragh on National Stakes day, when he faced a demanding headwind. His attitude is endearing and, even if he is not good enough to win the Newmarket Guineas, he should win more Group races in 2012.

Nephrite Aidan O'Brien

Being by Pivotal, Nephrite was surprisingly easy to back on his Curragh debut when the ground was particularly testing for two-year-olds. However, he cantered through the race and won in the manner of a class act. When pitched into combat against Born To Sea in the Kilavullan, the half-brother to Golden Jubilee winner Cape Of Good Hope made light work of his more exalted rival, leaving him for dead and winning snugly. Nephrite's ability to handle ease in the ground should stand him in good stead at some stage during this season but he ought to be fine on better ground and is clearly already Group class.

Famous Name Dermot Weld

This horse will probably never win a Group 1 but he has been able to take some soft Group 2s and Group 3s down the years,

registering a remarkable 14 career successes – and there are more to come. Now a seven-year-old, he has won more than £1m in prize-money and seems sure to add more this season. Dermot Weld has generally placed him to excellent effect and he would be a wise pick.

Emulous *(above)* Dermot Weld

Dermot Weld and Pat Smullen believed the best was to come from Emulous when she won the Equestrian Stakes at the Curragh in May. By Dansili, like Famous Name, Khalid Abdullah's five-year-old landed another Group 3 (at Fairyhouse) before comfortably taking the Matron Stakes to record a Group 1 success by an impressive three lengths. That victory suggested Emulous has a rare ability to travel and cruise through strongly run mile races. She ought to get further and can make a major impact in 2012, with the Matron an obvious target later on.

Saddler's Rock John Oxx

Saddler's Rock emerged as a stayer of virtually unlimited potential when winning the Doncaster Cup last September at the tender age of three and having made his debut only in May. The manner of how he went about his business suggested the Gold Cup trip at Royal Ascot will improve him, as John Oxx ekes out more progress with experience. Staying races in Ireland such as the Vintage Crop at Navan and the Saval Beg at Leopardstown, as well as the Irish Leger and Gold Cup, would be obvious targets. It would be no surprise if he usurped Fame And Glory in the staying division this year.

Treasure Beach Aidan O'Brien

Given that So You Think is reportedly to return to Australia for stud duties, that leaves a gap for one of his middle-distance juniors from Ballydoyle. Quite whether Treasure Beach will make a serious mark at Group 1 level this season remains to be seen but the fact that he remains in training is a pointer to plans for 2012. He will likely be kept busy and that could include trips to America.

Maybe Aidan O'Brien

Europe's leading juvenile filly in 2011, being by Galileo, ought to give Aidan O'Brien and his bosses a dilemma of a nice type this year: which races to avoid? She should have the pace for the Guineas. Whether she gets the Oaks trip remains to be seen, but there are loads of targets for this likeable filly.

Wading Aidan O'Brien

This daughter of Montjeu seems to have an admirable temperament and it will be fascinating to see what trip she proves best over in 2012. It is likely she will develop into an Oaks filly and could also go for the Yorkshire Oaks. She should pay her way for Ten to Follow players.

Plethora of big names have the credentials to challenge for top honours

Scott Burton assesses the strength in depth France will bring to the scene this season

WHILE the major French yards have traditionally eschewed top-level competition for many of their future stars at two, leaving most of the major questions to be posed at the beginning of a horse's three-year-old career, last season might have bucked the trend somewhat.

Dabirsim emerged as a genuine Group 1 juvenile from the previously unheralded stable of Christophe Ferland. Richard Gibson's former assistant handled all the pressure with the consummate air of a man going places, a pressure that won't have in any way decreased with owner Simon Springer's decision to put up Frankie Dettori for the ride in the Prix Morny and the Prix Jean-Luc Lagardere.

In becoming the first horse since Arazi to do that double, he poses an intriguing question – can the son of Japanese sire Hat Trick progress into a Classic-winning three-year-old?

Ferland has opted for the home comforts of Longchamp at which to answer that question, with the promise of a trip to Britain later in the season if all goes well.

Ferland is based away from the goldfish bowl of Chantilly down near Bordeaux, and the traditional king of the south-west Jean-Claude Rouget could also be due a revival after a somewhat subdued 2011 by his standards.

Abtaal demolished a smart field in the

Group 3 Prix Thomas Bryon, which included subsequent Group 1 winner French Fifteen, and could be the star of Rouget's squad.

Among a slew of once- and twice-raced colts, Rouget picked out Deauville winner **Beauvoir** among his favourites in a recent interview, while Breeders' Cup also-ran **Dear Lavinia** remains exciting on the distaff side.

In addition, there is hope that the Aga Khan's Prix du Jockey Club third **Baraan** can return from an extended spell on the sidelines to fight for middle-distance honours at four.

Freddy Head begins the post-Goldikova era well armed to plunder more Group 1 prizes, not least with little sister **Galikova**. The Prix Vermeille heroine appeared to have had one too many hard races in the Arc but remains an exciting flagbearer for Alain and Gerard Wertheimer.

The famous blue and white silks will also be carried aboard Head's primary Classic hopefuls. **Sofast** twice came out on the wrong side of the argument against Dabirsim last term, but the Rock Of Gibraltar colt will have an early chance to redress the balance in the Prix Fontainebleau.

Zantenda was a disappointing favourite in the Prix Marcel Boussac in October but Head retains plenty of faith in the Prix d'Aumale winner and will aim her at the Poule d'Essai des Pouliches rather than the 1,000 Guineas.

Joining Galikova at the top table among the older horses are Prix Maurice de Gheest winner **Moonlight Cloud** and **Havant**, unsighted since finishing down the field in last year's Oaks for Sir Michael Stoute.

Criquette Head-Maarek will be something of a wild card this Classic season, having had most of last year wiped out by a persistent virus.

Of the few two-year-olds to get to the track, Khalid Abdullah's **Preferential** showed class and determination to win her maiden at Saint-Cloud over a mile and should stay further.

The Juddmonte colours will also be followed with interest aboard the unraced **Postale**, who is described by her trainer as "physically magnificent".

Head-Maarek ranks alongside Sir Henry Cecil in her handling of Classic fillies, and another Chantilly trainer who could have an exciting crop of females is Robert Collet.

Last season's revelation was **Immortal Verse**, who is scheduled to make her seasonal bow at the scene of her first Group 1 triumph at Royal Ascot. Last seen in Europe when failing to get to grips with Frankel off the back of an interrupted preparation, the daughter of Pivotal has a devastating turn of foot when at her best.

The same owner's **Wizz Kid** could be a player in the sprint division, having been relatively lightly campaigned at three.

Perhaps most exciting of all is the three-year-old Whipper filly **Topeka**, who rattled off four successes last autumn in good style.

Sporting the chocolate and white hoops of Gerry Oldham made famous by the great Sagaro, Topeka will start off in the Prix Imprudence, after which Collet will choose between Newmarket and Longchamp for her Guineas assignment.

Three more Chantilly yards that know all about Classic success can each boast at least one hopeful based on their highly promising juvenile careers.

Jean-Marie Beguigne sent out Lawman to land the 2007 Prix du Jockey Club and now trains the next generation of the family in the shape of Prix de Conde winner **Loi**, a possible for Epsom according to his trainer.

Pascal Bary will also be looking to build on Group 3 success with Prix des Reservoirs heroine **Boldogsag**, who was unbeaten in three starts last season.

Beauty Parlour won a pair of Saint-Cloud conditions races by a combined total of 11½ lengths without being asked a serious question by Christophe Soumillon, and trainer Elie Lellouche must be hopeful she can follow the example of Aquarelliste and Bright Sky onto the Classic roll of honour for the Wildenstein family.

Finally to the two greatest French trainers of their generation, and the two hardest to get a handle on at this early stage of the year.

Both Andre Fabre and his great rival Alain de Royer-Dupre enter the season stocked with any number of homebred three-year-olds, many of whom didn't reach the track at all in 2011.

The problem of unearthing the best among them is illustrated by the fact that Fabre is responsible for 48 of the initial 221 entries in the Prix de Diane.

Of the master trainer's Classic hopefuls to race last year, **Petite Noblesse** began to make a dent in the €240,000 she cost Coolmore with a smooth success on her only start at Deauville in July.

Dual Classic winner **Golden Lilac** returns with a clean bill of heath after her brilliant 2011 was cut short by a virus and is reported to be in great shape by owner Dietrich von Boetticher.

One with a lower profile who could make up into a very smart four-year-old over middle distances is **King Of Arnor**, who couldn't cope with Reliable Man in the Prix Niel but has always looked more of a long-term project.

Reliable Man will be a powerful presence for Royer-Dupre as well, albeit that it now seems established that the son of Dalakhani doesn't operate on firm going. He was extremely impressive in the Jockey Club and the Niel and will contest top honours as his owners seek to establish his credentials as a stallion prospect.

Among the green-clad army from the Aga Khan, Royer-Dupre can call on last season's Arc runner-up **Shareta**, who can't have it fast enough, while among the Classic generation last year's maiden winners Maradini and Sagawara were no doubt just the tip of the iceberg.

With targets in Britain Dabirsim is impossible to leave out of calculations

Scott Burton with his ten to keep on eye on – some trained in France and some elsewhere

G IVEN the locations of the bonus races in the Ten to Follow competition, an over-reliance on French-trained horses might not seem the best tactic. I have tried to include horses who might have a chance of venturing beyond the home comforts of Longchamp and Chantilly, as well as a few British and Irish-trained entrants who have caught the eye from this side of La Manche.

Cirrus Des Aigles
Corine Barande-Barbe

Cirrus Des Aigles ended 2011 as officially the top-rated horse in France and the six-year-old could be a potential points machine in the Ten to Follow.

Despite an early-season jaunt to Dubai, the tough and classy son of Even Top is expected to turn out for plenty of the summer and autumn main events. Owing to French disdain for geldings in Group 1s, opportunities are limited at home and races like the Prince of Wales's Stakes, Eclipse, King George and Juddmonte International could come on to the radar for trainer Corine Barande-Barbe before a possible defence in the Qipco Champion Stakes at Ascot.

Dabirsim Christophe Ferland

Even despite the decision of Christophe Ferland to go down the French Guineas route, Dabirsim remains impossible to keep off the list. The manner in which the joint European champion two-year-old finished in the Prix Jean-Luc Lagardere last season is hard to shake from the memory.

What's more, Ferland is committed to coming to Britain sooner rather than later with the son of Hat Trick in order to further establish his stallion credentials, which considerably lessens the risk of his inclusion.

He was all muscle and power last season and, even if Dabirsim fails at the highest level over Classic distances, the Morny winner would be a fascinating addition in the second half of the season if reverting to sprinting.

Loi Jean-Marie Beguigne

Loi went into winter quarters following an impressive display in the Group 3 Prix de Conde at Longchamp, with Classic-winning trainer Jean-Marie Beguigne teasing the press with the notion that the strong galloper might be more of an Epsom horse than one for Chantilly on the first weekend in June.

The son of Lawman is reported to have wintered well and will start in the Prix la Force followed by the Prix Greffulhe at Saint-Cloud (won last season by Pour Moi). Those two races will tell us a lot and connections will also look at the relative strengths of the two Derbies before a target is decided.

With the likely assistance of Beguigne's long-time ally Olivier Peslier, Loi can take the rise in class in his stride.

Reliable Man Alain de Royer-Dupre

Reliable Man can prove himself one of the better winners in recent editions of the Prix du Jockey Club, with trainer Alain de Royer-Dupre likely to target the biggest races from a mile and a quarter to a mile and a half in Europe with the son of Dalakhani.

While a second crack at the Arc is the long-term goal (assuming there is no repeat of last season's quick ground), it is worth noting his international syndicate of owners is headed by the anglophile Swedes Sven and Carina Hanson, who are not wholly shackled by French loyalty to Longchamp on the first weekend in October.

Topeka Robert Collet

Robert Collet produced Immortal Verse to land two Group 1s over a mile last season (including the bonus Coronation Stakes) and he could have another in her mould in Topeka. After taking three turns to get off the mark, she quickly made up into a smart filly with a real turn of foot.

While the form of her wins in Listed and Group 3 company might not bear comparison with some of last term's best form among the juvenile fillies, her electric acceleration should remain a potent weapon and she looks right in the mix for whichever version of the Guineas Collet chooses.

Wizz Kid Robert Collet

Collet's Wizz Kid gets the nod over Freddy Head's Moonlight Cloud in the sprint division, in which both will contest plenty of the big speed prizes. Preference is for the four-year-old daughter of Whipper, who was fifth in the Abbaye and then chased home Deacon Blues in the Champions Sprint at Ascot.

Her veteran trainer loves to take a tilt at the big English meetings and has promised she will be up to taking more racing this season.

Of the remaining selections, some have a stronger French connection than others . . .

Bonfire Andrew Balding

Andrew Balding's colt had shaped with plenty of promise when scoring on his Salisbury debut, and both trainer and jockey felt he would have beaten French Fifteen comfortably in the Group 1 Criterium International at Saint-Cloud had Jimmy Fortune not been locked on the rail until the final half-furlong.

Born To Sea John Oxx

Former Arc-winning trainer and now French press room stalwart Jean Lesbordes remains a fervent supporter of Born To Sea, despite his reverse in the Killavullan Stakes at Leopardstown. Having been responsible for the mother of them all, Urban Sea, during her racing career, Lesbordes' enthusiasm for the son of Invincible Spirit is infectious.

Victory in the 2,000 Guineas would more than pay for his inclusion and given the stamina and sheer class on his remarkable dam's side, you can't say for certain where he might end up.

Mandaean Mahmood Al Zarooni

Mandaean was breathtaking in winning his Longchamp maiden, a race his then trainer Andre Fabre won with Rewilding and Hurricane Run. He may not have pleased everyone with his errant passage up the home straight in the Criterium de Saint-Cloud, but the ground was desperate that day and he remains a middle-distance prospect to be filed under 'very exciting' now he's been transferred to Newmarket under the care of Mahmood Al Zarooni.

Wading Aidan O'Brien

You didn't have to be anywhere near Newmarket to be impressed by the manner of Wading's performance in the Rockfel Stakes. Whether Aidan O'Brien attempts to win a mile Classic with her before stepping up to middle distances is anyone's guess, but it will be disappointing if she isn't running at the highest level as a three-year-old.

If it's a thrill you want for your money then Captain is one to have on your side

Brian Morgan with ten quiet achievers he expects to improve on what they have shown so far

Captain Dunne Tim Easterby

I've been addicted to following the minimum-trip specialists ever since I developed my first speed ratings, so it's good to start this year's list with a fine example of the genre. This seven-year-old gelding has been with Middleham Park Racing and Tim Easterby all his career, which has brought him 23 wins and places from 49 starts.

Captain Dunne appears to be significantly better on good to firm ground – he's yet to win on good in 17 attempts but has been victorious on his one try at soft, albeit in a minor race some time ago. Perhaps just a pound or two short of Class 1 and really a four-furlong-and-nine-tenths expert who struggles to get home over five and a half furlongs unless it's downhill, Captain Dunne is regarded by connections as very fast.

He relishes the chance to blaze away from the front on a sprinter-friendly track and has plenty of heart for the fight when tackled for the lead. Last year's highlight was his success under 9st 10lb in the Epsom's Dash, in which he had lost out only narrowly once before.

He performs particularly well at Beverley, Chester, Epsom and Thirsk and is two out of two at Southwell, so he must be supported if he returns there. Granted a fast five-furlong event with no juice in the ground, Captain Dunne will always give you a thrill for your money.

Colonel Mak David Barron

Last season this likeable Makbul gelding made the transition to the edges of the top level of sprinters and, with many of his sire's stock continuing to improve with maturity, he could make the breakthrough this season.

Now five and from a good sprinting family, he has been raced almost exclusively over six furlongs and on a straight track – he couldn't get near the front rank over five furlongs and the evidence for staying seven is inconclusive.

He achieved his best QA rating last August at Ffos Las and next time out looked a stand-out each-way bet in the Ayr Gold Cup, where he rewarded each-way support by finishing fourth at 16-1.

He might need a little sympathy from the handicapper and a mark in the mid-90s would see him remain competitive.

Along with Ayr, he has a distinct liking for Hamilton, where his form figures are 112. He is built to carry big weights if appearing there under a welter burden.

He was tried on the all-weather at Lingfield and Southwell in January but didn't seem over-enamoured with the surface and is best avoided on the artificial tracks unless contrary evidence emerges. Let's stick to supporting him over a straight six on good or softer ground.

Jonny Mudball Tom Dascombe

Jonny Mudball saw racecourse action only twice last term, tasting hot Group 3 company at Newmarket at the end of April and running a blinder to finish a close third over an inadequate five furlongs, and

Speed machine Captain Dunne (1) can continue to deliver over the minimum distance

disappointing over the same distance at Longchamp a fortnight later before an extended break. He'll come back fresh and hopefully just as fast this year. He's my high-end Quiet Achiever for 2012.

La Fortunata Mike Murphy

This lovely sprinting five-year-old mare is one of Lucky Story's best progeny. She likes a sound surface and her career record on going with 'firm' in the description is three wins and six places from 13 outings. In addition, her four all-weather appearances have brought three runner-up slots at Kempton. She has been tried only three times at six furlongs: the first of those brought a win against three rivals on the grass at Lingfield, while the others were her most recent appearances, where she won a fillies' handicap at Newmarket and then weakened a fair way out in a classy affair at Goodwood. The jury is still out on whether she truly gets much more than the minimum trip in a highly

competitive event, but on breeding she should.

She ended last season on a mark of 87, just 4lb higher than she began. Her last success before that, in August 2010, was off a mark of 75 but she had gone close from 82, 81 and 79 and needs to be cut only a little slack from the handicapper to be on a decent mark again.

Nippy La Fortunata loves a good test of speed at the likes of Epsom, Goodwood and Kempton. Remember her when the going is on the firm side.

Licence To Till Mark Johnston

The epitome of his trainer's mission statement of 'Always Trying', this five-year-old gelding by Breeders' Cup Mile winner War Chant went 15 runs without a win last season before coming good twice in the space of eight autumnal days in handicaps at Dundalk and York. Already in 2012 he's grabbed third prize in a decent handicap at

Lingfield and then schmoozed with the jet set for a couple of singularly unsuccessful efforts on the snow at St Moritz. An afternoon at Wolverhampton suddenly doesn't somehow seem the same.

There were already plenty of travelling miles on Licence To Till's cv, with his career having taken him from Brighton to Musselburgh for a healthy return of six wins and 15 places. Happy out in front or racing prominently, like many of his Middleham peers, he shares their sheer determination not to be overtaken before the line.

He seems relatively undeterred by underfoot conditions, stays at least 11 furlongs and goes particularly well on the all-weather surfaces.

Life And Soul Amanda Perrett

This half-brother to Sha Tin Group 1 winner Mr Medici is clearly not in that league but still has a lot to offer at his own level. He has shown a liking for Ascot and for Lingfield's Polytrack. Effective over a mile and a quarter, he races mostly at a mile and a half nowadays, and a shortish four-year-old campaign saw just six runs that yielded a trio of third places in handicaps at Newmarket, Windsor and Ascot.

He has dropped a few pounds in the handicap and looks to be back on a winning mark. Life And Soul runs well fresh and could score on his return if forward enough. If he emulates Mr Medici by improving with age, some decent handicaps should be within his reach and it could be that an extra couple of furlongs will work the oracle.

Mulaqen Marcus Tregoning

This four-year-old Haafhd colt, who is a half-brother to Group 2-placed Sir Lando, has had just five races in two seasons. An imposing sort, Mulaqen has always looked the type to do better with age and his trainer has clearly decided not to rush him.

He raced during the last campaign as though he could improve for an attempt at cup distances, with all three runs coming over a mile and a half in May, June and July. He won his maiden at Kempton in impressive fashion first time out, gamely out-battling odds-on favourite Keys, who went on to land handicaps at Ascot and Newbury. Mulaqen's subsequent two handicap runs, both on turf, seemed to show that a mile and a half at Musselburgh was too tight for him and that the same distance at Ascot suited fast finishers better.

He will have strengthened up a lot during his break and there is any amount of unfulfilled potential ready to be tapped into. Likely to act on any surface and capable of winning from a mile and a half to an extended two miles, he is a colt to look out for.

Nasri David Nicholls

This six-year-old gelding is with his third trainer, having previously been stabled with Brian Meehan and David Simcock, and is in what many judges would view as the best place for his pace to be fully exploited.

Effective over both six and seven furlongs, his best win percentage is over six, but my ratings show little difference between the two trips. Last season he won two from eight outings and bagged a couple of handy place prizes too, rising 11lb in the weights. While he could well have improved sufficiently over the winter to defy that hike, he may need to come down just a bit before he can get his head back in front again.

Like most offspring of Kyllachy, he does well with some cut in the ground and acts well on good or good to firm ground. Nasri has performed with distinction on tracks as varied as Goodwood, Newmarket, Hamilton and Musselburgh – in fact he has a 100 per cent record north of the border, which is worth noting. It would be a brave man who wagered against him having another fine campaign.

Novirak James Fanshawe

The darkest of the Quiet Achievers for the 2012 campaign, this well-bred four-year-old has seen the track only three times. Unimpressive outings at Kempton and

Pintura (centre) has plenty going for him in Doncaster's Lincoln Handicap

Folkestone last August, in which he came seventh each time and was beaten a total of 70 lengths, could hardly have prepared any observer for the sight of a Pegasus Stables winner at Folkestone the next month at 100-1.

Was it immaturity or perhaps just an instant dislike of an artificial racing surface that can explain his first two starts? Either way, Novirak is bred to be suited by middle distances. He's a half-brother to Group 3 winner Strawberry Dale, so was entitled to have a decent chance in that Class 5 maiden over a mile and a quarter, and he took it well.

Reported to have grown and matured over the winter, he should have bags of improvement to come and can move up through the ranks this summer.

Pintura David Simcock

If you're looking to follow a horse for all seasons, your search could well end with this five-year-old Efisio gelding. Initially with Mick Channon, with whom he won two from 11, Pintura stays a mile and a quarter and is highly effective over a mile – the halfway house of nine furlongs seems just about ideal for him. A career record of five wins and 12 places from 31 starts is testament to his level of consistency, while his liking for tracks as diverse as Haydock and Goodwood displays genuine versatility.

Yet to win outside Class 3, he has been knocking on the door in Class 2 and, while having a good record in cheekpieces, runs well enough without them.

A winless return last term doesn't tell the whole story as he finished within a length of the winner in competitive handicaps at Chester, Goodwood, Newbury and York.

He holds a Lincoln entry and, off his mark of 99, is currently set to carry 8st 13lb. That stretching mile at Doncaster could be right up his street nowadays and he finished best of all the horses drawn in single figures in last year's renewal: the only caveat is that each of his wins has come after a return to action of between seven and 23 days.

His ability to act on any ground (including heavy) makes him a lot easier than many to find the right opportunities for and this, allied to his flexibility in trip, leads me to anticipate David Simcock will be able to place Pintura to good advantage this season.

'He could be a contender for cup races and could put it to Fame And Glory'

Nick Watts of the Racing & Football Outlook with his idea of the big points scorers

YOU could make a list entirely made up from Aidan O'Brien's stable if you wanted to – and it would probably go pretty close to winning the Ten to Follow competition.

Such is the trainer's strength in depth it seems inconceivable he won't win at least one British Classic, thereby ending a drought that goes back to Henrythenavigator's 2008 2,000 Guineas win.

Camelot is a must among the colts. He is already perceived as a Derby winner by many, but recent money for him in the 2,000 Guineas market suggests he could go there first.

We've been here before – think St Nicholas Abbey – but there appears to be a supreme air of confidence at Ballydoyle that he is the real deal. You cannot leave him out.

As a back-up to Camelot in the Derby, O'Brien's **David Livingston** is worthy of inclusion. He was a most progressive juvenile and ended his campaign by scooping the Group 2 Beresford Stakes late in the season at the Curragh.

Many pundits put that win down to an ill-judged ride from Johnny Murtagh on Akeed Mofeed, but that is unfair on the winner, who opened up a healthy lead turning for home and always looked like holding on.

He's likely to be seen out early in one of the Irish Derby trials and could excel over middle distances, particularly when there is cut in the ground.

It's not just the colts where O'Brien is strong. **Kissed** is an intriguing filly who won on her debut at Navan in eyecatching fashion and could develop into an Oaks contender.

She's bred for the job, being closely related to last year's Derby winner Pour Moi, and should get an Oaks trip with little difficulty.

For the 1,000 Guineas O'Brien has a plethora of options with one of the best looking to be **Twirl,** a sister to Misty For Me.

Any horse who wins a maiden by six and a half lengths has to possess a degree of ability, and that's the distance Twirl beat her rivals in a Leopardstown maiden last November. Whether she comes to hand in time for the 1,000 Guineas remains to be seen, but she could emerge as a strong contender for her domestic Classics.

Fame And Glory could be the stayer to follow, but in the spirit of adventure let's go with John Gosden's **Arctic Cosmos**.

The 2010 St Leger winner had a truncated campaign last season owing to injury but in the two outings he managed the ability seemed to be still there. On his seasonal return he was second behind Quest For Peace at Ascot before finishing sixth in the Canadian International at Woodbine.

If Gosden gets a clear run with him this time he is a contender for all the cup races and could put it up to Fame And Glory at Ascot, thereby preventing the Ballydoyle stayer from winning two in a row.

As for sprinters, it's an open category after Deacon Blues was ruled out for the season just as this book went to print. There is no

Plenty of reasons to expect Derby trip to bring out the best in Camelot

Nancy Sexton with ten whose breeding suggests we can expect great things

Born To Sea
b c Invincible Spirit - Urban Sea (Miswaki)

The final foal out of 1993 Arc heroine Urban Sea, Born To Sea is a half-brother to two champions – Galileo and Sea The Stars. Another half-brother, Black Sam Bellamy, was a Group 1 winner over 1m4f, while half-sisters All Too Beautiful and Melikah were placed in the Oaks. This is a family that has excelled over 1m4f but, as Born To Sea is by a speed influence in Invincible Spirit, he may find trips at around 1m his optimum.

Camelot *b c Montjeu - Tarfah (Kingmambo)*

On breeding Camelot should only improve as he steps up in distance. He is one of 25 Group 1 winners by Montjeu, who has rightly earned a reputation as Europe's premier Derby sire with sons Motivator, Authorized and Pour Moi each successful in the Epsom Classic. It is worth remembering Motivator and Authorized were also successful in the Racing Post Trophy, the race in which Camelot impressed so much last October.

A half-brother to 1m2f winner Ideal, Camelot is out of Dahlia Stakes winner Tarfah and descends from the 1975 Cheshire and Lancashire Oaks winner One Over Parr.

Dabirsim
br c Hat Trick - Rumored (Royal Academy)

Dabirsim's victories in the Prix Morny and Prix Jean-Luc Lagardere placed the spotlight firmly on his young Kentucky-based sire Hat Trick, an eight-time winner between 1m and 1m1f in Japan and Hong Kong who was Japan's champion miler of 2005. Dabirsim is from the first-crop by Hat Trick, a rare American-based son of Japanese sire sensation Sunday Silence, whose son Divine Light provided the 1,000 Guineas heroine Natagora in 2008.

Dabirsim's dam has produced three sprint winners in the US, including stakes-placed Preferred Yield. However, as Rumored is a half-sister to 1m1f Group 3 winner Fathayer and out of Oaks d'Italia heroine Bright Generation, Dabirsim should find a mile – and perhaps further – within his range.

Discourse
br f Street Cry - Divine Dixie (Dixieland Band)

One of several Godolphin Classic prospects by Street Cry, the sire of 13 Group/Grade 1 winners between 6f and 2m, Sweet Solera Stakes winner Discourse owns an American – and dirt – pedigree of the highest order. She is a half-sister to 2005 Grade 1 Blue Grass Stakes winner Bandini and out of a Listed-placed half-sister to useful sprinter and prominent sire Stormy Atlantic. Her granddam Hail Atlantis won the 1990 Grade 1 Santa Anita Oaks while her fourth dam, Moccasin, was US Horse of the Year.

The 1,000 Guineas is Discourse's most likely chance of Classic success. However, Bandini excelled over 1m1f while another half-sibling, Virginia Minstrel, is a useful American hurdler, suggesting she should be effective over further as well.

reason why **Margot Did** can't enjoy more Group-race glory, however.

She gets on famously with Hayley Turner and together the pair won York's Nunthorpe in great style. Borderlescott won the race in successive years recently and you wouldn't rule out Margot Did doing likewise as she always runs well on the Knavesmire.

Medicean Man officially improved 13lb last year and he's also worthy of inclusion in the sprinting division. He's now won three times at Ascot and clearly loves the place, so he could be an interesting contender for the King's Stand if he keeps improving.

Roger Charlton's **Cry Fury** was a lightly raced handicapper last season and could have more to give – maybe in Group races. He was down the field in the Cambridgeshire last season but is better than that and shouldn't be written off.

Strong Suit *(above)* has yet to win at Group 1 level but he can amend that statistic this season granted fast ground. He could go back to France for some of their Group 1s – he was a close third in the Prix Jean Prat last year.

Finally . . . it has to be **Frankel**. He was unbeaten last season, never really looked like being beaten, and it's likely to be the same story this year. Opposition could well be thin on the ground as trainers look for easier pickings and he should score regularly and heavily. He simply cannot be omitted.

Harbour Watch
b c Acclamation - Gorband (Woodman)

Unbeaten Richmond Stakes winner Harbour Watch headed a group of eight stakes-winning juveniles in 2011 by Acclamation, who was a high-class sprinter and is regarded as a speed influence. If Harbour Watch succeeds in the 2,000 Guineas, he will become only the third of his 16 Pattern winners to score at stakes level over a mile or further.

His female family offers hope that he can last a mile; a descendant of blue hen Fall Aspen, he is a half-brother to a Group 3 winner in South Africa over a mile and out of a half-sister to 1m2f Group 2 winner Kabool and 1m6f Listed winner Sharaf Kabeer.

Lyric Of Light
b f Street Cry - Suez (Green Desert)

Suez looked destined to take a hand in the 2005 Classics when second in the Cheveley Park Stakes but never made it back to the track for Godolphin. Perhaps her second foal, unbeaten Fillies' Mile heroine Lyric Of Light, will put that record straight.

A daughter of Godolphin's Dubai World Cup winner Street Cry, Lyric Of Light descends from a famous Meon Valley family as a great-granddaughter of Reprocolor, who features in the backgrounds of 37 stakes winners including Opera House, Kayf Tara and Caspar Netscher.

Lyric Of Light already stays further than her dam did and it wouldn't be surprising to see her also effective at around 1m2f.

Maybe *b f Galileo - Sumora (Danehill)*

Last year's champion two-year-old filly is yet another advert for the Galileo-Danehill cross, which produced Frankel as well as Teofilo and Roderic O'Connor.

Maybe should be able to take the step up to a mile in her stride but her pedigree provides mixed messages as to whether she can cope with further. Although she is another top-notcher by middle-distance influence Galileo, she is out of a 5f Listed winner who is related to Group 3-winning sprinter Archway. On the other hand, Sumora is also a half-sister to last year's Oaks heroine Dancing Rain and related to 1992 Derby winner Dr Devious.

Parish Hall
b c Teofilo - Halla Siamsa (Montjeu)

Last year's Dewhurst winner is inbred to Sadler's Wells, which suggests he should improve as he steps up in trip. Champion juvenile Teofilo never got the chance to tackle beyond 7f but at the time of writing, he is already the sire of four winners over a mile or beyond including one over 1m4f. In addition, Parish Hall is the first foal out of a 1m2f winner by Montjeu from the family of Ascot Gold Cup winner Enzeli.

Power *b c Oasis Dream - Frappe (Inchinor)*

Although a top-class sprinter, Oasis Dream has sired Pattern winners over a variety of distances, ranging from sprinter Prohibit to 1m4f Group 1 winner Midday. Therefore, while Power showed plenty of speed during his first season on the track, it wouldn't be surprising to see the colt improve when stepped up to a mile, especially as he is a half-brother to a Ribblesdale Stakes winner in Thakafaat. Power's juvenile form, which included victory in the National Stakes, entitles him to line up in the 2,000 Guineas.

Was *b f Galileo - Alluring Park (Green Desert)*

A 1.2 million guineas yearling purchase by Coolmore, Was served notice she could justify that price tag with a smooth debut victory over a mile at the Curragh.

By the all-conquering Galileo, Was is a half-sister to 7f Listed winner Janood and closely related to champion two-year-old and Derby winner New Approach, who is a half-brother to her dam. This is a family with its share of speed – Alluring Park is a sister to high-class sprinter Shinko Forest and was Listed-placed over 6f – but Galileo's influence could see Was emulate New Approach by developing into an Epsom Classic candidate.

Sirius a bright prospect who can make successful leap to Group company

Horse-by-horse profiler **Dylan Hill** with his list of those who stand out most

Camelot Aidan O'Brien

Let St Nicholas Abbey act as a warning to anyone who expects Camelot to sweep all before him this season. I would be a little concerned if Aidan O'Brien decides to send him to the 2,000 Guineas given that so few of Montjeu's progeny are able to make an impact over a mile in their three-year-old season. Ultimately, though, it's hard to question O'Brien's judgement and there is no evidence to suggest he will prove as fragile as his last brilliant Racing Post Trophy winner. Camelot looked something special at Doncaster and looks by far the most likely to dominate the middle-distance scene.

Discourse Mahmood Al Zarooni

Last season's three-year-old fillies were an extremely moderate bunch, which suggests this year's Classic generation should have plenty of opportunities against their elders later in the season. Therefore it may be wise to include two or even three fillies of that age in Ten To Follow lists, and this Godolphin recruit looks the best of them. She was brilliant when winning the Sweet Solera at Newmarket last season and was rated better at home than Fillies' Mile winner Lyric Of Light before suffering an injury. Her trainer Mahmood Al Zarooni showed a fine touch with Blue Bunting last season.

Excelebration Aidan O'Brien

Excelebration never had much of a chance against Frankel last season, finishing behind Sir Henry Cecil's superstar three times. However, he won the Group 1 Prix du Moulin at Longchamp and looks comfortably the next-best older miler. It is possible that Aidan O'Brien will eke out some more improvement from him following his purchase by Coolmore and it would help his prospects massively if Frankel moves up in trip, which has been strongly mooted.

Frankel Sir Henry Cecil

An absolute must for anyone having a serious crack at the Ten To Follow competition. Frankel is one of the all-time greats, already with five Group 1 wins to his name, and he looks sure to add several more to his tally this year. He showed his incredible raw ability when destroying the opposition in the 2,000 Guineas and seemed to progress mentally as the season went on, settling much better before producing powerful bursts to run away with the Sussex Stakes and the Queen Elizabeth II Stakes.

Harbour Watch Richard Hannon

There was a lack of star quality at the inaugural Future Champions Day at Newmarket last October when the two Group 1 races were won by Crusade and Parish Hall, reinforcing the notion that Harbour Watch was the best juvenile seen in Britain and Ireland. He missed the Dewhurst after a setback but had already posted a good enough level of form to win that race, having counted Caspar Netscher among his victims when easing home in the Richmond Stakes at Glorious Goodwood. He's not certain to be back in time for the 2,000 Guineas but should soon prove himself a top-class miler either way.

Hoof It Mick Easterby

Don't make the mistake of writing off Hoof It just because he failed to hit the target in his first two attempts at Group 1 level last season. Hoof It looked ready to break through at the top level following his brilliant win in the Stewards' Cup, but was unlucky to finish only sixth in the Nunthorpe – he had little chance from a bad draw given the trip was always likely to be on the short side for him – and should have won the Haydock Sprint Cup when he didn't get a clear run at the death.

Saddler's Rock John Oxx

Four-year-olds struggle to make an impact in the Ascot Gold Cup but Saddler's Rock is one who could go close and looks likely to rack up more points than favourite Fame And Glory, who seems best when fresh these days. John Oxx will be keen to get plenty of runs into Saddler's Rock to give him more experience and he certainly has the ability to remain a force in top staying races, having landed the Doncaster Cup so impressively last season.

Sirius Prospect Dean Ivory

Along with Hoof It, this one has the ability to make hay in the sprint division this season. He was seriously progressive last year, winning each of his last four starts, and he showed blistering speed to land the Coral Sprint Trophy at York when he came from almost last to first in the blink of an eye. He took a step up to

Listed grade in his stride on his final outing, cosily beating Mayson by a neck with a lot more up his sleeve. It would be no surprise to see Group races come his way.

So You Think Aidan O'Brien

Plenty of people were disappointed with So You Think last season, which was perhaps inevitable given the fanfare that greeted his arrival at Aidan O'Brien's yard in the spring. However, it is still no mean feat to win three Group 1 races and finish second in another two and So You Think seems guaranteed to rack up plenty more points this year. He also seems more adaptable in terms of trip than he was allowed to demonstrate last season – he has reportedly shown the speed of a miler on the gallops yet also finished like a train when fourth in the Arc.

Wading Aidan O'Brien

Another three-year-old filly worthy of serious consideration, Wading may prove the best of Aidan O'Brien's plethora of horses in that division. She was an outstanding winner of the Rockfel Stakes at Newmarket last season and that race has been an outstanding trial for the 1,000 Guineas in recent times. There has to be a slight doubt about whether she will have the speed for that Classic given that she is by Montjeu, but there will be many more opportunities for her over further.

Excelebration with his former trainer Marco Botti

Keep strategy simple and you shouldn't be too far wide of the mark

Flat Guide editor **David Dew** with some ideas on selecting your squad for the Ten to Follow

K
EEP it simple is good advice when it comes to picking your Ten to Follow team. With an enormous 200 points, **Frankel** was king of the scoreboard last year and, having ended his juvenile campaign with four wins, including the Group 1 Dewhurst, he was near enough an automatic selection for many entrants. His huge haul meant that to claim a top-ten finish in last year's competition you needed more than 910 points, but Frankel contributed to more than a fifth of that tally and got many people well on their way.

The second leading scorer last year, with 164 points, was **So You Think**. Although 12 months ago he was yet to race in Britain, he had chalked up five Group 1 wins in Australia and, having joined Aidan O'Brien, was another logical selection.

So, without being too adventurous, picking that pair would have netted well over a third of the total needed to be in with a shout of grabbing a share of a fortune.

Be sure to include them again as they can bag any number of big races, including several of the all-important bonus races that offer an additional 25 points. And here are some suggestions for others who are worthy candidates to make up the ten before the bonus window opens on July 8 . . .

With 29 inclusions, Aidan O'Brien has more horses in the competition than any other trainer, so he has to be first port of call

when it comes to finding potential names for any list. He also has the ante-post favourite for the first four Classics.

There was much to like about the way **Camelot** stormed home in the Racing Post Trophy at Doncaster at the end of last season. He is favourite for the 2,000 Guineas and the Derby and looks a must. Enthusiasm might be tempered by the fact that St Nicholas Abbey is the only winner of that race since 2007 who has won again in Britain, but it would be a great surprise if Camelot failed to earn his supporters points in the Ten to Follow. Including him gives coverage to several bonus races.

Power won four of his six races at two, including the Group 1 National Stakes – a race previously won by New Approach, who went on to win the Derby and Champion Stakes, and Mastercraftsman, who won the Irish 2,000 Guineas and St James's Palace Stakes at Royal Ascot the following season. Also trained by O'Brien, Power will surely be kept apart from his stablemate and looks nailed on to pick up plenty of points.

Ballydoyle also houses **Maybe**, who was unbeaten in five starts last year, graduating from winning a maiden to scoring in Listed, Group 3, Group 2 and in Group 1 company when winning the Moyglare Stud Stakes at the Curragh, a race that has thrown up Irish 1,000 Guineas winners Again and Misty For Me in recent seasons.

She is favourite for the 1,000 Guineas and is difficult to ignore. The same goes for stablemate **Wading**, who is also prominent in the betting for the first fillies' Classic and favourite for the Oaks.

She signalled her promising future when

winning the Group 2 Rockfel Stakes at Newmarket in October. That race might not have a great recent record when it comes to fillies in their Classic year, but the Racing Post Rating of 115 she earned has been bettered only once in the last ten years and that was by Finsceal Beo, who went on to win the 1,000 Guineas and the Irish equivalent at the Curragh in 2007.

Moving away from O'Brien's crack team, one to consider closely is John Gosden's **Masked Marvel**. He might have ended his season with a no-show in the Arc, but he was impressive in staying on well to win the Leger on his previous start and earned a Racing Post Rating of 124. The last Leger winner to achieve that figure was Conduit, in 2008, and he went on to win twice at the Breeders' Cup and also won a Group 1 at Ascot. That, added to Gosden's prowess with this type of horse, bodes well for Masked Marvel's chances this season.

Saddler's Rock might have missed out on running as a two-year-old, but after his first couple of runs last season at three he never looked back. He graduated from winning a maiden to a handicap and ended by running away with the Doncaster Cup. He could prove a formidable force in the top staying races this summer, especially as he is open to further improvement after just six starts.

Dabirsim had five starts in France last season and won every time, including Group 1s at Deauville and Longchamp. We don't yet know whether he will stay a mile or more, but the way he has done his winning suggests he will. His trainer is keen to have a crack at some of the big races in Britain, so he looks a live one for Ten to Follow lists with the possibility of picking up some bonus points along the way.

Finally, last season might have been disappointing for Sir Michael Stoute by his standards, but his **Sea Moon** still won a Group 2 and was runner-up in the Breeders' Cup Turf. He looks a good thing for success at the highest level this season.

Ante-post 2,000 Guineas and Derby favourite Camelot can bag plenty of points for Ten to Follow players this season

Promising debut suggests Hero won't be long in getting off the mark

Racing Post Ratings expert **Simon Turner** puts forward his ten to sparkle this season

Cardinal Walter David Simcock

David Simcock has an interesting prospect on his hands in Cardinal Walter, who shaped with notable promise behind a red-hot favourite at Redcar on his only start in 2011. Far from knocked about that day, this half-brother to Group 2 winner Manieree was doing some good late work over seven furlongs, a trip that will almost certainly prove too sharp for him. He appeals as the type to improve plenty during 2012 and is one to keep a close eye on.

Counsel Sir Michael Stoute

There was distinct promise in each of Counsel's three runs as a juvenile and he is expected to step forward significantly this year. Out of a sister to Leger winner Brian Boru, the 200,000gns son of Dansili showed fair ability on all three runs, going on close home on his debut at Leicester before not being knocked about at either Windsor or Yarmouth. He looks sure to do better and appeals as the sort to do really well in handicaps as he steps up in trip.

Dickie's Lad Kevin Ryan

There are few better trainers around than Kevin Ryan, who has an interesting sprinter on his hands in the form of Dickie's Lad. Unplaced on his only two-year-old start,

the son of Diamond Green showed significant improvement to rout a field of maidens on his seasonal debut last year and ran with credit in defeat at York's Ebor meeting among other places. Likely to be more the finished article this year, he should pay his way in decent sprint handicaps.

Forgotten Hero Charlie Hills

There are always plenty of promising debut efforts to analyse during the autumn at Newmarket and it was hard not to be impressed by the effort of Forgotten Hero, who really caught the eye when third behind stablemate Ellaal in October. The son of High Chaparral was travelling well from a long way out and made some impressive headway from a modest position to leave the impression he would do a lot better in the future. He looks a likely early-season maiden winner for his powerful stable.

Frankel Sir Henry Cecil

Having been firmly in Frankel's corner since his second start I've no wish to desert him this year. The odds of reward will not always be great but he looks sure to score heavily in the Ten to Follow competition and will prove hard to beat. There should be some exciting days as his ever-popular trainer steps him up to a mile and a quarter. Already boasting a superb RPR of 139, it is feasible he could break into the 140s this season.

Pearl Secret (opposite) David Barron

As racecourse debuts go, Pearl Secret's was

flawless. Representing the powerful Pearl Bloodstock team, the son of Compton Place breezed through a good sprint maiden at York before readily powering clear in the style of a colt with much more to offer. His opening handicap mark in the mid-80s looks fair and it is quite possible he will prove an awful lot better than that in time.

Sea Moon Sir Michael Stoute

The world looked to be Sea Moon's oyster after his romp in the Great Voltigeur at York's Ebor meeting, where he posted an RPR of 126. He was unable to build on that effort in two subsequent efforts in the St Leger and Breeders' Cup Turf but ran with great credit to finish in the money in those top-level races. It is not hard to envisage him doing better again for his excellent trainer and he can score at the highest level this year.

Seven Veils Sir Mark Prescott

This sister to an Italian Oaks winner looked anything but the finished article in three starts in 2011 but showed more than enough on her second start to suggest she can pay her way in handicaps this year. Sir Mark Prescott's prowess with three-year-old handicappers is the stuff of legend and in Seven Veils he has an interesting horse to work with.

Solar View Sir Mark Prescott

Three runs in just 25 days qualified Solar View for a rating and he shaped with promise while completing his quick-fire handicap education, notably when not looking entirely comfortable around Wolverhampton's tight turns on his second start. He is from a family that can improve with age and it would be a surprise if this well-bred son of Galileo cannot show significant improvement and win races this year.

Welsh Bard Sir Mark Prescott

Three maiden appearances towards the end of 2011 leaves Welsh Bard potentially well handicapped for this year's assignments and the son of Dylan Thomas is one to keep in mind for the busy summer period. An opening handicap mark in the low 60s looks fair given the merit of his final performance at Wolverhampton and he should be respected when making his handicap debut.

RACING POST RATINGS TOP TWO-YEAR-OLDS OF 2011

KEY: Horse name, Best RPR figure Finishing position when earning figure
(Details of race where figure was earned)

Aaraas 96 3 (7f, Leop, Yld, Oct 30)
Abishena (IRE) 94 2 (1m, Newm, Gd, Oct 29)
After (IRE) 96 9 (6f, Curr, Yld, Aug 7)
Akeed Mofeed 114 2 (1m, Curr, Hvy, Sep 25)
Alkazim (IRE) 94 4 (7f, Newm, GF, Oct 1)
Alla Speranza 97 2 (1m 1f, Leop, Yld, Nov 6)
Alsindi (IRE) 103 1 (7f, Newm, GF, Sep 23)
Among Equals 98 1 (6f, Cork, GF, Jul 31)
An Ghalanta (IRE) 95 3 (6f, Curr, Sft, Sep 10)
Angels Will Fall (IRE) 107 1 (6f, Asco, GS, Jul 23)
Apollo (IRE) 98 1 (7f, Curr, Yld, Jul 17)
Artistic Jewel (IRE) 98 1 (6f, Newm, Gd, Oct 28)
Astrology (IRE) 108 3 (7f, Curr, Gd, Aug 20)
B Fifty Two (IRE) 103 8 (6f, Newm, Gd, Oct 8)
Balty Boys (IRE) 110 4 (6f, Newm, Gd, Oct 8)
Bana Wu 105 4 (7f, Newm, Gd, Oct 8)
Bannock (IRE) 108 1 (6f, York, Gd, Oct 8)
Bapak Chinta (USA) 106 1 (5f, Asco, GS, Jun 16)
Bayleyf (IRE) 101 4 (6f, Kemw, SD, Sep 3)
Best Terms 114 1 (6f, York, GS, Aug 18)
Bible Black (IRE) 99 1 (7f, Dunw, SD, Oct 7)
Bling King 94 2 (6f 18y, Ches, GF, Jul 31)
Blue White Fire (IRE) 96 2 (7f, Galw, Gd, Jul 30)
Bogart 107 1 (6f, Redc, GF, Oct 1)
Boomerang Bob (IRE) 102 2 (5f, Asco, GS, Jun 16)
Boris Grigoriev (IRE) 97 2 (5f, Curr, Yld, Aug 20)
Born To Sea (IRE) 106 2 (7f, Leop, Yld, Oct 30)
Bronterre 115 4 (7f, Newm, Gd, Oct 8)
Buffalo Billy (IRE) 96 3 (7f, Dunw, SD, Oct 7)
Burwaaz 110 2 (5f, Donc, Gd, Sep 9)
Caledonia Lady 105 3 (5f, Donc, Gd, Sep 9)
Caledonian Spring (IRE) 106 1 (1m, Hayd, GF, Sep 3)
Call To Battle (IRE) 101 1 (1m 1f, Leop, Yld, Nov 6)
Camelot 119 1 (1m, Donc, Gd, Oct 22)
Campanology 95 7 (6f 110y, Donc, Gd, Sep 8)
Captain Obvious (IRE) 97 2 (7f, Dunw, SD, Oct 7)
Caspar Netscher 114 1 (6f 8y, Newb, Gd, Sep 17)
Chandlery (IRE) 110 2 (7f, Newj, GF, Jul 9)
Charles The Great (IRE) 102 1 (5f 34y, Newb, Gd, Jul 16)
Chunky Diamond (IRE) 100 2 (6f, Donc, Gd, Oct 22)
Coquet 95 1 (1m, Newm, Gd, Oct 29)
Coral Wave (IRE) 105 1 (7f, Curr, Hvy, Sep 25)
Coupe De Ville (IRE) 104 1 (7f, Newm, GF, Oct 1)
Criostal (IRE) 98 7 (7f, Curr, Gd, Aug 28)
Crius (IRE) 110 1 (7f, Newm, GF, Sep 22)
Crown Dependency (IRE) 99 4 (5f, Good, Gd, Jul 26)
Crusade (USA) 114 1 (6f, Newm, Gd, Oct 8)
Daddy Long Legs (USA) 114 1 (1m, Newm, GF, Sep 24)
David Livingston (IRE) 115 1 (1m, Curr, Hvy, Sep 25)
Discourse (USA) 113 1 (7f, Newj, Gd, Aug 6)
Dozy (IRE) 98 1 (5f, Beve, GF, May 25)
Dragon Pulse (IRE) 117 2 (7f, Curr, Sft, Sep 10)
East Meets West (IRE) 95 3 (7f 100y, Tipp, GF, Aug 5)
Ektihaam (IRE) 98 1 (7f, Donc, Gd, Sep 9)
Elkhart (IRE) 97 5 (7f, Good, Gd, Jul 27)
Entifaadha 107 1 (7f, York, GS, Aug 17)
Eureka (IRE) 101 1 (6f, Donc, Gd, Sep 7)
Ewell Place (IRE) 96 3 (6f, York, GS, Aug 18)
Excelette (IRE) 99 2 (6f, Redc, GF, Oct 1)
Experience (USA) 99 2 (6f, Curr, Gd, Aug 28)
Factory Time (IRE) 107 6 (7f, Newm, Gd, Oct 8)
Fallen For You 111 2 (1m, Donc, Gd, Sep 9)
Falls Of Lora (IRE) 94 1 (1m, Asco, Gd, Sep 3)
Family One (FR) 100 (6f, Newm, Gd, Oct 8)
Farhaan (USA) 100 5 (1m, Newm, GF, Sep 24)

Farraaj (IRE) 107 1 (7f 16y, Sand, Gd, Sep 14)
Fencing (USA) 111 3 (1m, Donc, Gd, Oct 22)
Fillionaire 95 3 (7f, Newb, GF, Oct 22)
Firdaws (USA) 98 3 (1m, Newm, GF, Sep 23)
Fire Lily (IRE) 109 2 (7f, Curr, Gd, Aug 28)
Forevertheoptimist (IRE) 97 1 (5f 6y, Sand, Gd, Jul 1)
Fort Bastion (IRE) 104 2 (7f, York, GS, Aug 17)
Foxtrot Romeo (IRE) 102 4 (6f 8y, Newb, Gd, Sep 17)
Frederick Engels 111 1 (6f, Newj, Gd, Jul 7)
French Emperor (IRE) 98 1 (6f, Naas, Gd, Aug 1)
Fulbright 95 3 (7f, Donc, Gd, Oct 22)
Furner's Green (IRE) 113 4 (7f, Curr, Sft, Sep 10)
Gamilati 108 1 (6f, Newj, Gd, Jul 8)
Gatepost (IRE) 105 5 (6f, Asco, Gd, Jun 14)
Gentlemans Code (USA) 94 4 (5f, Asco, Gd, Jun 14)
Gerfalcon 99 1 (6f, Ripo, GS, Aug 29)
Gold City (IRE) 98 2 (6f, Donc, Gd, Sep 7)
Gooseberry Fool 96 3 (7f, Leop, Gd, Jul 14)
Graphic (IRE) 97 1 (7f, Kemw, SD, Sep 14)
Gray Pearl 109 3 (7f, Newm, Gd, Oct 8)
Gusto 101 1 (6f, Donc, Gd, Oct 22)
Harbour Watch (IRE) 117 1 (6f, Good, GF, Jul 29)
Hazaz (IRE) 98 3 (7f, Newb, GF, Oct 22)
Hello Glory 95 6 (6f, Newm, Gd, Sep 24)
Hestian (IRE) 103 1 (5f, Dunw, SD, Sep 23)
Hexagonal (IRE) 96 2 (5f, Ayr, GS, Sep 16)
Homecoming Queen (IRE) 104 2 (7f, Curr, Hvy, Sep 25)
Illaunglass (IRE) 98 3 (6f, Asco, GS, Jun 17)
Inetrobil (IRE) 103 2 (6f, Asco, GS, Jun 17)
Ishvana (IRE) 95 4 (7f, Leop, Yld, Oct 30)
Janey Muddles (IRE) 102 6 (7f, Newm, Gd, Oct 8)
Justineo 105 4 (6f, York, GS, Aug 19)
Kinetica 98 3 (7f, Newj, Gd, Aug 6)
Kinglet (USA) 99 1 (1m, Kemw, SD, Oct 12)
Kohala (IRE) 99 1 (5f 34y, Newb, Gd, Aug 12)
La Collina (IRE) 114 1 (6f, Curr, Yld, Aug 7)
Lady Wingshot (IRE) 99 4 (7f, Curr, Hvy, Sep 25)
Last Bid 96 2 (5f, York, Gd, Aug 20)
Learn (IRE) 106 4 (1m, Donc, Gd, Oct 22)
Leqqaa (USA) 97 2 (1m, Newm, Gd, Oct 19)
Lethal Force (IRE) 105 4 (6f, Asco, Gd, Jun 14)
Letsgoroundagain (IRE) 101 1 (1m 4y, Pont, Gd, Oct 17)
Lightening Pearl (IRE) 111 1 (6f, Newm, Gd, Sep 24)
Lilbourne Lad (IRE) 112 2 (6f, Newm, Gd, Oct 8)
Lily's Angel (IRE) 101 2 (7f, Newj, Gd, Aug 6)
Lord Ofthe Shadows (IRE) 101 1 (1m, Newm, Gd, Oct 19)
Lyric Of Light 113 1 (1m, Newm, GF, Sep 23)
Mary Fildes (IRE) 99 7 (7f, Newm, Gd, Oct 8)
Maybe (IRE) 114 1 (7f, Curr, Gd, Aug 28)
Mehdi (IRE) 99 1 (6f, Newj, GS, Aug 27)
Minal 96 6 (7f, Good, Gd, Jul 27)
Minidress 95 4 (7f, Newm, GF, Sep 23)
Miss Lahar 100 2 (5f, Asco, Gd, Oct 1)
Miss Work Of Art 102 4 (6f, Newm, GF, Sep 24)
Misty Conquest (IRE) 96 2 (6f, Sali, Gd, Sep 1)
Mojave (IRE) 96 1 (1m 2f, Newm, Gd, Oct 29)
Moon Pearl (USA) 98 4 (6f 110y, Donc, Gd, Sep 8)
Most Improved (IRE) 116 3 (7f, Newm, Gd, Oct 8)
My Propeller (IRE) 100 1 (5f, York, Gd, Aug 20)
My Queenie (IRE) 96 5 (7f, Good, GS, Aug 27)
Nayarra (IRE) 99 3 (7f, Newm, GF, Sep 23)
Nephrite 110 1 (7f, Leop, Yld, Oct 30)
Nero Emperor (IRE) 98 1 (5f, Dunw, SD, Nov 18)
North Star Boy (IRE) 96 4 (6f 8y, Newb, GF, Jul 15)
On The Dark Side (IRE) 95 5 (5f, Good, Gd, Jul 26)
Parish Hall (IRE) 118 1 (7f, Newm, Gd, Oct 8)
Pea Shooter 98 1 (5f 89y, York, Gd, Sep 4)
Pearl Mix (IRE) 97 4 (7f, Newj, GF, Jul 9)

RACING POST RATINGS TOP TWO-YEAR-OLDS OF 2011

Perennial 101 2 (1m, Newm, Gd, Oct 8)
Pimpernel (IRE) 110 2 (7f, Newm, Gd, Oct 8)
Ponty Acclaim (IRE) 104 1 (5f, Asco, Gd, Oct 1)
Power 118 1 (7f, Curr, Sft, Sep 10)
Princess Sinead (IRE) 104 3 (7f, Curr, Hvy, Sep 25)
Producer 97 4 (7f, Newb, GF, Oct 22)
Pyman's Theory (IRE) 97 1 (5f 6y, Sand, GS, May 26)
Questing 100 2 (7f, Newm, GF, Sep 23)
Quote Of The Day (IRE) 95 1 (1m, Nava, Sft, Oct 5)
Rakasa 100 2 (7f, Good, GS, Aug 27)
Rebellious Guest 99 1 (6f, Wind, GS, Aug 8)
Red Duke (USA) 111 2 (7f, Donc, GF, Sep 10)
Red Seventy 99 6 (7f, Newm, GF, Sep 22)
Redact (IRE) 109 2 (6f 8y, Newb, Gd, Sep 17)
Redoutable (IRE) 95 7 (7f, Curr, Yld, Aug 7)
Regal Realm 106 2 (6f, Asco, GS, Jul 23)
Remember Alexander 105 1 (7f, Leop, Sft, Jul 21)
Repeater 95 2 (1m 2f, Newm, Gd, Oct 29)
Reply (IRE) 111 3 (6f, Newm, Gd, Oct 8)
Requinto (IRE) 110 1 (5f, Donc, Gd, Sep 9)
Rex Imperator 95 5 (5f, Asco, Gd, Oct 1)
Riviera Poet (IRE) 106 5 (7f, Curr, Gd, Aug 20)
Rockinante (FR) 105 1 (1m, Newm, Gd, Oct 8)
Roger Sez (IRE) 106 1 (6f, Ayr, Sft, Sep 17)
Roman Soldier (IRE) 109 2 (6f, Asco, Gd, Jun 14)
Rubina (IRE) 101 4 (7f, Curr, Gd, Aug 28)
Ruby's Day 96 6 (5f, Asco, Gd, Jun 15)
Russelliana 104 2 (6f, Newj, Gd, Jul 8)
Saigon 109 6 (6f, Newm, Gd, Oct 8)
Sajwah (IRE) 100 1 (6f, Sali, Gd, Sep 1)
Salford Art (IRE) 97 4 (1m, Newm, GF, Sep 23)
Samitar 109 2 (1m, Newm, GF, Sep 23)
Secretary Of State (IRE) 97 1 (1m, List, Sft, Sep 12)
Semayyel 96 2 (7f, Newb, GF, Oct 22)

Shumoos (USA) 106 2 (5f, Asco, Gd, Jun 15)
Silver Sycamore (USA) 95 1 (7f, Leop, Gd, Sep 3)
Silverheels (IRE) 102 4 (6f, Good, GF, Jul 29)
Soon (IRE) 98 6 (7f, Curr, Yld, Aug 7)
Spiritual Star (IRE) 106 7 (7f, Newm, Gd, Oct 8)
St Barths 105 3 (6f, Asco, Gd, Jun 14)
Stepper Point 95 1 (5f 110y, Warw, Gd, Aug 29)
Stonefield Flyer 100 1 (6f, Donc, Gd, Jul 14)
Storming Bernard (USA) 96 7 (7f, Newm, GF, Sep 22)
Strait Of Zanzibar (USA) 104 6 (7f, Curr, Gd, Aug 20)
Sunday Times 110 2 (6f, Newm, GF, Sep 24)
Swerve 99 1 (6f 60y, List, Sft, Sep 12)
Switcher (IRE) 96 4 (6f, Asco, GS, Jun 17)
Takar (IRE) 99 1 (7f, Leop, Yld, Nov 6)
Talwar (IRE) 107 1 (7f 16y, Sand, Sft, Aug 20)
Tell Dad 104 1 (7f, Newb, GF, Oct 22)
Telwaar 100 2 (7f, Newb, Gd, Aug 13)
Tenth Star (IRE) 106 2 (1m, Newm, GF, Sep 24)
Teolane (IRE) 101 1 (6f, Naas, GF, Jun 6)
Top Cop 95 8 (6f 110y, Donc, Gd, Sep 8)
Tough As Nails (IRE) 111 3 (6f, Curr, Yld, Aug 7)
Tower Rock (IRE) 96 3 (1m 1f, Leop, Yld, Nov 6)
Trumpet Major (IRE) 114 5 (7f, Newm, Gd, Oct 8)
Validus 95 1 (1m, Kemw, SD, Sep 2)
Vault (IRE) 100 7 (7f, Curr, Gd, Aug 20)
Vocational (USA) 104 2 (6f, Kemw, SD, Sep 3)
Wading (IRE) 115 1 (7f, Newm, Gd, Oct 8)
West Leake Diman (IRE) 106 7 (6f, Newm, Gd, Oct 8)
Whip Rule (IRE) 98 4 (1m, Newm, Gd, Oct 8)
Wrote (IRE) 105 3 (1m, Newm, GF, Sep 24)
Yellow Rosebud (IRE) 105 2 (7f, Curr, Yld, Aug 7)
Zip Top (IRE) 111 2 (1m, Donc, Gd, Oct 22)
Zumbi (IRE) 102 3 (7f, York, GS, Aug 17)

RPR TOP THREE-YEAR-OLDS AND OLDER HORSES OF 2011

KEY: Horse name, Best RPR figure Finishing position when earning figure
(Details of race where figure was earned)

Aaim To Prosper (IRE) 110 6 (2m, Good, GF, Jul 28)
Acclamazing (IRE) 105 2 (7f, Asco, GF, May 6)
Across The Rhine (USA) 111 3 (1m, Curr, Yld, Sep 11)
Addictive Dream (IRE) 107 1 (6f, Ripo, Gd, Jun 1)
Admiral Of The Red (IRE) 103 3 (1m 6f, Curr, Sft, Jun 25)
Afsare 114 2 (1m 4f, Newj, GS, Jun 25)
Akmal 108 3 (1m 5f 61y, Newb, GF, May 14)
Al Kazeem 115 2 (1m 3f 5y, Newb, Gd, Sep 17)
Al Shemali 105 2 (1m 4f, Newm, GF, Sep 23)
Alainmaar (FR) 117 1 (1m 4f, Asco, GF, May 7)
Alanza (IRE) 112 1 (7f, Donc, Gd, Sep 8)
Albaasil (IRE) 106 2 (1m, Asco, GS, Jul 23)
Albaqaa 103 4 (1m 1f, Newm, Gd, Oct 8)
Alkimos (IRE) 110 2 (1m 2f, Asco, GS, Jun 16)
All Action (USA) 105 1 (1m 2f, Asco, Gd, Jul 9)
All The Aces (IRE) 104 4 (1m 2f 7y, Sand, Gd, Jul 1)
Allied Powers (IRE) 111 2 (1m 5f 89y, Ches, GF, May 6)
Amico Fritz (GER) 109 6 (6f, Asco, Sft, Jun 18)
Amour Propre 114 1 (5f, Curr, Gd, Aug 28)
Anam Allta (IRE) 115 1 (7f 100y, Tipp, Hvy, Oct 2)
Anatolian 103 1 (1m 4f, Newm, GF, Sep 24)
Ancient Cross 107 4 (5f 140y, Donc, GF, Sep 10)
Anmar (USA) 111 3 (1m 2f 6y, Newb, Gd, Jul 16)
Anne Of Kiev (IRE) 107 1 (6f, Hayd, GF, May 21)
Antara (GER) 108 1 (1m 114y, Epso, Gd, Jun 3)
Aoife Alainn (IRE) 105 4 (1m 2f, Curr, Gd, Aug 7)
Apache (IRE) 108 3 (1m 6f, York, Gd, Aug 20)

Arctic (IRE) 104 5 (5f, Curr, Gd, Jun 26)
Arctic Cosmos (USA) 113 2 (1m 4f, Asco, Gd, Oct 1)
Arganil (USA) 105 1 (5f, Souw, SD, Jan 25)
Arlequin 108 2 (1m 2f 88y, York, GS, Aug 17)
Ask Jack (USA) 106 4 (1m, Curr, Gd, Jun 26)
Askar Tau (FR) 113 5 (2m 4f, Asco, GS, Jun 16)
Atlantic Sport (USA) 106 5 (7f, Asco, GS, Jul 23)
Auld Burns 109 2 (1m 2f 95y, Hayd, Gd, Aug 6)
Averroes (IRE) 105 1 (1m 4f, Asco, GS, Aug 6)
Await The Dawn (USA) 125 1 (1m 2f 75y, Ches, GF, May 5)
Awsaal 104 1 (1m 4f, York, Gd, Jul 8)
Awzaan 108 3 (7f, York, Gd, May 21)
Axiom 104 4 (7f, Asco, Gd, Oct 15)
Balcarce Nov (ARG) 106 3 (1m, Donc, Gd, Apr 16)
Balducci 107 4 (1m 67y, Wind, Gd, Jun 25)
Ballybacka Lady (IRE) 104 6 (1m, Leop, Gd, Sep 3)
Banimpire (IRE) 114 1 (1m 2f, Curr, Gd, Aug 7)
Banksters Bonus (IRE) 107 1 (1m 4f 190y, Dowr, Sft, Jun 18)
Banna Boirche (IRE) 103 4 (1m, Cork, GF, Jul 31)
Barack (IRE) 107 2 (1m 100y, Kill, Gd, Aug 23)
Barbican 116 1 (1m 4f, Kemw, SD, Nov 30)
Barefoot Lady (IRE) 110 5 (1m 1f 192y, Good, GF, Jul 30)
Bated Breath 122 2 (6f, Hayd, GF, Sep 3)
Bauer (IRE) 110 1 (1m 6f, Hayd, GF, Sep 3)
Bay Knight (IRE) 104 2 (7f 100y, Tipp, Hvy, Oct 2)
Bea Remembered 104 1 (1m 2f 60y, Donc, Gd, Jun 3)
Beachfire 111 1 (1m 2f, Asco, GS, Jun 17)
Beacon Lodge (IRE) 115 3 (1m, Good, GS, Aug 27)
Beaten Up 123 1 (1m 4f 5y, Newb, GF, Oct 22)
Belgian Bill 104 4 (1m, Asco, GS, Jun 16)

RPR TOP THREE-YEAR-OLDS AND OLDER HORSES OF 2011

Belle Royale (IRE) 112 1 (1m 2f 75y, Ches, GS, Sep 24)
Below Zero (IRE) 103 1 (7f, Leop, Gd, Sep 3)
Bergo (GER) 111 3 (2m 88y, York, Gd, Aug 20)
Best Hello 103 4 (1m 2f, Leop, Gd, May 8)
Bewitched (IRE) 113 1 (7f, Leop, GF, May 29)
Beyond Desire 106 4 (5f 34y, Newb, Gd, Sep 17)
Bible Belt (IRE) 114 2 (1m 4f, Asco, Gd, Oct 15)
Black Spirit (USA) 110 2 (1m 2f 7y, Sand, Gd, Apr 23)
Blanche Dubawi (IRE) 106 1 (6f, Newm, GF, Oct 1)
Blissful Moment (USA) 105 2 (1m 4f, Asco, Sft, Jun 18)
Blue Bajan (IRE) 116 3 (2m, Good, GF, Jul 28)
Blue Bunting (USA) 120 1 (1m 4f, York, GS, Aug 18)
Bob Le Beau (IRE) 110 3 (1m 4f, Leop, Gd, Aug 4)
Bohemian Melody 108 1 (6f, Donc, Gd, Oct 21)
Bonnie Brae 103 1 (7f, Donc, Sft, Nov 5)
Boom And Bust (IRE) 103 1 (1m, Good, GF, Jul 29)
Borderlescott 113 4 (5f, Hayd, GF, May 21)
Brae Hill (IRE) 104 1 (7f, Newj, GF, Jul 9)
Brave Prospector 107 1 (5f 216y, Wolv, SD, Feb 4)
Bravo Echo 107 1 (1m, Kemw, SD, Jan 23)
Brevity (USA) 106 3 (1m 14y, Sand, Sft, Aug 20)
Bridge Of Gold (USA) 112 2 (1m 4f 5y, Newb, GF, Apr 16)
Bridgefield (USA) 105 1 (1m, Newj, Gd, Jul 7)
Brigantin 114 3 (2m 4f, Asco, GS, Jun 16)
Bronze Cannon (USA) 109 2 (1m 4f, Kemw, SD, Sep 3)
Brown Panther 119 2 (1m 6f 132y, Donc, GF, Sep 10)
Brushing 106 8 (1m 4f, Asco, Gd, Oct 15)
Bubble Chic (FR) 109 1 (1m 1f, Newm, Gd, Oct 8)
Bullet Train 110 8 (1m, Asco, Gd, Oct 15)
Burj Nahar 106 1 (1m 2f, Newj, Gd, Jun 25)
Burning Thread (IRE) 104 1 (5f, Muss, GF, Jun 4)
Buthelezi (USA) 105 4 (1m 5f 61y, Newb, Gd, Aug 13)
Buxted (IRE) 108 5 (1m 6f, York, GF, May 13)
Cai Shen (IRE) 109 1 (1m 2f 60y, Donc, Gd, Sep 7)
Campanologist (USA) 117 2 (1m 2f 110y, Curr, Gd, May 22)
Canford Cliffs (IRE) 130 1 (1m, Asco, Gd, Jun 14)
Cape Dollar (IRE) 106 3 (1m 14y, Sand, Gd, Jul 2)
Captain Dunne (IRE) 111 1 (5f, Epso, GF, Jun 4)
Captain John Nixon 103 1 (2m, Kemw, SD, Jun 29)
Captain Ramius (IRE) 107 1 (7f, Newj, Gd, Aug 6)
Carlton House (USA) 121 3 (1m 4f 10y, Epso, GF, Jun 4)
Casual Glimpse 108 3 (1m, Donc, GF, Sep 10)
Cavalryman 114 2 (1m 4f, Newj, GS, Jun 25)
Ceilidh House 103 3 (1m 2f 188y, Warw, Gd, Jun 13)
Celerina (IRE) 103 2 (5f, Ayr, Sft, Jun 18)
Census (IRE) 118 1 (1m 5f 61y, Newb, Gd, Aug 13)
Chachamaidee (IRE) 116 2 (1m, Newm, GF, Sep 24)
Chain Lightning 106 2 (1m 2f 60y, Donc, Gd, Sep 8)
Chef 105 2 (1m, Good, GF, Jul 29)
Cheviot (USA) 103 3 (6f, Curr, Sft, Oct 9)
Chiberta King 111 2 (2m, Newm, GF, Sep 22)
Chilworth Lad 114 1 (7f, Redc, GF, Oct 1)
Cill Rialaig 108 6 (1m 4f, Asco, Gd, Oct 15)
Circumvent 107 2 (1m 2f, Linw, SD, Nov 12)
Cirrus Des Aigles (FR) 130 1 (1m 2f, Asco, Gd, Oct 15)
Citrus Star (USA) 105 1 (7f, Linw, SD, Oct 27)
City Leader (IRE) 114 1 (1m 1f 192y, Good, GF, May 21)
Cityscape 123 3 (1m, Asco, Gd, Jun 14)
Claiomh Solais (IRE) 110 4 (1m, Curr, Gd, May 22)
Class Is Class 105 1 (1m 2f 95y, Hayd, Gd, Aug 6)
Classic Punch 105 1 (1m 2f, Newj, Gd, Aug 6)
Clinical 105 1 (1m, Linw, SD, Oct 27)
Clowance 116 3 (1m 4f 10y, Epso, Gd, Jun 3)
Club Oceanic 107 1 (1m 2f 60y, Donc, Gd, Sep 8)
Cocozza (USA) 103 5 (1m 2f, Curr, Gd, Aug 7)
Colombian (IRE) 105 2 (1m 3f 183y, Leic, GF, Oct 24)
Colonel Mak 106 1 (6f, Ffos, GS, Aug 26)
Colonial (IRE) 112 1 (7f 26y, Warw, Gd, Aug 29)

Colour Vision (FR) 113 3 (2m, Asco, Gd, Oct 15)
Con Artist (IRE) 103 1 (1m 2f 18y, Epso, Gd, Sep 25)
Confessional 105 2 (5f, Hayd, GS, Sep 24)
Confront 111 1 (1m 208y, York, Gd, Jun 11)
Contredanse (IRE) 103 3 (1m 2f 88y, York, GS, Jul 22)
Creekside 104 1 (1m, Leop, Gd, Jun 16)
Critical Moment (USA) 107 4 (1m 2f 75y, Ches, GF, May 5)
Croisultan (IRE) 106 3 (6f, Curr, Sft, Sep 11)
Crystal Capella 121 1 (1m 4f, Newj, Gd, Jul 7)
Crystal Gal (IRE) 103 1 (1m, Hayd, Gd, Aug 6)
Dafeef 112 2 (7f, Donc, GF, Sep 10)
Dahindar (IRE) 104 2 (1m, Dunw, SD, Apr 8)
Dalghar (FR) 107 6 (7f, Good, Gd, Jul 26)
Dan Excel (IRE) 114 5 (1m 4f, Curr, Gd, Jun 26)
Dance And Dance (IRE) 116 5 (1m, Good, GF, Jul 29)
Dancing Rain (IRE) 118 1 (1m 4f, Asco, Gd, Oct 15)
Dandino 117 1 (1m 4f, Newm, GF, Apr 30)
Dansili Dancer 109 2 (1m 2f, Linw, SD, Mar 26)
Dare To Dance (IRE) 111 1 (1m 2f, Ayr, Sft, Sep 27)
Dark Promise 109 1 (1m, Newm, GF, Sep 23)
Darley Sun (IRE) 104 8 (2m, Asco, Gd, Oct 15)
Deacon Blues 125 1 (6f, Curr, Yld, Aug 7)
Debussy (IRE) 109 4 (1m 4f, Asco, GS, Jul 23)
Definightly 108 2 (6f, Curr, Sft, Sep 11)
Defining Year (IRE) 106 2 (1m 2f, Leop, Yld, Oct 30)
Delegator 117 1 (6f, York, Gd, May 11)
Desert Law (IRE) 109 2 (6f, Asco, GS, Aug 6)
Desert Poppy (IRE) 105 3 (6f, Asco, Gd, Oct 1)
Dever Dream 111 2 (7f, Donc, Gd, Sep 8)
Dick Turpin (IRE) 123 1 (1m, Asco, Gd, Jul 9)
Dinkum Diamond (IRE) 111 2 (5f, Donc, Gd, Sep 7)
Distant Memories (IRE) 113 2 (1m 2f 75y, Ches, GF, May 5)
Docofthebay (IRE) 109 2 (7f 32y, Wolw, SD, Mar 12)
Dominant (IRE) 115 3 (1m 2f 88y, York, Gd, Jul 23)
Doncaster Rover (USA) 113 2 (6f, Newc, GS, Jun 25)
Dorcas Lane 106 3 (1m 3f 200y, Hayd, GF, Jul 2)
Dordogne (IRE) 104 1 (1m 3f 106y, Ling, GF, May 7)
Dream Ahead (USA) 124 1 (6f, Newj, GF, Jul 9)
Dream Eater (IRE) 104 5 (1m 2f 75y, Ches, GF, May 5)
Drunken Sailor (IRE) 118 1 (1m 5f 61y, Newb, GF, May 14)
Dubai Prince (IRE) 114 1 (1m 1f, Newb, GS, Sep 16)
Dubawi Gold 120 4 (1m, Asco, Gd, Oct 15)
Duchess Dora 107 2 (5f, Asco, Gd, Jul 24)
Duff (IRE) 105 2 (1m, Leop, Gd, Jun 16)
Duncan 119 1 (1m 6f, Curr, Sft, Sep 10)
Dunelight (IRE) 110 1 (7f 32y, Wolw, SD, Mar 12)
Dungannon 103 1 (5f, Asco, GS, Aug 6)
Dux Scholar 115 2 (1m 2f, Newm, Gd, Oct 29)
Ecliptic (USA) 111 1 (6f 212y, Sali, Gd, Oct 10)
Edinburgh Knight (IRE) 106 1 (1m, Kemw, SD, Nov 23)
Eleanora Duse (IRE) 109 6 (1m 2f 88y, York, Gd, Jul 23)
Electrolyser (IRE) 107 3 (2m 78y, Sand, Gd, Jul 2)
Elnawin 113 1 (6f, Sali, Sft, Jun 12)
Elusive Pimpernel (USA) 111 2 (1m 2f 95y, Hayd, Gd, Aug 6)
Elzaam (AUS) 117 1 (6f 8y, Newb, GF, May 13)
Emerald Commander (IRE) 114 1 (1m 4y, Pont, GF, Jul 24)
Emiyna (USA) 109 2 (1m, Leop, Gd, Aug 11)
Empowering 104 3 (1m, Naas, Sft, Oct 16)
Emulous 120 1 (1m, Leop, Gd, Sep 3)
Eternal Heart (IRE) 106 6 (2m, Asco, Gd, Oct 15)
Eton Forever (IRE) 110 1 (1m, Donc, Gd, Apr 2)
Eton Rifles (IRE) 109 1 (6f, Curr, Sft, Oct 9)
Evens And Odds (IRE) 105 1 (6f, Thir, Gd, Apr 9)
Excelebration (IRE) 129 2 (1m, Asco, Gd, Oct 15)
Fallen Idol 113 1 (1m 2f 7y, Sand, GS, Aug 20)
Fame And Glory 121 1 (2m 4f, Asco, GS, Jun 16)
Famous Name 123 1 (1m 1f, Leop, Sft, Jul 21)
Fanunalter 118 2 (1m, Asco, Gd, Jul 9)

RPR TOP THREE-YEAR-OLDS AND OLDER HORSES OF 2011

Fareer 112 8 (1m, York, Gd, May 12)
Farhh 107 1 (1m, Newm, Gd, Oct 29)
Ferdoos 118 1 (1m 3f 200y, Hayd, GF, May 28)
Fictional Account (IRE) 106 4 (1m 6f, Leop, GF, May 29)
Field Day (IRE) 108 6 (1m 1f 192y, Good, GF, Jul 30)
Field Of Dream 106 2 (7f 9y, Leic, GF, Apr 16)
Field Of Miracles (IRE) 110 2 (1m 4f, Asco, GS, Jun 16)
Finicius (USA) 103 2 (1m, Leop, GF, Apr 10)
Fiorente (IRE) 111 2 (1m 4f, Good, Gd, Jul 26)
Firebeam 109 1 (7f, Hayd, GS, Sep 13)
First City 112 3 (1m, Newj, Gd, Jul 8)
Flambeau 113 1 (7f 9y, Leic, GF, Apr 16)
Flowers Of Spring (IRE) 105 1 (1m 1f 100y, Gowr, Gd, Sep 24)
Folly Bridge 104 1 (7f, Newm, Gd, May 27)
Fontley 105 3 (1m, Asco, GF, May 7)
Forjatt (IRE) 105 2 (7f, Newj, GF, Aug 11)
Forte Dei Marmi 112 3 (1m 2f 75y, Ches, GF, May 5)
Fox Hunt (IRE) 118 6 (1m 6f, York, Gd, Aug 20)
Frankel 139 1 (1m, Asco, Gd, Oct 15)
Free Agent 105 3 (2m, Asco, GF, Apr 27)
Freedom (IRE) 105 1 (1m 2f 150y, Dunw, SD, Sep 30)
French Navy 115 1 (1m 1f 192y, Good, GS, Sep 10)
Fulgur 106 1 (1m 2f, Newj, Gd, Jul 7)
Fury 109 2 (1m 14y, Sand, GS, May 26)
Future Generation (IRE) 109 4 (1m, Curr, Gd, Aug 28)
Galileo's Choice (IRE) 111 1 (1m 2f, Leop, Gd, Sep 3)
Gemstone (IRE) 105 6 (1m 4f, Curr, Yld, Jul 17)
Genius Beast (USA) 110 1 (1m 2f 7y, Sand, Gd, Apr 24)
Genki (IRE) 117 4 (6f, Hayd, GF, Sep 3)
Gertrude Bell 111 3 (1m 4f, Asco, Gd, Oct 15)
Glen's Diamond 107 1 (1m 2f 75y, Ches, GF, May 6)
Global City 105 3 (6f, Linw, SD, Nov 12)
Glor Na Mara (IRE) 105 3 (7f, Leop, GF, May 29)
Goldikova (IRE) 126 2 (1m, Asco, Gd, Jun 14)
Gramercy (IRE) 106 2 (7f, Asco, Gd, Sep 3)
Green Destiny (IRE) 121 1 (1m 3f 5y, Newb, Gd, Sep 17)
Group Therapy 112 3 (5f, Good, GF, Jul 28)
Halfsin (IRE) 106 1 (1m 2f, Newj, GS, Jul 16)
Halicarnassus (IRE) 108 5 (1m 4f, Good, GF, Jul 29)
Hamish Mcgonagall 117 2 (5f, York, GS, Aug 19)
Handassa 104 4 (1m 2f, Leop, Yld, Oct 30)
Harlestone Times (IRE) 106 1 (1m 4f, Good, GF, May 21)
Harris Tweed 118 2 (1m 4f, Asco, Sft, Jun 18)
Hawaafez 104 1 (1m 4f, Newm, Gd, Oct 28)
Hawkeyethenoo (IRE) 110 1 (7f, Asco, GF, May 7)
Haziyna (IRE) 103 2 (1m 4f, Rosc, GF, Jul 4)
High Ruler (USA) 104 2 (1m 2f 150y, Dunw, SD, Sep 30)
High Standing (USA) 105 3 (7f, Good, Gd, Aug 28)
High Twelve (IRE) 110 1 (1m 2f, Asco, GS, Jul 22)
Highland Castle 113 1 (1m 6f 21y, Sali, Gd, Sep 1)
History Note (IRE) 108 6 (1m, Curr, Gd, May 22)
Hitchens (IRE) 117 3 (6f, Newj, GF, Jul 9)
Holberg (UAE) 107 3 (2m 78y, Sand, GS, May 26)
Hoof It 124 1 (6f, Good, GF, Jul 30)
Hooray 109 1 (7f, Epso, Gd, Jun 3)
Horseradish 109 2 (6f, York, GF, May 13)
Hot Prospect 112 2 (1m 2f 6y, Newb, Gd, Jul 16)
Hujaylea (IRE) 110 2 (7f, Leop, Gd, Sep 3)
Humidor (IRE) 113 1 (5f, Donc, Gd, Sep 7)
Hunter's Light (IRE) 116 1 (1m 1f 192y, Good, Sft, Sep 21)
Hurricane Higgins (IRE) 105 4 (1m 5f, Newj, Gd, Jul 7)
I Love Me 108 4 (1m, Asco, GS, Jun 17)
I'm A Dreamer (IRE) 115 1 (1m 1f, Newm, GF, May 1)
Icon Dream (IRE) 103 2 (1m 6f, Good, GF, Jul 30)
Immortal Verse (IRE) 118 3 (1m, Asco, Gd, Oct 15)
Imperial Guest 103 1 (6f, Asco, GF, May 7)
Imperial Pippin (USA) 104 2 (1m 4f, Newm, GF, Sep 22)
Imperial Rome (IRE) 109 1 (7f, Curr, GF, May 2)

Indian Days 117 1 (1m 4f 5y, Newb, GF, Apr 16)
Inler (IRE) 109 4 (7f, Hayd, GF, May 28)
Internationaldebut (IRE) 108 1 (6f, Donc, Gd, Sep 8)
Investissement 108 3 (1m 6f, York, Gd, Aug 20)
Invincible Ash (IRE) 110 1 (5f, Curr, Gd, Jun 26)
Invincible Soul (IRE) 104 3 (1m, Good, GF, May 30)
Invisible Man 111 3 (1m, Asco, Gd, Jun 15)
Inxile (IRE) 118 1 (5f, Tipp, GF, Aug 5)
Irish Flame (SAF) 116 1 (1m 3f, Kemw, SD, Nov 10)
Iver Bridge Lad 111 2 (6f, Newm, GF, Apr 14)
Izzi Top 106 3 (1m 4f 10y, Epso, Gd, Jun 3)
Jackaroo (IRE) 106 1 (1m 2f 150y, Dunw, SD, Aug 14)
Jacqueline Quest (IRE) 105 2 (7f, Good, Gd, Aug 28)
Jan Vermeer (IRE) 108 2 (1m 2f, Curr, Sft, Jun 24)
Jet Away 116 1 (1m 2f 88y, York, Gd, Oct 7)
Jimmy Styles 111 1 (6f, Donc, Gd, Apr 2)
Joe Packet 107 3 (7f, Newb, GS, Sep 16)
Johnny Castle 103 3 (7f, Donc, Gd, Sep 7)
Jonny Mudball 108 3 (5f, Newm, GF, Apr 30)
Joshua Tree (IRE) 115 2 (1m 2f, Newj, Gd, Aug 13)
Joviality 109 4 (1m, Newj, Gd, Jul 8)
Jukebox Jury (IRE) 119 1 (1m 6f, Curr, Sft, Sep 10)
Julienas (IRE) 105 1 (1m, Asco, Gd, Jun 15)
Jutland 104 1 (1m 1f 192y, Good, Gd, Jul 26)
Kakatosi 109 2 (7f, York, Gd, May 21)
Kaldoun Kingdom (IRE) 103 3 (5f, Muss, GF, Jun 4)
Kansai Spirit (IRE) 107 3 (1m 4f, York, GF, May 13)
Kasbah Bliss (FR) 110 7 (2m 4f, Asco, GS, Jun 16)
Katla (IRE) 105 2 (6f, Fair, Gd, Jul 10)
Khor Sheed 107 1 (7f 26y, Warw, GF, Jun 23)
Kiama Bay (IRE) 106 2 (1m 4f, York, GS, Aug 19)
King Of Dixie (USA) 106 2 (1m, Kemw, SD, Sep 15)
King Of Jazz (IRE) 104 2 (1m, Hayd, Gd, May 21)
King Torus (IRE) 113 1 (1m, Hayd, GF, Sep 3)
Kings Gambit (SAF) 111 2 (1m 1f 170y, Ripo, Gd, Apr 7)
Kingsgate Native (IRE) 107 3 (5f, Hayd, GF, May 21)
Kirthill (IRE) 104 1 (1m 2f 6y, Newb, GF, Oct 22)
Kissable 104 2 (1m 4f, Curr, Sft, Oct 9)
Laaheb 114 4 (1m 4f, Asco, Sft, Jun 18)
Laajooj (IRE) 108 1 (1m 2f, Newm, Gd, May 28)
Labarinto 104 1 (1m 1f 192y, Good, Gd, Jul 28)
Ladies Are Forever 111 1 (6f, York, Gd, Jul 8)
Laughing (IRE) 104 1 (1m 3f, Leop, Yld, Jun 9)
Laughing Lashes (USA) 113 4 (1m 4f, Curr, Yld, Jul 17)
Law Of The Range 107 3 (7f, Good, GF, Jul 29)
Lay Time 111 1 (1m 14y, Sand, Gd, Sep 14)
Lechevalier Choisi (IRE) 106 3 (7f, York, Gd, Aug 20)
Lexi's Hero (IRE) 108 2 (6f, Newj, Gd, Jul 8)
Libranno 117 3 (6f, Asco, Gd, Oct 15)
Light From Mars 106 1 (1m, Newb, GF, Apr 16)
Lightning Cloud (IRE) 103 1 (7f, Donc, Gd, Sep 7)
Lolly For Dolly (IRE) 115 1 (1m, Asco, Gd, Jun 15)
Look At Me (IRE) 106 1 (1m 100y, Cork, Sft, Oct 15)
Lord Of The Stars (USA) 103 2 (7f, Epso, Gd, Jun 3)
Lost In The Moment (IRE) 115 2 (2m, Good, GF, Jul 28)
Louis The Pious 103 3 (6f, Asco, Gd, Sep 30)
Lowther 108 1 (1m 141y, Wolw, SD, Mar 12)
Loyalty 106 1 (1m, Linw, SD, Dec 17)
Luisant 108 3 (6f, Curr, Sft, Mar 20)
Mac Love 105 5 (1m 114y, Epso, GF, Jun 4)
Mac's Power (IRE) 107 2 (6f 8y, Newb, GF, May 14)
Mahbooba (AUS) 108 1 (1m 4f, Newm, GF, Sep 23)
Majestic Myles (IRE) 114 2 (7f, York, Gd, Aug 20)
Malcheek (IRE) 106 3 (7f 32y, Wolw, SD, Mar 12)
Malthouse (GER) 106 2 (1m 3f 16y, Hami, Gd, Jul 14)
Man Of Action (USA) 107 1 (1m, Donc, GF, Sep 10)
Manassas (IRE) 104 1 (7f, Asco, Sft, Jun 17)
Manieree (IRE) 116 1 (1m 2f, Curr, Yld, Sep 11)

RPR TOP THREE-YEAR-OLDS AND OLDER HORSES OF 2011

Manighar (FR) 113 4 (2m 4f, Asco, GS, Jun 16)
Maqaasid 111 3 (1m, Newm, GF, May 1)
Maraheb 105 1 (1m, Hayd, GS, Aug 4)
Margot Did (IRE) 118 1 (5f, York, GS, Aug 19)
Markab 112 2 (6f 8y, Newb, Gd, Jul 16)
Marksmanship (IRE) 110 2 (1m 4f, Leop, Gd, Aug 4)
Masamah (IRE) 118 2 (5f 34y, Newb, Gd, Sep 17)
Masked Marvel 124 1 (1m 6f 132y, Donc, GF, Sep 10)
Mayson 105 2 (6f, Donc, Sft, Nov 5)
Measuring Time 108 3 (1m 1f 192y, Good, GS, Sep 10)
Medicean Man 113 2 (5f, Asco, GS, Aug 6)
Meeznah (USA) 115 1 (1m 6f 132y, Donc, Gd, Sep 8)
Memphis Tennessee (IRE) 119 3 (1m 4f, Curr, Gd, Jun 26)
Merchant Of Dubai 105 5 (1m 4f 17y, Hami, Gd, May 13)
Mia's Boy 106 1 (1m 141y, Wolw, SD, Dec 10)
Midday 123 1 (1m 2f 88y, York, Gd, May 12)
Mijhaar 111 2 (1m 2f, Newj, Gd, Jul 7)
Mikhail Glinka (IRE) 106 4 (1m 14y, Sand, Gd, Sep 14)
Mirror Lake 104 2 (1m 4f 5y, Newb, Gd, Jul 31)
Misty For Me (IRE) 119 1 (1m 2f, Curr, Sft, Jun 25)
Modeyra 108 2 (1m 14y, Sand, Sft, Aug 20)
Modun (IRE) 113 1 (1m 4f, Kemw, SD, Sep 3)
Mohedian Lady (IRE) 108 1 (1m 4f, Newm, GF, Sep 22)
Mon Cadeaux 104 2 (7f 2y, Ches, Gd, Jul 9)
Monsieur Chevalier (IRE) 117 2 (6f, Asco, Sft, Jun 18)
Monsieur Joe (IRE) 104 3 (5f, Asco, GF, May 6)
Montaff 110 2 (2m 19y, Newc, GS, Jun 25)
Moonlight Cloud 113 5 (6f, Asco, Gd, Oct 15)
Morache Music 108 1 (6f, Asco, GS, Aug 6)
Moran Gra (USA) 107 2 (1m, Curr, Gd, Aug 28)
Moriarty (IRE) 104 2 (1m 2f, Curr, Gd, May 22)
Motivado 105 4 (1m 6f, Hayd, GS, Sep 24)
Motrice 112 3 (2m 2f, Donc, Gd, Sep 9)
Mount Athos (IRE) 108 4 (1m 3f 200y, Hayd, GF, Jul 2)
Move In Time 106 1 (5f, Asco, Gd, Oct 1)
Moyenne Corniche 110 1 (1m 6f, York, Gd, Aug 20)
Music Show (IRE) 110 5 (1m, Newm, GF, Sep 24)
Musir (AUS) 110 3 (7f, Newb, Gd, Aug 13)
Mutahadee (IRE) 106 3 (1m 2f, Curr, Gd, Aug 7)
Myplacelater 106 2 (1m 2f 88y, York, GS, Jul 22)
Nahrain 107 1 (1m 14y, Sand, Gd, Jul 2)
Namecheck (GER) 107 1 (1m, Newj, GS, Jul 16)
Namibian (IRE) 115 1 (1m 4f, Good, Gd, Jul 26)
Nanton (USA) 108 4 (1m 1f, Newm, GF, Sep 24)
Naqshabban (USA) 111 2 (1m 2f 6y, Newb, Gd, Sep 17)
Nasri 104 1 (6f 5y, Hami, Sft, Sep 19)
Nathaniel (IRE) 126 1 (1m 4f, Asco, GS, Jul 23)
Nationalism 111 1 (1m 67y, Wind, Gd, Jun 25)
Native Khan (FR) 118 5 (1m 4f 10y, Epso, GF, Jun 4)
Native Ruler 117 2 (1m 4f, Newm, GF, Apr 30)
Navajo Chief 113 1 (1m, York, GS, Aug 18)
Nebula Storm (IRE) 107 2 (1m 5f, Nava, Yld, Apr 17)
Neebras (IRE) 116 4 (1m, Asco, Gd, Jun 14)
Nehaam 113 4 (2m, Asco, Gd, Oct 15)
New Deerfield 115 1 (7f, Newm, GF, May 14)
New Planet (IRE) 105 6 (6f, York, Gd, Jun 11)
Nideeb 112 1 (1m 2f, Linw, SD, Mar 26)
Night Carnation 113 1 (5f 6y, Sand, Gd, Apr 24)
Noble Storm (USA) 114 1 (5f 34y, Newb, GF, Apr 15)
Nocturnal Affair (SAF) 111 1 (5f 140y, Donc, GF, Sep 10)
Northgate (IRE) 105 1 (1m 4f 195y, Dowr, Gd, Sep 9)
Norville (IRE) 104 1 (6f, Wind, Gd, Jun 25)
Notable Graduate (IRE) 105 2 (1m 3f, Leop, Yld, Jun 9)
Nova Hawk 110 2 (1m, Asco, GS, Jun 17)
Oasis Dancer 104 1 (5f 216y, Wolw, SD, Dec 10)
Ocean War 108 1 (1m 2f, Newm, GF, Apr 30)
Off Chance 104 5 (1m, York, Gd, May 12)
Opera Gal (IRE) 104 1 (1m 3f 135y, Wind, GS, Aug 27)

Opinion Poll (IRE) 120 1 (2m 88y, York, Gd, Aug 20)
Oracle (IRE) 114 3 (1m, Curr, GF, May 21)
Our Joe Mac (IRE) 105 1 (1m 2f 88y, York, GS, Aug 17)
Our Jonathan 117 1 (6f, Ayr, Sft, Sep 17)
Overdose 116 4 (5f, Asco, Gd, Jun 14)
Overturn (IRE) 110 7 (2m, Good, GF, Jul 28)
Pabusar 109 2 (6f, Newj, Gd, Jul 23)
Packing Tycoon (IRE) 108 3 (1m 4f, Asco, GS, Jun 17)
Parlour Games 104 1 (1m 6f, York, Gd, Aug 20)
Passion For Gold (USA) 115 1 (1m 4f, Good, GF, May 21)
Pastoral Player 114 1 (7f, Asco, Gd, Oct 1)
Pausanias 109 2 (7f, Newj, GS, Jun 25)
Penitent 111 3 (1m 67y, Wind, Gd, May 9)
Pepper Lane 107 1 (6f, Ripo, GS, Aug 13)
Perfect Tribute 108 1 (7f, Ling, GF, May 7)
Petara Bay (IRE) 111 1 (1m 6f, Good, GF, Jul 30)
Pink Symphony 104 1 (1m 4f, Cork, GF, Jul 31)
Pintura 105 3 (1m, York, GS, Aug 18)
Pirateer (IRE) 104 1 (1m, Curr, Gd, Jun 26)
Pisco Sour (USA) 113 1 (1m 2f, Asco, GS, Jun 16)
Planteur (IRE) 116 4 (1m 2f, Asco, Gd, Jun 15)
Poet 118 2 (1m 2f 7y, Sand, GS, May 26)
Poet's Voice 117 6 (1m, Asco, Gd, Oct 15)
Polly's Mark (IRE) 109 2 (1m 4f, Good, GF, Apr 30)
Polytechnicien (USA) 115 2 (1m 1f, Newm, GF, Apr 14)
Poplin 103 2 (1m 2f, Newm, GF, Oct 1)
Pour Moi (IRE) 123 1 (1m 4f 10y, Epso, GF, Jun 4)
Premio Loco (USA) 117 3 (1m, Newb, GF, May 14)
Primaeval 107 1 (7f, Kemw, SD, Nov 16)
Prime Defender 113 1 (6f, Donc, Gd, Jul 30)
Primevere (IRE) 107 1 (1m 1f 198y, Sali, GF, Aug 10)
Prince Bishop (IRE) 110 1 (1m 4f, Kemw, SD, Nov 2)
Prince Siegfried (FR) 116 1 (1m 2f 7y, Wind, GS, Aug 27)
Principal Role (USA) 114 3 (1m 1f 192y, Good, GF, Jul 30)
Prohibit 121 1 (5f, Asco, Gd, Jun 14)
Prompter 107 3 (1m 4f, York, GS, Aug 19)
Proponent (IRE) 106 3 (1m 1f, Newm, GF, Sep 24)
Prospect Wells (FR) 103 4 (1m 6f, York, Gd, May 21)
Puff (IRE) 106 1 (6f, Newj, GF, Jun 24)
Pyrrha 104 3 (7f, Ling, GF, May 7)
Quest For Peace (IRE) 116 1 (1m 4f, Asco, Gd, Oct 1)
Quest For Success (IRE) 107 1 (6f 5y, Hami, GF, Jul 15)
Questioning (IRE) 112 2 (1m, Hayd, GF, Sep 3)
Radharcnafarraige (IRE) 103 1 (6f, Leop, Gd, Jun 9)
Rain Delayed (IRE) 109 2 (5f 34y, Newb, GF, Apr 15)
Rajsaman (FR) 114 3 (1m, Good, Gd, Jul 27)
Ransom Note 118 1 (1m, Newm, GF, Sep 23)
Rasmy 108 6 (1m 4f, Good, Gd, Jul 29)
Rave (IRE) 109 3 (1m, Asco, GS, Jul 23)
Recital (FR) 118 1 (1m 2f, Leop, Gd, May 8)
Red Cadeaux 118 3 (1m 6f, Curr, Sft, Sep 10)
Red Gulch 108 1 (1m, Kemw, SD, Sep 3)
Red Jazz (USA) 115 2 (7f, Good, Gd, Jul 26)
Redford 107 3 (7f, Hayd, Gd, May 7)
Redwood 112 4 (1m 4f, Good, GF, Jul 29)
Regal Parade 115 2 (6f, York, Gd, May 11)
Regent Street (IRE) 107 2 (1m 2f, Leop, GF, Apr 10)
Rerouted (USA) 108 2 (7f, Newm, GF, Apr 13)
Resurge (IRE) 107 1 (1m 2f 18y, Epso, Gd, Jun 3)
Rewilding 130 1 (1m 2f, Asco, Gd, Jun 15)
Rhythm Of Light 106 1 (1m, Asco, Gd, Jun 15)
Rich Tapestry (IRE) 105 4 (1m 2f, Leop, GF, Apr 10)
Riggins (IRE) 105 1 (1m, Linw, SD, Nov 12)
Right Step 104 2 (1m 2f 18y, Epso, Gd, Jun 3)
Rimth 106 4 (7f, Good, GF, Jul 29)
Rio De La Plata (USA) 119 3 (1m, Good, Gd, Jul 27)
Rite Of Passage 113 3 (1m 6f, Leop, GF, May 29)
River Jetez (SAF) 108 5 (1m, Newj, Gd, Jul 8)

RPR TOP THREE-YEAR-OLDS AND OLDER HORSES OF 2011

Rock A Doodle Doo (IRE) 105 4 (1m 4f, Asco, Sft, Jun 18)
Rock And Roll Kid (IRE) 105 1 (1m 1f, Leop, Gd, Sep 3)
Rock Critic (IRE) 104 1 (1m 100y, Galw, Gd, Jul 28)
Rock Jock (IRE) 104 1 (6f 18y, Ches, GF, Jul 31)
Roderic O'connor (IRE) 117 1 (1m, Curr, GF, May 21)
Roicead (USA) 107 3 (5f, Curr, Gd, Aug 28)
Rose Blossom 105 3 (6f, York, Gd, Jul 8)
Rose Bonheur 107 2 (6f, Asco, Gd, Oct 1)
Roxy Flyer (IRE) 106 6 (1m 6f, Good, GF, Jul 28)
Royal Rock 117 4 (6f, Asco, Gd, Oct 15)
Sabotage (UAE) 108 5 (1m 4f, Newj, GS, Jun 25)
Saddler's Rock (IRE) 122 1 (2m 2f, Donc, Gd, Sep 9)
Sadeek's Song (USA) 107 1 (1m 3f 183y, Leic, GF, Oct 24)
Sadler's Risk (IRE) 104 4 (1m 4f 66y, Ches, GF, May 5)
Sahara Sun (CHI) 109 6 (1m 2f 60y, Donc, Gd, Sep 7)
Sahpresa (USA) 119 1 (1m, Newm, GF, Sep 24)
Sajjhaa 115 2 (1m 2f 88y, York, Gd, May 12)
Santo Padre 106 3 (6f, Curr, GF, May 21)
Sapphire (IRE) 113 1 (1m 4f, Curr, Sft, Oct 9)
Saptapadi (IRE) 113 5 (1m 2f 88y, York, Gd, Jul 23)
Sarrsar 109 1 (1m, Asco, GS, Aug 6)
Sea Moon 126 1 (1m 4f, York, GS, Aug 17)
Sea Of Heartbreak (IRE) 107 3 (1m 3f 5y, Newb, Gd, Sep 17)
Secrecy 112 1 (1m, Donc, Gd, Jul 14)
Secret Asset (IRE) 104 1 (5f 89y, York, GS, Aug 17)
Secret Witness 105 2 (6f, Linw, SD, Nov 12)
Seeharn (IRE) 104 2 (6f, Curr, Sft, Oct 9)
Sense Of Purpose (IRE) 108 1 (1m 4f, Leop, Gd, Aug 4)
Set The Trend 116 2 (1m, Good, GS, Aug 27)
Set To Music 110 2 (1m 6f 132y, Donc, Gd, Sep 8)
Seta 107 2 (1m, Newm, GF, Sep 23)
Seville (GER) 121 2 (1m 4f, Curr, Gd, Jun 26)
Shamali 110 2 (1m 4f, Asco, GF, May 7)
Shankardeh (IRE) 112 2 (1m 6f, Good, GF, Jul 28)
Sharaayeen 104 2 (1m 4f, Newm, GF, May 1)
Shimraan (FR) 110 4 (1m 2f 6y, Newb, Gd, Jul 16)
Side Glance 119 1 (1m 67y, Wind, Gd, May 9)
Sikeeb (IRE) 105 6 (7f, Asco, Gd, Jun 15)
Silaah 106 1 (6f, Kemw, SD, Jan 5)
Simon De Montfort (IRE) 106 3 (1m 2f 7y, Wind, GS, Aug 27)
Sirius Prospect (USA) 115 1 (6f, York, Gd, Oct 8)
Sirvino 104 2 (1m 3f 135y, Wind, GS, Aug 27)
Six Of Hearts 109 1 (6f 63y, Curr, Gd, Jun 26)
Skilful 111 1 (1m, Hayd, GS, Sep 24)
Slumber 114 1 (1m 2f, Newm, Gd, Oct 29)
Smartcity (USA) 104 3 (1m 2f, Curr, Gd, May 22)
Smarty Socks (IRE) 108 2 (7f, Asco, Gd, Oct 1)
Snow Fairy (IRE) 125 3 (1m 2f, Asco, Gd, Oct 15)
So You Think (NZ) 129 1 (1m 2f 7y, Sand, Gd, Jul 2)
Society Rock (IRE) 119 1 (6f, Asco, Sft, Jun 18)
Solar Sky 105 2 (2m, Asco, GS, Jun 17)
Sole Power 120 1 (5f, Hayd, GF, May 21)
Son Of The Cat (USA) 106 1 (6f, Good, GF, Jul 30)
Sooraah 104 2 (1m, Linw, SD, Oct 27)
Spanish Duke (IRE) 110 1 (1m 2f 18y, Epso, Gd, Apr 20)
Specific Gravity (FR) 104 4 (1m 2f, Asco, GS, Jun 16)
Splash Point (USA) 111 5 (7f, Asco, Gd, Jun 15)
Sri Putra 118 3 (1m 2f 7y, Sand, Gd, Jul 2)
St Moritz (IRE) 112 2 (1m 4y, Pont, GF, Jul 24)
St Nicholas Abbey (IRE) 124 1 (1m 4f 10y, Epso, Gd, Jun 3)
Star Witness (AUS) 119 2 (5f, Asco, Gd, Jun 14)
Start Right 108 2 (1m 14y, Sand, Gd, Jul 2)
Steele Tango (USA) 110 3 (1m 4f, Good, GF, May 21)
Strawberrydaiquiri 114 3 (1m, Newm, GF, Sep 24)
Strong Suit (USA) 126 1 (7f, Newm, Gd, Oct 8)
Stunning View (IRE) 104 1 (1m 100y, Galw, Gd, Jul 26)
Sud Pacifique (IRE) 106 1 (1m 1f 207y, Beve, GS, Aug 27)
Suits Me 106 3 (1m 2f, Linw, SD, Nov 12)

Sweet Lightning 114 1 (1m, Donc, Gd, Apr 2)
Sweet Sanette (SAF) 114 3 (5f, Asco, Gd, Jun 14)
Swingkeel (IRE) 104 1 (2m 5f 159y, Asco, Sft, Jun 18)
Swiss Dream 105 2 (6f, Newm, GF, Sep 22)
Tactician 113 2 (1m 6f, York, Gd, Aug 20)
Tajneed (IRE) 111 2 (6f, York, Gd, Jul 23)
Tangerine Trees 116 1 (5f, Beve, GS, Aug 27)
Taqleed (IRE) 108 1 (1m 2f 6y, Newb, Gd, Sep 17)
Tartan Gigha (IRE) 105 2 (1m 141y, Wolw, SD, Mar 12)
Tastahil (IRE) 116 2 (2m 2f 147y, Ches, GF, May 4)
Tazahum (USA) 116 2 (1m 208y, York, GS, Aug 19)
Tazeez (USA) 110 2 (1m 2f 7y, Sand, Gd, Jul 1)
Ted Spread 107 2 (1m 4f 8y, Pont, Gd, Jun 19)
The Betchworth Kid 104 4 (2m, Asco, GF, Apr 27)
The Cheka (IRE) 113 1 (7f, Hayd, GF, May 28)
The Rectifier (USA) 112 3 (1m, Sali, Gd, Aug 11)
Theology 109 3 (1m 5f 89y, Ches, GF, Aug 20)
Theyskens' Theory (USA) 112 1 (1m 14y, Sand, Sft, Aug 20)
Tiddliwinks 114 3 (6f, York, Gd, May 11)
Timepiece 116 1 (1m, Newj, Gd, Jul 8)
Times Up 116 1 (2m, Newm, GF, Sep 22)
Together (IRE) 114 2 (1m, Newm, GF, May 1)
Tominator 105 4 (1m 6f 132y, Donc, Gd, Sep 9)
Toolain (IRE) 108 3 (7f, Asco, GF, May 6)
Treasure Beach 122 1 (1m 4f, Curr, Gd, Jun 26)
Triple Aspect (IRE) 109 5 (6f, York, Gd, May 11)
Twice Over 126 1 (1m 2f 88y, York, GS, Aug 17)
Unaccompanied (IRE) 104 2 (1m 2f, Leop, Yld, Nov 6)
Utley (USA) 108 3 (7f, Newm, GF, Apr 13)
Vadamar (FR) 114 7 (1m 4f 10y, Epso, GF, Jun 4)
Verdant 108 4 (1m 4f, Newj, GS, Jun 25)
Vesuve (IRE) 109 2 (1m 2f, Ayr, Sft, Sep 17)
Viscount Nelson (USA) 117 1 (1m 2f, Curr, GF, Jun 3)
Vita Nova (IRE) 119 2 (1m 4f, York, GS, Aug 18)
Vivacious Vivienne (IRE) 104 2 (1m 6f, Leop, GF, May 29)
Vulcanite (IRE) 106 5 (1m 4f 5y, Newb, GF, Oct 22)
Waffle (IRE) 113 2 (6f, Asco, Sft, Jun 18)
Wannabe King 104 1 (1m 14y, Sand, Gd, Apr 23)
War Artist (AUS) 112 7 (6f, Newj, GF, Jul 9)
Waydownsouth (IRE) 105 3 (1m 2f, Asco, GS, Jun 17)
Webbow (IRE) 104 2 (7f, Good, GS, Aug 27)
Western Aristocrat (USA) 111 3 (7f, Asco, Gd, Jun 15)
What A Charm (IRE) 105 1 (1m 4f, List, Hvy, Sep 14)
When Not Iff (IRE) 104 1 (7f, Gowr, GF, May 1)
Whiplash Willie 110 2 (1m 6f, York, Gd, Aug 20)
Wigmore Hall (IRE) 117 9 (1m 2f, Asco, Gd, Oct 15)
Wild Coco (GER) 114 1 (1m 4f, Newj, GS, Jul 16)
Wild Wind (GER) 110 2 (1m, Curr, Yld, Sep 11)
Willing Foe (USA) 104 4 (1m 2f 6y, Newb, GF, Oct 22)
Winker Watson 104 6 (6f, Newc, GS, Jun 25)
Wizz Kid (IRE) 115 2 (6f, Asco, Gd, Oct 15)
Wonder Of Wonders (USA) 113 3 (1m 4f, York, GS, Aug 18)
Workforce 128 2 (1m 2f 7y, Sand, Gd, Jul 2)
World Heritage 104 4 (1m 4f, Asco, GF, May 7)
Worthadd (IRE) 123 2 (1m, Newb, GF, May 14)
Xilerator (IRE) 105 1 (7f 50y, Ayr, Sft, Sep 17)
Yaa Wayl (IRE) 107 1 (7f, Newb, GF, Jun 30)
Yaseer (IRE) 108 4 (1m 4f, Good, Gd, Jul 26)
York Glory (USA) 106 1 (5f, York, Gd, Aug 20)
Zabarajad (IRE) 108 2 (7f, Curr, GF, May 2)
Zain Al Boldan 105 1 (1m 3f 106y, Ling, GF, May 7)
Zaminast 109 1 (1m 2f, Leop, Yld, Oct 30)
Zanughan (IRE) 105 1 (1m 4f, Galw, Gd, Aug 29)
Zeitoper 106 2 (1m 2f 60y, Donc, Gd, Sep 7)
Zero Money (IRE) 108 1 (5f, Hayd, GF, Sep 3)
Zoffany (IRE) 120 2 (1m, Asco, Gd, Jun 14)
Zuider Zee (GER) 108 1 (1m 4f, Donc, Sft, Nov 5)

Far from Beyond belief that maiden winner could turn into Leger candidate

Dave Edwards with ten whose efforts on the clock suggest they should be worth following

Beyond Conceit Tom Tate

Dwarfed his rivals in the paddock when joint-favourite on his debut over 7f at Redcar in August but was outpaced in the closing stages and came home third behind Asatir. A 250,000 guineas purchase, he was also third when unsuited by a muddling pace over a mile at Haydock later in the month but proved a different proposition when never headed at the same track in October. Relishing the extended ten furlongs and stronger gallop, he clocked comparatively the quickest time on the card, a notable achievement for a then juvenile. Middle distances will suit this season and connections hope he could be a St Leger candidate.

Camberley Two Roger Charlton

Shrewdly placed to complete a sparkling six-timer last season, he improved from a mark of 53 to 79 on official ratings but may still be competitive off his latest mark of 85. It will be tougher this time but he has a willing attitude and, while all his wins were over seven furlongs and a mile, there is every reason to believe he can progress further when upped in trip. Proven on ground ranging from good to firm to good to soft, he could enjoy another profitable campaign.

Colour Vision Saeed Bin Suroor

Held his form remarkably well for Mark Johnston last season and could develop into a Cup horse for Godolphin. Ideally suited by a test of stamina, he improved by 2st during 2011. He won at Pontefract in October and finished third in the Cesarewitch just five days later. And a week after that he took the same berth on Champions Day at Ascot behind Fame And Glory. The sectionals revealed his final furlong split of 12.55sec was not only the pick of the race but was in fact bettered all day by just two horses, Cirrus Des Aigles and Snow Fairy – first and second in the Champion itself – a fine testament to his talents.

Halling's Quest Hughie Morrison

An imposing, lightly raced colt, he had time fans drooling when powering home by eight lengths on the sand in October. It may have been only at Southwell but not many horses earn a Topspeed figure of 91 at the track, especially as a two-year-old. Slowly away on his Salisbury bow in September, he had clearly learned plenty and earned standout figures on the sand, all the more remarkable given the manner of his success. Runner-up Third Half boosted the form the following month and he looks an exciting colt who could be going places.

Intransigent Andrew Balding

Has raced only twice but has the potential to develop into a decent sprinter this summer. Well backed, he ran below expectations on his debut at Salisbury in October and beat just three of the ten runners home. Already a gelding, he was a different proposition on Lingfield's Polytrack six weeks later, scoring smoothly with plenty left in the locker. A half-brother to former useful sprinter Border Music, he looks sure to improve and may exploit a favourable handicap mark.

Mayson Richard Fahey

Having twice been successful as a youngster he returned from a near year absence at Ripon in August, bumping into a well-treated and in-form Pepper Lane and finished third. He was below par on soft ground in the Ayr Gold Cup the following month and then took minor honours in a Listed heat at Ascot. He was later fourth behind Nocturnal Affair before producing a lifetime best on the clock at Doncaster's final meeting when beating all bar high-flying Sirius Prospect. All in all, he showed enough from five outings without a win last season to suggest he can end his lean spell.

Robemaker John Gosden

After six bites at the cherry he broke his duck on easy ground at Yarmouth in July and was not knocked about as he tried to recover from being hampered at the start at Newmarket a month later, beating just one home. He hit the woodwork in a couple of subsequent outings and on ground faster than ideal acquitted himself well when sixth to Farhh back at Newmarket on his final start. That effort warranted a personal best on the stopwatch, which augurs well for his future prospects.

Rugged Cross Henry Candy

Although no match for the winner, he made an eyecatching debut at Newbury in July and put his experience to good use to take the most valuable juvenile maiden of the season at York in August. Always handy, he hit the front about a furlong from home and strode purposefully clear to beat a decent field in good style. The jury remains out on the true worth of the form but he clocked decent time and this promising colt can make an impact in top middle-distance contests.

Shubaat Roger Varian

Unraced as a juvenile, he made a successful debut over a mile and a half at Doncaster in June 2010 and was clearly well regarded as favourite backers never had a moment's anxiety. Two subsequent reverses were clearly not in the script but following an absence of more than a year he reappeared in a handicap at Newbury last September and took minor honours. He has a pronounced knee action but connections have persevered and this unexposed five-year-old could make up for lost time, particularly when upped to a mile and three-quarters.

Spifer Luca Cumani

Although a four-year-old, he has had only a handful of starts and broke his duck in a Newbury maiden in May. Despite three narrow reverses he went up 10lb in the handicap, which will at least open up more opportunities this season. He should have won a hot Newmarket handicap but after overcoming traffic problems he veered left and handed the initiative to Tanfeeth. Unfortunately he displayed a similar trait with a similar outcome at Ascot in September when Barbican was the beneficiary. Hopefully as he matures he will prove capable of ending his frustrating sequence.

'He had time fans drooling when powering home by eight lengths on the sand in October. It may have been only at Southwell but not many horses earn a figure of 91 at the track'

TOPSPEED'S TOP TWO-YEAR-OLDS OF 2011

KEY: Horse name, Best Topspeed figure Finishing position when earning figure
(Details of race where figure was earned)

Abishena (IRE) 90 2 (1m, Newm, Gd, Oct 29)
Absolute Crackers (IRE) 86 2 (1m, Curr, Sft, Oct 9)
After (IRE) 90 2 (6f 63y, Curr, Sft, Jul 17)
Akeed Mofeed 87 2 (1m, Curr, Hvy, Sep 25)
Al Khan (IRE) 88 5 (7f, York, GS, Aug 17)
Alejandro (IRE) 85 1 (6f 18y, Ches, GF, Jul 31)
Alice's Dancer (IRE) 84 1 (5f 218y, Leic, Gd, Sep 19)
Alsindi (IRE) 85 1 (7f, Newm, GF, Sep 23)
Amazing Storm (IRE) 85 1 (6f, Wind, Gd, Aug 8)
An Ghalanta (IRE) 88 1 (5f, Curr, Yld, Aug 20)
Arnold Lane (IRE) 84 2 (5f 161y, Bath, GF, Aug 20)
Artistic Jewel (IRE) 89 1 (6f, Newm, Gd, Oct 28)
Astrology (IRE) 86 1 (1m, Leop, Gd, Aug 11)
Athens (IRE) 88 1 (1m, List, Sft, Sep 13)
B Fifty Two (IRE) 87 8 (6f, Newm, Gd, Oct 8)
Balty Boys (IRE) 97 4 (6f, Newm, Gd, Oct 8)
Bana Wu 95 4 (7f, Newm, Gd, Oct 8)
Bannock (IRE) 100 1 (6f, York, Gd, Oct 8)
Bapak Chinta (USA) 105 1 (5f, Asco, GS, Jun 16)
Bear Behind (IRE) 85 2 (5f, Folk, GF, May 26)
Beau Amadeus (IRE) 89 1 (6f, Naas, Sft, Oct 16)
Beaufort Twelve 85 1 (7f, Newm, Gd, Oct 28)
Best Terms 111 1 (6f, York, GS, Aug 18)
Betty Fontaine (IRE) 86 7 (6f, Newj, Gd, Jul 8)
Bible Black (IRE) 85 3 (5f, Curr, Yld, Aug 20)
Bling King 86 3 (7f 2y, Ches, Gd, Sep 9)
Bogart 102 1 (6f, York, GS, Aug 18)
Boomerang Bob (IRE) 101 2 (5f, Asco, GS, Jun 16)
Boris Grigoriev (IRE) 91 3 (6f 63y, Curr, Sft, Jul 17)
Brocklebank (IRE) 85 1 (6f, York, Gd, May 21)
Bronterre 104 4 (7f, Newm, Gd, Oct 8)
Bronze Angel (IRE) 84 4 (7f, Good, GF, Jul 29)
Bubbly Ballerina 84 3 (5f, York, GF, May 13)
Burwaaz 100 2 (5f, Good, Gd, Jul 26)
Caledonia Lady 98 3 (5f, Asco, Gd, Jun 15)
Caledonian Spring (IRE) 98 4 (7f, York, GS, Aug 17)
Call To Battle (IRE) 88 1 (1m, Curr, Sft, Oct 9)
Camelot 90 1 (1m, Donc, Gd, Oct 22)
Caspar Netscher 110 1 (6f 8y, Newb, Gd, Sep 17)
Chandlery (IRE) 102 2 (7f, Newj, GF, Jul 9)
Charles The Great (IRE) 99 3 (5f, Good, Gd, Jul 26)
Chil The Kite 84 1 (1m, Good, GS, Aug 27)
Chunky Diamond (IRE) 90 2 (6f, Donc, Gd, Oct 22)
Commissar 91 1 (5f, Newm, GF, May 1)
Coquet 92 1 (1m, Newm, Gd, Oct 29)
Coupe De Ville (IRE) 93 1 (7f, Newm, GF, Oct 1)
Cravat 92 1 (7f 2y, Ches, Gd, Sep 9)
Crius (IRE) 96 1 (7f, Newm, GF, Sep 22)
Crown Dependency (IRE) 98 4 (5f, Good, Gd, Jul 26)
Crusade (USA) 102 1 (6f, Newm, Gd, Oct 8)
Daddy Long Legs (USA) 85 1 (1m, Newm, GF, Sep 24)
David Livingston (IRE) 98 3 (7f, Curr, Sft, Sep 10)
Diala (IRE) 85 1 (7f, Newm, Gd, Oct 19)
Discourse (USA) 100 1 (7f, Newj, Gd, Aug 6)
Dragon Pulse (IRE) 103 2 (7f, Curr, Sft, Sep 10)
Dreamwriter (USA) 90 1 (6f 8y, Newb, Gd, Aug 13)
El Lail (USA) 85 1 (1m, York, Gd, Oct 7)
Encke (USA) 86 2 (1m, Donc, Gd, Sep 8)
Entifaadha 106 1 (7f, York, GS, Aug 17)
Esentepe (IRE) 88 3 (1m, Newm, Gd, Oct 29)
Eureka (IRE) 89 6 (6f, Good, GF, Jul 29)
Ewell Place (IRE) 90 3 (6f, York, GS, Aug 18)
Excelette (IRE) 89 2 (5f 34y, Newb, Gd, Aug 12)
Experience (IRE) 92 1 (6f, Curr, Sft, Jun 25)
Factory Time (IRE) 95 6 (7f, Newm, Gd, Oct 8)

Fallen For You 108 2 (1m, Donc, Gd, Sep 9)
Falls Of Lora (IRE) 90 1 (6f 110y, Donc, GF, Jun 4)
Farraaj (IRE) 88 2 (7f, Newm, GF, Sep 22)
Fatcatinthehat 85 3 (1m, Leop, Yld, Oct 30)
Fencing (USA) 93 1 (7f, Newb, Gd, Aug 13)
Firdaws (USA) 88 3 (1m, Newm, GF, Sep 23)
Fire Lily (IRE) 100 2 (6f, York, GS, Aug 18)
Fort Bastion (IRE) 102 2 (7f, York, GS, Aug 17)
Foxtrot Romeo (IRE) 96 4 (6f 8y, Newb, Gd, Sep 17)
Frederick Engels 106 1 (5f, Asco, Gd, Jun 14)
Free Verse 86 1 (6f, Wind, Gd, Jul 18)
Frontier (GER) 85 1 (1m, Nava, Sft, Oct 19)
Fulbright 91 3 (7f, Donc, Gd, Oct 22)
Furner's Green (IRE) 97 4 (7f, Curr, Sft, Sep 10)
Gabrial's Gift (IRE) 88 1 (1m, Kemw, SD, Aug 24)
Gamilati 106 1 (6f, Newj, Gd, Jul 8)
Gatepost (IRE) 98 5 (6f, Asco, Gd, Jun 14)
Gentlemans Code (USA) 94 4 (5f, Asco, Gd, Jun 14)
Gerfalcon 90 3 (6f, York, GS, Aug 18)
Gifted Girl (IRE) 85 4 (1m, Newm, Gd, Oct 29)
Goldoni (IRE) 85 1 (7f, Good, GF, Jul 29)
Graphic (IRE) 86 1 (7f, Kemw, SD, Sep 14)
Gray Pearl 100 3 (7f, Newm, Gd, Oct 8)
Gusto 91 1 (6f, Donc, Gd, Oct 22)
Halling's Quest 91 1 (1m, Souw, SD, Oct 24)
Harbour Watch (IRE) 109 1 (6f, Good, GF, Jul 29)
Harvard N Yale (USA) 89 1 (1m, Newj, Gd, Aug 12)
Hazaz (IRE) 93 3 (7f, Newb, GF, Oct 22)
Hazel Lavery (IRE) 86 1 (7f, Newb, GS, Sep 16)
Hello Glory 87 3 (6f, York, GS, Aug 18)
Homecoming Queen (IRE) 100 1 (1m, Curr, Sft, Oct 9)
I Have A Dream 87 2 (1m, Leop, Yld, Oct 30)
Illaunglass (IRE) 95 3 (6f, Asco, GS, Jun 17)
Inetrobil (IRE) 102 2 (6f, Asco, GS, Jun 17)
Janey Muddles (IRE) 91 6 (7f, Newm, Gd, Oct 8)
Jupiter Storm 85 1 (7f 214y, Brig, GF, Oct 20)
Kohala (IRE) 92 1 (5f 34y, Newb, Gd, Aug 12)
Kune Kune 90 1 (6f, Kemw, SD, Nov 17)
Lady Gorgeous 85 1 (6f 8y, Newb, GF, Jul 15)
Ladys First 85 2 (6f 18y, Ches, GF, Aug 20)
Last Bid 87 2 (5f, York, Gd, Aug 20)
Leqqaa (USA) 93 2 (1m, Newm, Gd, Oct 19)
Lethal Force (IRE) 100 4 (6f, Asco, Gd, Jun 14)
Letsgoroundagain (IRE) 88 1 (1m 4y, Pont, Gd, Oct 17)
Lightening Pearl (IRE) 100 1 (6f, Curr, Gd, Aug 28)
Lilbourne Lad (IRE) 99 2 (6f, Newm, Gd, Oct 8)
Lily's Angel (IRE) 88 5 (6f, Asco, GS, Jun 17)
Limetree Lady 91 1 (5f, Cork, GF, Aug 22)
Lord Ofthe Shadows (IRE) 99 3 (7f, Good, GF, Jul 29)
Lyric Of Light 109 1 (1m, Donc, Gd, Sep 9)
Madhmoonah 90 1 (7f, Curr, Sft, Sep 10)
Magic City (IRE) 93 1 (5f 34y, Newb, GF, Apr 15)
Main Sequence (USA) 89 1 (1m 1f, Newm, Gd, Oct 19)
Mary Fildes (IRE) 88 7 (7f, Newm, Gd, Oct 8)
Maybe (IRE) 99 1 (7f, Asco, Sft, Jun 18)
Mehdi (IRE) 88 3 (7f, Newm, GF, Oct 1)
Mezmaar 88 1 (5f 218y, Leic, Gd, Sep 19)
Mickdaam (IRE) 85 1 (7f, York, Gd, Oct 8)
Miss Lahar 87 2 (6f, York, Gd, Oct 8)
Miss Work Of Art 95 2 (6f, York, GS, Aug 18)
Mojave (IRE) 88 1 (1m 2f, Newm, Gd, Oct 29)
Most Improved (IRE) 106 3 (7f, Newm, Gd, Oct 8)
Mr Majeika (IRE) 85 3 (5f 218y, Leic, Gd, Sep 19)
My Propeller (IRE) 91 1 (5f, York, Gd, Aug 20)
Nephrite 88 1 (6f, Curr, Sft, Sep 25)
Nero Emperor (IRE) 93 1 (5f, Dunw, SD, Nov 18)
Noor Zabeel (USA) 88 1 (6f, York, Gd, May 12)
North Star Boy (IRE) 85 7 (6f, Asco, Gd, Jun 14)

TOPSPEED'S TOP TWO-YEAR-OLDS OF 2011

On The Dark Side (IRE) 94 5 (5f, Good, Gd, Jul 26)
Ortac Rock (IRE) 86 2 (7f, Donc, Gd, Oct 22)
Overpowered 88 1 (7f, Newj, GF, Jul 9)
Parish Hall (IRE) 109 1 (7f, Newm, Gd, Oct 8)
Pearl Mix (IRE) 88 1 (7f, Kemw, SD, Jun 22)
Perennial 88 1 (1m, Donc, Gd, Sep 8)
Pickled Pelican (IRE) 94 1 (1m 3y, Yarm, GF, Sep 13)
Pimpernel (IRE) 103 1 (7f, Newm, GF, Sep 24)
Power 107 2 (7f, Newm, Gd, Oct 8)
Powerful Wind (IRE) 88 1 (5f, Warw, GF, Aug 23)
Pride And Joy (IRE) 86 1 (7f 16y, Sand, Sft, Aug 20)
Producer 91 4 (7f, Newb, GF, Oct 22)
Pyman's Theory (IRE) 95 1 (5f 6y, Sand, GS, May 26)
Radiomarelli (USA) 85 3 (6f, Newj, Gd, Jul 23)
Rakasa 85 1 (6f, Good, Gd, Jul 27)
Rawaafed (IRE) 85 3 (1m, Donc, Gd, Sep 8)
Rebellious Guest 89 1 (6f, Wind, GS, Aug 8)
Red Art (IRE) 87 5 (6f, York, GS, Aug 18)
Red Duke (USA) 103 1 (7f, Newj, GF, Jul 9)
Redact (IRE) 105 2 (6f 8y, Newb, Gd, Sep 17)
Regal Realm 92 4 (1m, Donc, Gd, Sep 9)
Repeater 86 2 (1m 2f, Newm, Gd, Oct 29)
Reply (IRE) 98 3 (6f, Newm, Gd, Oct 8)
Requinto (IRE) 105 1 (5f, Good, Gd, Jul 26)
Requisition (IRE) 87 1 (1m 100y, Galw, Gd, Aug 29)
Rex Imperator 87 1 (6f 15y, Nott, GF, Aug 12)
Rigoletta (IRE) 85 2 (7f, Leop, Gd, Jun 9)
Rockinante (FR) 91 1 (1m, Newm, Gd, Oct 8)
Roman Soldier (IRE) 106 2 (6f, Asco, Gd, Jun 14)
Ruby's Day 88 6 (5f, Asco, Gd, Jun 15)
Rugged Cross 90 1 (7f, York, GS, Aug 19)
Russelliana 100 2 (6f, Newj, Gd, Jul 8)
Saigon 104 3 (6f 8y, Newb, Gd, Sep 17)
Sajwah (IRE) 94 5 (6f, Newj, Gd, Jul 8)

Salacia (IRE) 85 2 (7f, Newm, Gd, Oct 29)
Salford Art (IRE) 86 4 (1m, Newm, GF, Sep 23)
Samitar 105 1 (6f, Asco, GS, Jun 17)
Samminder (IRE) 87 2 (5f 218y, Leic, Gd, Sep 19)
Secretary Of State (IRE) 94 1 (1m, List, Sft, Sep 12)
Shumoos (USA) 99 3 (6f, Newj, Gd, Jul 8)
Silverheels (IRE) 92 4 (6f, Good, GF, Jul 29)
Somasach (USA) 85 2 (6f, Curr, Sft, Jun 25)
Spiritual Star (IRE) 94 7 (7f, Newm, Gd, Oct 8)
St Barths 101 3 (6f, Asco, Gd, Jun 14)
Starboard 89 1 (7f, Redc, Gd, Nov)
Stepper Point 85 1 (5f 110y, Warw, Gd, Aug 29)
Stonefield Flyer 97 2 (5f, Asco, Gd, Jun 14)
Storming Bernard (USA) 89 1 (7f, Linw, SD, Nov 19)
Sunday Times 94 5 (7f, Newm, Gd, Oct 8)
Switcher (IRE) 93 4 (6f, Asco, GS, Jun 17)
Takar (IRE) 88 1 (7f, Leop, Yld, Nov 6)
Talwar (IRE) 99 1 (7f 16y, Sand, Sft, Aug 20)
Tell Dad 100 1 (7f, Newb, GF, Oct 22)
Telwaar 85 2 (7f, Newb, Gd, Aug 13)
The Fugue 90 1 (7f, Newm, Gd, Oct 29)
Thomasgainsborough (IRE) 88 1 (1m, Leop, Yld, Oct 30)
Tough As Nails (IRE) 99 2 (5f, Curr, GF, May 21)
Trumpet Major (IRE) 103 5 (7f, Newm, Gd, Oct 8)
Twirl (IRE) 92 1 (7f, Leop, Yld, Nov 6)
Validus 90 1 (1m, Kemw, SD, Sep 2)
Vocational (USA) 93 6 (5f, Good, Gd, Jul 26)
Wading (IRE) 107 1 (7f, Newm, Gd, Oct 8)
West Leake Diman (IRE) 91 7 (6f, Newm, Gd, Oct 8)
Wrote (IRE) 94 1 (7f, Galw, Gd, Aug 29)
Yellow Rosebud (IRE) 88 1 (7f, Leop, Gd, Jun 9)
Zip Top (IRE) 87 3 (7f, Newm, GF, Sep 22)
Zumbi (IRE) 100 3 (7f, York, GS, Aug 17)

TOPSPEED'S TOP THREE-YEAR-OLDS AND OLDER HORSES OF 2011

KEY: Horse name, Best Topspeed figure Finishing position when earning figure
(Details of race where figure was earned)

Aaman (IRE) 72 2 (1m 6f, Souw, SD, Jan 31)
Abi Scarlet (IRE) 62 1 (6f, Souw, SD, Jan 24)
Abigails Angel 64 2 (1m, Linw, SD, Jan 13)
Absa Lutte (IRE) 69 4 (5f 20y, Wolw, SD, Feb 7)
Accumulate 62 4 (1m 4f 50y, Wolw, SD, Feb 17)
Ace Master 60 4 (7f, Souw, SD, Feb 23)
Ace Of Spies (IRE) 67 2 (7f, Souw, SD, Feb 23)
Admirable Duque (IRE) 69 1 (1m 4f, Souw, SD, Jan 24)
Adranian (IRE) 66 3 (6f, Linw, SD, Feb 22)
Akasaka (IRE) 67 2 (1m, Dunw, SD, Feb 10)
Al Aqabah (IRE) 61 8 (7f, Linw, SD, Jan 4)
Al Freej (IRE) 61 2 (6f, Linw, SD, Jan 14)
Alben Star (IRE) 90 2 (6f, Linw, SD, Jan 21)
Aldermoor (USA) 68 1 (6f, Linw, SD, Feb 25)
Alhaban (IRE) 67 2 (7f, Linw, SD, Jan 13)
All Nighter (IRE) 76 1 (1m, Linw, SD, Jan 14)
Almadaa 70 2 (6f, Dunw, SD, Feb 10)
Amazing Win (IRE) 64 2 (6f, Kemw, SD, Feb 23)
Amitola (IRE) 76 1 (1m, Linw, SD, Feb 4)
An Saighdiur (IRE) 62 1 (6f, Dunw, SD, Feb 17)
Angel Gabrial (IRE) 61 3 (7f 32y, Wolw, SD, Jan 9)
Angelo Poliziano 61 2 (5f 20y, Wolw, SD, Jan 6)
Appealing (IRE) 69 1 (7f 32y, Wolw, SD, Jan 6)
April Fool 77 1 (7f, Kemw, SD, Jan 12)
Aqua Ardens (GER) 63 1 (6f, Souw, SW, Feb 7)
Aquarian Spirit 60 5 (1m 1f 103y, Wolw, SS, Feb 4)
Aquilifer (IRE) 63 4 (1m, Linw, SD, Jan 28)

Aragorn Icon (IRE) 69 5 (1m, Dunw, SD, Feb 17)
Aragorn Rouge 78 2 (1m, Dunw, SD, Feb 24)
Archelao (IRE) 64 8 (1m 2f, Linw, SD, Feb 15)
Archie Rice (USA) 81 1 (1m 1f 103y, Wolw, SD, Jan 19)
Arctic Lynx (IRE) 71 2 (6f, Kemw, SD, Feb 22)
Argentine (IRE) 63 1 (5f, Souw, SD, Jan 2)
Art Scholar (IRE) 74 5 (1m 4f, Linw, SD, Feb 4)
Arte Del Calcio 65 3 (7f 32y, Wolw, SD, Jan 30)
Arteus 72 (6f, Linw, SD, Jan 21)
Artisan 75 1 (1m 3f, Souw, SD, Feb 21)
Ascendant 65 5 (2m 119y, Wolw, SD, Jan 5)
Attain 74 2 (1m, Linw, SD, Feb 11)
Atticus Finch (IRE) 74 2 (7f, Dunw, SD, Jan 27)
Available (IRE) 70 1 (5f, Linw, SD, Feb 18)
Aviso (GER) 67 3 (1m 2f, Linw, SD, Feb 15)
Avonrose 62 (6f, Souw, SW, Feb 7)
Baby Strange 69 5 (5f, Linw, SD, Feb 25)
Bahamian Lad 62 1 (7f 32y, Wolw, SD, Feb 20)
Baileys Strider 61 5 (7f 32y, Wolw, SD, Jan 20)
Baitsileir (IRE) 64 5 (1m 2f 150y, Dunw, SD, Jan 13)
Bandstand 76 1 (6f, Souw, SW, Feb 7)
Bareback (IRE) 60 6 (7f, Kemw, SD, Jan 12)
Battleoftrafalgar 70 2 (1m 4f, Linw, SD, Feb 18)
Bawaardi (IRE) 80 4 (7f 32y, Wolw, SS, Feb 4)
Beachwood Bay 69 1 (7f, Souw, SD, Feb 23)
Bedouin Bay 61 4 (1m 4f, Souw, SD, Jan 24)
Belinsky (IRE) 60 1 (6f, Kemw, SD, Jan 11)
Bella Ophelia (IRE) 61 1 (5f, Souw, SD, Jan 12)
Beneath 62 3 (1m 4f 50y, Wolw, SD, Feb 2)
Berlusca (IRE) 68 3 (7f, Kemw, SD, Feb 1)

TOPSPEED'S TOP THREE-YEAR-OLDS AND OLDER HORSES OF 2011

Bianca De Medici 62 3 (7f, Kemw, SD, Feb 1)
Big Creek (IRE) 59 2 (1m 4f, Kemw, SD, Jan 15)
Billy Red 68 5 (5f, Kemw, SD, Feb 22)
Billyford (IRE) 61 1 (7f, Dunw, SD, Jan 6)
Black Baccara 63 4 (5f, Linw, SD, Jan 18)
Black Iceman 63 1 (1m 4f 50y, Wolw, SD, Feb 2)
Black N Brew (USA) 66 6 (1m, Dunw, SD, Feb 24)
Blown It (USA) 70 2 (5f, Linw, SD, Jan 13)
Blue Moon 73 4 (1m, Souw, SD, Jan 1)
Blueberry Fizz (IRE) 60 2 (7f, Kemw, SD, Feb 16)
Boa 59 3 (1m 4f 50y, Wolw, SD, Feb 17)
Bold Ring 64 8 (7f, Kemw, SD, Jan 22)
Bookiesindex Boy 61 3 (5f, Souw, SD, Jan 12)
Boudoir (IRE) 63 1 (7f, Kemw, SD, Jan 15)
Bow River Arch (USA) 72 2 (1m 4f, Souw, SD, Jan 1)
Brenin Taran 77 1 (5f, Linw, SD, Feb 22)
Bronze Angel (IRE) 70 1 (1m, Linw, SD, Jan 14)
Broughton Sands 69 2 (1m 4f, Linw, SD, Jan 28)
Broughtons Paradis (IRE) 62 3 (1m 3f, Kemw, SD, Jan 24)
Brunello 63 3 (1m 6f, Souw, SD, Jan 31)
Brunston 78 1 (1m 4f 50y, Wolw, SD, Feb 17)
Brynfa Boy 62 7 (6f, Linw, SD, Feb 18)
Bull Five 60 6 (1m 2f, Linw, SD, Jan 14)
Burke's Rock 75 1 (1m, Linw, SD, Feb 11)
Burnhope 62 4 (7f 32y, Wolw, SD, Jan 20)
Buxfizz (USA) 64 7 (1m 2f, Linw, SD, Feb 15)
By Invitation (USA) 60 1 (6f, Kemw, SD, Jan 4)
C P Joe (IRE) 60 4 (2m 119y, Wolw, SD, Jan 27)
Cadeaux Pearl 74 1 (5f, Kemw, SD, Jan 11)
Cadgers Brig 62 3 (1m 5f 194y, Wolw, SD, Jan 23)
Cailin Coillteach 64 1 (7f, Dunw, SD, Feb 7)
Caldercruix (USA) 73 3 (6f, Souw, SW, Feb 7)
Caledonia Princess 61 4 (6f, Linw, SD, Jan 27)
Call To Reason (IRE) 65 3 (1m, Souw, SD, Jan 1)
Canadian Danehill (IRE) 65 1 (5f, Souw, SS, Feb 16)
Cape Of Storms 61 1 (5f 216y, Wolw, SD, Jan 19)
Capone (IRE) 86 1 (5f 216y, Wolw, SD, Feb 3)
Captain Dimitrios 67 1 (6f, Linw, SD, Jan 7)
Captain Scooby 75 3 (5f, Kemw, SD, Feb 15)
Casa Bex 63 4 (6f, Kemw, SD, Jan 11)
Cashelgar (IRE) 97 6 (1m 2f, Linw, SD, Jan 14)
Casual Mover (IRE) 80 1 (1m 2f, Linw, SD, Feb 15)
Catalyze 70 4 (6f, Linw, SD, Feb 18)
Cativo Cavallino 60 2 (1m, Linw, SD, Feb 24)
Cats Eyes 60 1 (5f, Kemw, SD, Feb 1)
Cave Artist (IRE) 60 2 (1m 2f 150y, Dunw, SD, Jan 27)
Chabada (JPN) 73 1 (1m 5f 194y, Wolw, SD, Jan 23)
Chambles 61 3 (7f, Kemw, SD, Jan 12)
Chapellerie (IRE) 64 4 (7f, Kemw, SD, Jan 12)
Chebona Bula 68 2 (1m 4f, Dunw, SD, Feb 10)
Chester Deelyte (IRE) 60 2 (7f 32y, Wolw, SD, Feb 13)
Chilli Green 77 2 (7f, Linw, SD, Jan 25)
Chjimes (IRE) 65 4 (6f, Linw, SD, Feb 4)
Chookie Avon 59 6 (7f 32y, Wolw, SD, Feb 20)
Choral 67 2 (7f, Linw, SD, Jan 4)
Chosen Forever 68 (1m 1f 103y, Wolw, SD, Jan 19)
City Legend 62 4 (7f, Linw, SD, Jan 4)
Clean Bowled (IRE) 61 1 (1m 141y, Wolw, SD, Feb 9)
Clear Ice (IRE) 63 5 (6f, Linw, SD, Feb 18)
Clear Praise (USA) 77 3 (5f, Linw, SD, Feb 11)
Cliffords Reprieve 67 2 (6f, Linw, SD, Feb 18)
Clockmaker (IRE) 90 3 (1m, Linw, SD, Jan 21)
Close To The Edge (IRE) 78 4 (6f, Souw, SW, Feb 7)
Colonel Mak 62 9 (6f, Linw, SD, Jan 7)
Colour Guard 60 1 (7f, Souw, SW, Feb 10)
Comadoir (IRE) 64 4 (7f, Kemw, SD, Jan 22)
Confidence (USA) 74 3 (1m 4f, Dunw, SD, Jan 27)
Cool Athlete (IRE) 74 3 (1m, Dunw, SD, Feb 24)

Copper Canyon 76 4 (1m 2f, Linw, SD, Feb 15)
Copper Dock (IRE) 60 6 (6f, Dunw, SD, Feb 17)
Cotton Trader (USA) 67 2 (1m 3f, Souw, SD, Feb 21)
Country Road (IRE) 62 2 (1m 5f 194y, Wolw, SD, Jan 19)
Court Applause (IRE) 71 1 (5f 20y, Wolw, SD, Feb 24)
Cristaliyev 62 5 (7f, Linw, SD, Feb 4)
Crocodile Bay (IRE) 59 1 (7f, Linw, SD, Feb 4)
Crunched 77 1 (1m 4f, Linw, SD, Feb 18)
Crystal Gal (IRE) 77 9 (1m, Linw, SD, Feb 18)
Ctappers 64 3 (1m 4f, Linw, SD, Feb 25)
Cut And Thrust (IRE) 67 5 (7f, Kemw, SD, Jan 22)
Cut The Cackle (IRE) 64 1 (6f, Linw, SD, Feb 4)
Cyflymder (IRE) 69 2 (7f 32y, Wolw, SD, Feb 6)
Da'quonde 62 3 (5f 20y, Wolw, SD, Feb 24)
Dancing Freddy (IRE) 76 3 (5f, Souw, SD, Jan 3)
Dancing Maite 73 3 (5f 216y, Wolw, SD, Feb 2)
Dancing Welcome 71 1 (5f 216y, Wolw, SD, Jan 9)
Daniel Thomas (IRE) 61 1 (1m 141y, Wolw, SD, Feb 3)
Dark Castle 76 2 (6f, Kemw, SD, Jan 25)
Dasho 64 3 (6f, Kemw, SD, Jan 26)
Dazzling Valentine 72 4 (1m 2f, Kemw, SD, Jan 11)
Decider (USA) 63 5 (5f, Linw, SD, Jan 13)
Den's Gift (IRE) 70 5 (1m, Kemw, SD, Feb 11)
Derivatives (IRE) 61 2 (6f, Souw, SD, Jan 24)
Desert Strike 82 4 (6f, Linw, SD, Jan 21)
Devote Myself (IRE) 62 4 (1m, Linw, SD, Feb 11)
Diamond Charlie (IRE) 68 6 (5f, Linw, SD, Feb 25)
Diamond Vine (IRE) 70 3 (6f, Linw, SD, Feb 4)
Dickie Le Davoir 70 1 (6f, Souw, SD, Jan 3)
Diplomatic (IRE) 66 1 (7f, Kemw, SD, Feb 16)
Discoverer (IRE) 77 1 (7f, Kemw, SD, Feb 8)
Divine Rule (IRE) 59 3 (7f, Linw, SD, Feb 17)
Docofthebay (IRE) 73 4 (6f, Linw, SD, Feb 25)
Dorothy's Dancing (IRE) 66 1 (6f, Kemw, SD, Feb 23)
Double Carpet (IRE) 60 5 (7f 32y, Wolw, SD, Jan 9)
Dozy Joe 72 5 (7f, Kemw, SD, Jan 4)
Drawnfromthepast (IRE) 76 2 (5f, Linw, SD, Feb 22)
Dream Catcher (SWE) 61 3 (1m 5f 194y, Wolw, SD, Feb 17)
Dressed In Lace 70 2 (6f, Kemw, SD, Jan 4)
Drive Home (USA) 63 1 (7f 32y, Wolw, SD, Jan 13)
Dubai Bounty 59 5 (1m 1f 103y, Wolw, SD, Feb 13)
Dubai Sunshine (IRE) 65 1 (1m, Souw, SD, Jan 31)
Dubaianswer 59 1 (1m, Souw, SD, Feb 23)
Dunhoy (IRE) 73 2 (1m, Kemw, SD, Feb 11)
Dunmore Boy (IRE) 60 2 (5f 216y, Wolw, SD, Feb 10)
Dvinsky (USA) 70 1 (6f, Kemw, SD, Feb 11)
Earlsmedic 70 2 (5f 216y, Wolw, SD, Jan 6)
Echos Of Motivator 73 4 (1m 4f, Linw, SD, Jan 28)
Edgeworth (IRE) 71 2 (1m 2f, Linw, SD, Feb 15)
Efistorm 63 4 (7f 32y, Wolw, SD, Feb 13)
El Mcglynn (IRE) 62 2 (5f, Linw, SD, Feb 18)
Elijah Pepper (USA) 61 5 (1m 141y, Wolw, SD, Feb 2)
Elizabeth Coffee (IRE) 75 4 (1m 2f 150y, Dunw, SD, Feb 10)
Ellemujie 62 4 (1m 4f, Kemw, SD, Jan 15)
Elna Bright 71 2 (7f, Kemw, SD, Jan 22)
Elusive Express (IRE) 59 2 (7f, Dunw, SD, Jan 6)
Elwazeer (USA) 70 2 (1m, Dunw, SD, Feb 3)
Emerald Wilderness (IRE) 95 1 (1m 2f, Linw, SD, Jan 14)
Emma's Gift (IRE) 85 1 (1m 2f, Linw, SD, Feb 11)
Enery (IRE) 64 1 (1m 1f 103y, Wolw, SD, Feb 13)
Equation Of Time 62 1 (6f, Linw, SD, Feb 17)
Estonia 78 2 (5f, Kemw, SD, Feb 22)
Even Bolder 59 5 (6f, Linw, SD, Jan 28)
Even Stevens 87 1 (5f, Souw, SD, Jan 1)
Exemplary 78 3 (1m 4f, Linw, SD, Feb 4)
Ezra Church (IRE) 82 1 (7f, Souw, SD, Feb 2)
Fair Passion 82 1 (5f, Kemw, SD, Feb 22)
Fairy Wing (IRE) 66 1 (1m, Dunw, SD, Feb 24)

TOPSPEED'S TOP THREE-YEAR-OLDS AND OLDER HORSES OF 2011

Faithful Ruler (USA) 67 1 (7f 32y, Wolw, SD, Feb 6)
Fakhuur 77 9 (1m 2f, Linw, SD, Jan 14)
Falasteen (IRE) 68 2 (6f, Linw, SD, Jan 27)
Falcon's Reign (FR) 63 3 (7f 32y, Wolw, SD, Jan 20)
False Economy (IRE) 66 8 (1m 2f 150y, Dunw, SD, Feb 10)
Fantasy Fry 59 2 (7f, Souw, SD, Jan 24)
Faraway 63 3 (5f 216y, Wolw, SD, Jan 30)
Farmleigh House (IRE) 60 1 (6f, Dunw, SD, Jan 20)
Fear Nothing 65 2 (5f, Souw, SD, Jan 2)
Fibs And Flannel 62 1 (7f, Souw, SD, Jan 3)
First Avenue 71 6 (1m 4f, Linw, SD, Feb 4)
First Bid 59 2 (7f, Souw, SS, Feb 14)
First Class 62 1 (6f, Kemw, SD, Feb 23)
First In Command (IRE) 61 2 (5f, Souw, SS, Feb 16)
First Rock (IRE) 68 1 (1m 4f, Souw, SD, Jan 1)
Five Star Junior (USA) 85 6 (6f, Linw, SD, Jan 21)
Flavia Tatiana (IRE) 66 1 (1m 2f 150y, Dunw, SD, Jan 13)
Fleeting Moment (IRE) 68 1 (1m, Dunw, SD, Feb 17)
Fleetwoodsands (IRE) 76 1 (7f 32y, Wolw, SD, Jan 27)
Focail Maith 81 2 (1m 2f, Kemw, SD, Feb 1)
Follow The Flag (IRE) 88 2 (1m 2f, Linw, SD, Jan 14)
Forbidden City (IRE) 61 2 (7f, Dunw, SD, Feb 3)
Forceful Appeal (USA) 75 1 (1m, Linw, SD, Jan 28)
Forty Proof (IRE) 61 5 (6f, Linw, SD, Feb 4)
Fountain Of Honour (IRE) 59 (1m, Dunw, SD, Feb 3)
Four Better 75 1 (7f, Kemw, SD, Feb 1)
Franco Is My Name 83 2 (1m 4f, Linw, SD, Feb 4)
Fratellino 82 7 (6f, Linw, SD, Jan 21)
Fugitive Motel (IRE) 59 4 (1m, Linw, SD, Jan 14)
Full Toss 65 9 (1m 1f 103y, Wolw, SD, Jan 19)
Gabrial's Bounty (IRE) 70 1 (6f, Kemw, SD, Jan 18)
Gabrial's King (IRE) 62 1 (1m 1f 103y, Wolw, SD, Feb 7)
Gala Spirit (IRE) 61 2 (7f 32y, Wolw, SD, Feb 4)
Garstang 79 2 (7f 32y, Wolw, SD, Jan 27)
General Bunching (USA) 59 1 (1m 4f, Dunw, SD, Jan 20)
George Guru 80 1 (1m, Kemw, SD, Feb 11)
Ghostwing 87 1 (5f, Souw, SD, Jan 3)
Gin Twist 62 2 (5f 20y, Wolw, SD, Feb 20)
Global Village (IRE) 70 2 (7f, Souw, SD, Jan 2)
Gold Tobougg 61 2 (5f 216y, Wolw, SD, Jan 19)
Googlette (IRE) 66 4 (6f, Linw, SD, Jan 7)
Gorgeous Goblin (IRE) 59 7 (6f, Linw, SD, Feb 25)
Greensward 81 6 (1m, Linw, SD, Jan 21)
Greyfriarschorista 69 5 (1m 2f, Linw, SD, Jan 28)
Haadeeth 66 1 (6f, Linw, SD, Feb 11)
Haafhd Handsome 62 2 (7f, Linw, SD, Feb 3)
Hatta Stream (IRE) 71 2 (6f, Linw, SD, Jan 21)
Hawaana (IRE) 72 8 (1m 1f 103y, Wolw, SD, Jan 19)
Hawk Moth (IRE) 72 1 (7f 32y, Wolw, SD, Jan 30)
Hazzard County (USA) 94 3 (7f 32y, Wolw, SS, Feb 4)
He's Got Rhythm (IRE) 65 2 (7f, Dunw, SD, Jan 20)
Heir To The Mint (USA) 60 6 (1m, Dunw, SD, Feb 17)
Henry Bee 59 2 (5f 216y, Wolw, SD, Jan 19)
Henry Clay 70 1 (7f 32y, Wolw, SD, Jan 9)
Hidden Glory 76 4 (1m 1f 103y, Wolw, SD, Jan 19)
Hinton Admiral 79 1 (5f 216y, Wolw, SD, Feb 13)
Honey Of A Kitten (USA) 68 (1m 2f, Linw, SD, Jan 14)
Honourable Emperor (IRE) 75 1 (7f, Dunw, SD, Jan 27)
Hoover 68 4 (6f, Linw, SD, Feb 18)
Hunters Belt (IRE) 69 2 (1m 3f, Souw, SD, Jan 8)
Hurricane Hymnbook (USA) 60 2 (1m 3f, Kemw, SD, Jan 22)
I Confess 82 1 (1m 141y, Wolw, SD, Feb 11)
If I Were A Boy (IRE) 65 2 (1m 3f, Kemw, SD, Jan 24)
If Per Chance (IRE) 65 1 (1m, Dunw, SD, Feb 10)
Il Battista 63 3 (6f, Souw, SD, Jan 31)
Illustrious Forest 60 1 (1m 4f 50y, Wolw, SD, Feb 6)
Imprimis Tagula (IRE) 75 1 (7f, Souw, SS, Feb 14)
Imprudent Miss (IRE) 61 3 (1m 4f, Dunw, SD, Feb 10)

Imtithal (IRE) 66 3 (1m, Linw, SD, Feb 11)
Ingleby Arch (USA) 74 2 (7f, Souw, SS, Feb 14)
Into Wain (USA) 77 1 (1m 4f, Kemw, SD, Feb 23)
Iron Major (IRE) 72 4 (1m, Dunw, SD, Feb 10)
Island Legend (IRE) 81 2 (5f, Kemw, SD, Feb 15)
Island Melody (IRE) 60 2 (1m 1f 103y, Wolw, SD, Feb 13)
Italian Tom (IRE) 66 8 (6f, Linw, SD, Feb 18)
Ivory Jazz 66 4 (1m 2f, Linw, SD, Jan 14)
Jimmy Ryan (IRE) 74 1 (5f, Linw, SD, Jan 13)
Jo Boy 61 4 (7f, Kemw, SD, Jan 12)
Joe Eile (IRE) 61 2 (1m, Dunw, SD, Jan 27)
Johnnys Legacy (IRE) 71 2 (1m 4f, Dunw, SD, Jan 20)
Jonnie Skull (IRE) 60 1 (7f 32y, Wolw, SD, Feb 10)
July Days (IRE) 66 1 (7f 32y, Wolw, SD, Feb 4)
Jungle Bay 70 2 (7f, Kemw, SD, Feb 23)
Junoob 88 4 (1m 2f, Linw, SD, Jan 28)
Just Bond (IRE) 70 2 (1m 1f 103y, Wolw, SD, Feb 24)
Just Breathe (IRE) 62 2 (6f, Kemw, SD, Jan 18)
Justonefortheroad 61 7 (1m, Souw, SD, Jan 1)
Kai Mook 62 6 (1m 2f, Linw, SD, Feb 15)
Kakatosi 70 6 (7f, Kemw, SD, Jan 4)
Kalacan (IRE) 64 2 (1m, Dunw, SD, Feb 17)
Kames Park (IRE) 72 3 (1m 4f, Linw, SD, Feb 3)
Kangaroo Court (IRE) 78 1 (1m 4f, Linw, SD, Jan 28)
Katmai River (IRE) 64 2 (7f, Kemw, SD, Jan 22)
Katy's Secret 66 4 (6f, Souw, SD, Jan 31)
Kayalar (IRE) 62 1 (1m 5f, Linw, SD, Feb 15)
Kedleston (IRE) 62 1 (1m, Dunw, SD, Jan 13)
Key Ambition 69 2 (6f, Souw, SD, Jan 8)
Khajaaly (IRE) 74 3 (7f 32y, Wolw, SD, Feb 6)
Kickingthelilly 76 1 (7f, Kemw, SD, Feb 11)
King Of Aran (IRE) 72 5 (1m 2f 150y, Dunw, SD, Feb 10)
King Of Windsor (IRE) 63 7 (1m 2f, Kemw, SD, Feb 1)
Kiss A Prince 73 1 (1m 2f, Linw, SD, Jan 14)
Knockgraffon Lad (USA) 65 4 (1m, Dunw, SD, Feb 3)
Knowe Head (NZ) 70 5 (1m 1f 103y, Wolw, SD, Jan 19)
Kucharova (IRE) 60 2 (7f, Linw, SD, Feb 4)
Kylladdie 67 3 (6f, Linw, SD, Jan 27)
La Estrella (USA) 82 1 (1m 5f 194y, Wolw, SD, Jan 19)
Lady Caprice 69 1 (5f, Linw, SD, Jan 27)
Lady Mango (IRE) 65 2 (6f, Kemw, SD, Feb 23)
Laffan (IRE) 79 1 (6f, Souw, SD, Jan 10)
Lakota Ghost (USA) 60 2 (1m 5f 194y, Wolw, SD, Feb 17)
Lanarkshire (IRE) 59 4 (1m, Linw, SD, Feb 24)
Last Sovereign 59 3 (7f, Kemw, SD, Feb 22)
Lastkingofscotland (IRE) 77 1 (7f, Kemw, SD, Feb 11)
Laugh Out Loud 63 2 (7f 32y, Wolw, SD, Jan 20)
Layline (IRE) 88 1 (1m 4f, Linw, SD, Feb 4)
Le King Beau (USA) 62 5 (6f, Kemw, SD, Jan 18)
Leenavesta (USA) 62 3 (6f, Kemw, SD, Jan 4)
Legal Legacy 76 2 (7f 32y, Wolw, SD, Feb 6)
Legendary 67 2 (1m, Linw, SD, Feb 24)
Levitate 67 6 (7f, Souw, SD, Jan 2)
Liberal Lady 64 2 (5f, Kemw, SD, Jan 24)
Licence To Till (USA) 89 3 (1m 2f, Linw, SD, Jan 28)
Lil Ella (IRE) 62 1 (1m 4f 50y, Wolw, SD, Feb 20)
Lily's Star (IRE) 60 8 (1m, Dunw, SD, Feb 17)
Lisahane Bog 69 5 (1m 2f, Kemw, SD, Jan 11)
Little Garcon (USA) 85 5 (7f 32y, Wolw, SS, Feb 4)
Little Jazz 60 4 (1m 3f, Kemw, SD, Jan 24)
Lockantanks 86 4 (1m, Linw, SD, Jan 21)
Lord Kenmare (USA) 65 1 (1m, Dunw, SD, Jan 27)
Love You Louis 72 4 (5f, Souw, SD, Jan 3)
Loyal Royal (IRE) 71 2 (6f, Linw, SD, Jan 7)
Loyalty 84 7 (1m, Linw, SD, Feb 18)
Lujeanie 75 8 (6f, Linw, SD, Jan 21)
Lyric Poet (USA) 66 2 (1m 5f 194y, Wolw, SD, Jan 23)
Mafi (IRE) 73 1 (1m, Linw, SD, Feb 24)

TOPSPEED'S TOP THREE-YEAR-OLDS AND OLDER HORSES OF 2011

Magic Millie (IRE) 62 1 (1m 5f 194y, Wolw, SD, Feb 17)
Majuro (IRE) 80 8 (1m 2f, Linw, SD, Jan 14)
Malcheek (IRE) 66 5 (6f, Souw, SD, Jan 31)
Mambo Spirit (IRE) 71 2 (7f, Kemw, SD, Feb 22)
Marajaa (IRE) 76 1 (7f, Kemw, SD, Feb 22)
Marvo 62 5 (1m 2f, Linw, SD, Jan 14)
Masai Moon 71 9 (7f 32y, Wolw, SS, Feb 4)
Maslak (IRE) 65 1 (1m 4f, Linw, SD, Feb 3)
Master Of Dance (IRE) 61 2 (1m 141y, Wolw, SD, Feb 3)
Master Of Disguise 74 2 (5f 216y, Wolw, SD, Feb 13)
Masters Club 61 3 (7f, Linw, SD, Jan 4)
Mataajir (USA) 69 1 (1m, Souw, SD, Jan 1)
Matjar (IRE) 68 3 (1m, Dunw, SD, Feb 17)
Maverik 67 3 (7f, Souw, SD, Jan 2)
Mawaakef (IRE) 79 (1m 2f, Linw, SD, Jan 14)
May's Boy 63 4 (7f, Kemw, SD, Feb 11)
Mazij 64 3 (1m 4f, Souw, SD, Jan 24)
Mazovian (USA) 67 1 (7f, Souw, SS, Feb 16)
Mcconnell (USA) 63 1 (1m, Souw, SD, Feb 23)
Mccool Bannanas 62 3 (1m 141y, Wolw, SD, Feb 11)
Mcmonagle (USA) 65 3 (6f, Dunw, SD, Feb 17)
Megalala (IRE) 75 1 (1m 2f, Kemw, SD, Feb 1)
Memphis Man 60 5 (6f, Linw, SD, Feb 18)
Menadati (USA) 65 3 (1m 2f, Kemw, SD, Feb 1)
Mia's Boy 92 5 (1m, Linw, SD, Jan 21)
Mishrif (USA) 77 2 (7f, Kemw, SD, Feb 11)
Mister Green (FR) 62 5 (1m 2f, Linw, SD, Feb 15)
Mister Mackenzie 64 3 (6f, Kemw, SD, Jan 11)
Monadreen Dancer 59 6 (7f, Linw, SD, Feb 4)
Monsieur Jamie 61 7 (5f, Souw, SD, Jan 1)
Moral Issue 65 3 (7f, Kemw, SD, Jan 12)
Mosstown (IRE) 60 6 (1m 4f, Dunw, SD, Feb 10)
Mottley Crewe 82 3 (5f, Linw, SD, Feb 22)
Mountain Coral (IRE) 70 2 (6f, Dunw, SD, Feb 17)
Mr Red Clubs (IRE) 74 2 (1m, Linw, SD, Jan 14)
Mr Willis 81 3 (1m, Linw, SD, Feb 18)
Mull Of Killough (IRE) 89 1 (1m, Linw, SD, Jan 21)
Mullins Way (USA) 74 2 (1m 141y, Wolw, SD, Feb 2)
Munsarim (IRE) 70 1 (1m, Linw, SD, Jan 25)
Mutasareb (USA) 79 1 (1m 4f, Dunw, SD, Jan 20)
My Lord 68 3 (6f, Linw, SD, Feb 18)
Myboyalfie (USA) 78 1 (7f, Souw, SW, Feb 10)
Nacho Libre 61 2 (7f, Kemw, SD, Jan 18)
Naked Cowboy (IRE) 59 4 (1m, Dunw, SD, Feb 17)
Naoise (IRE) 61 1 (7f, Dunw, SD, Feb 3)
Naughtical 60 3 (7f, Kemw, SD, Jan 15)
Nazreef 80 4 (7f, Kemw, SD, Jan 4)
Needwood Ridge 66 2 (7f 32y, Wolw, SD, Jan 9)
Newport Arch 62 3 (1m 3f, Souw, SD, Jan 8)
Nezhenka 76 1 (2m 119y, Wolw, SD, Jan 27)
Nibani (IRE) 78 1 (1m 2f, Kemw, SD, Jan 11)
Night Lily (IRE) 82 1 (1m, Linw, SD, Feb 18)
Night Trade (IRE) 71 3 (6f, Linw, SD, Jan 21)
No Mean Trick (USA) 70 2 (5f, Souw, SD, Jan 3)
Norville (IRE) 88 4 (6f, Linw, SD, Jan 21)
Novabridge 69 1 (5f 20y, Wolw, SD, Feb 6)
Novellen Lad (IRE) 76 2 (6f, Linw, SD, Feb 11)
Nubar Boy 72 6 (6f, Linw, SD, Feb 18)
Numeral (IRE) 73 4 (1m, Linw, SD, Feb 18)
Oasis Dancer 84 1 (6f, Linw, SD, Jan 7)
Ocean Legend (IRE) 75 1 (7f, Kemw, SD, Feb 1)
Oil Strike 78 8 (7f 32y, Wolw, SS, Feb 4)
Olynard (IRE) 60 3 (7f, Kemw, SD, Feb 16)
One More Roman (IRE) 65 2 (5f 216y, Wolw, SD, Jan 30)
One Way Or Another (AUS) 70 4 (7f 32y, Wolw, SD, Feb 6)
Opus Maximus (IRE) 84 5 (1m 2f, Linw, SD, Jan 14)
Oratorian (IRE) 76 1 (6f, Kemw, SD, Jan 4)
Palace Moon 89 1 (6f, Linw, SD, Feb 11)

Pale Orchid (IRE) 84 1 (6f, Linw, SD, Feb 22)
Paperetto 59 6 (6f, Linw, SD, Jan 7)
Pat's Legacy (USA) 77 7 (7f 32y, Wolw, SS, Feb 4)
Peadar Miguel 62 4 (1m, Linw, SD, Feb 24)
Pearl Rebel 80 1 (7f, Kemw, SD, Jan 12)
Penangdouble O One 61 6 (2m 119y, Wolw, SD, Jan 27)
Perlachy 62 1 (5f 20y, Wolw, SD, Feb 3)
Pettochside 60 1 (5f 216y, Wolw, SD, Jan 5)
Picansort 72 2 (6f, Linw, SD, Feb 4)
Piccolo Express 66 1 (7f 32y, Wolw, SD, Feb 13)
Pick A Little 73 1 (6f, Souw, SD, Jan 31)
Pilgrim Dancer (IRE) 63 3 (6f, Souw, SD, Jan 31)
Piscean (USA) 92 3 (7f 32y, Wolw, SS, Feb 4)
Podgies Boy (IRE) 59 1 (7f, Souw, SD, Jan 10)
Postscript (IRE) 67 2 (1m 141y, Wolw, SD, Feb 11)
Prince Of Burma (IRE) 68 1 (1m, Linw, SD, Jan 25)
Prince Of Dance 63 8 (1m 1f 103y, Wolw, SD, Feb 24)
Prince Of Fire (GER) 79 2 (1m 2f 150y, Dunw, SD, Feb 10)
Prince Of Vasa (IRE) 63 3 (7f, Souw, SW, Feb 10)
Protaras (USA) 69 9 (1m 2f 150y, Dunw, SD, Feb 10)
Prussian 71 2 (1m, Linw, SD, Jan 14)
Pucon 59 1 (5f, Linw, SD, Jan 20)
Punching 67 2 (6f, Souw, SD, Feb 21)
Purple Affair (IRE) 59 3 (7f, Kemw, SD, Feb 11)
Push Me (IRE) 67 1 (1m, Linw, SD, Feb 18)
Queen Of Denmark (USA) 77 2 (1m 4f 50y, Wolw, SD, Feb 17)
Quinmaster (USA) 67 7 (1m, Dunw, SD, Feb 24)
Rapid Heat Lad (IRE) 75 1 (1m 4f, Linw, SD, Feb 25)
Rapid Water 59 7 (7f, Kemw, SD, Jan 22)
Rasheed 64 1 (2m, Kemw, SD, Feb 11)
Raucous Behaviour (USA) 87 3 (1m 2f, Linw, SD, Jan 14)
Reachforthebucks 70 1 (1m 1f 103y, Wolw, SD, Feb 13)
Red Cape (FR) 65 6 (5f 20y, Wolw, SD, Jan 6)
Red Shuttle 61 2 (1m 4f, Linw, SD, Jan 25)
Red Trump (IRE) 70 2 (7f 32y, Wolw, SD, Jan 30)
Redair (IRE) 62 1 (5f 20y, Wolw, SD, Feb 20)
Reggae Rock (IRE) 70 5 (1m 4f, Dunw, SD, Jan 27)
Reignier 69 6 (7f, Kemw, SD, Jan 22)
Requisite 67 6 (1m, Kemw, SD, Feb 11)
Restless Bay (IRE) 60 5 (5f 216y, Wolw, SD, Jan 13)
Reve De Nuit (USA) 88 2 (1m, Souw, SD, Jan 1)
Ridgeway Hawk 59 1 (6f, Souw, SD, Jan 24)
Riflessione 64 4 (5f 20y, Wolw, SD, Jan 6)
Right Divine 59 4 (7f, Kemw, SD, Feb 8)
Rightcar 60 1 (6f, Kemw, SD, Jan 26)
Rigid Rock (IRE) 64 5 (6f, Dunw, SD, Feb 10)
River Ardeche 60 2 (1m, Souw, SD, Feb 23)
Riverdale (IRE) 64 5 (7f 32y, Wolw, SD, Feb 6)
Rocky's Pride (IRE) 69 4 (1m, Dunw, SD, Feb 24)
Roedean (IRE) 70 1 (7f, Linw, SD, Feb 3)
Roman General (IRE) 67 3 (7f, Dunw, SD, Jan 27)
Roman Strait 63 2 (6f, Linw, SD, Feb 11)
Rosewood Lad 65 2 (2m 119y, Wolw, SD, Jan 27)
Royal Bajan (USA) 80 1 (5f, Kemw, SD, Jan 24)
Royal Box 60 5 (7f 32y, Wolw, SD, Jan 30)
Russian Ice 78 3 (1m, Linw, SD, Jan 13)
Rylee Mooch 55 6 (6f, Linw, SD, Feb 18)
Sail Home 63 1 (1m 3f, Kemw, SD, Jan 24)
Saint Boniface 60 3 (5f, Linw, SD, Jan 20)
Saint By Day (IRE) 65 2 (1m 4f, Dunw, SD, Feb 10)
Sam Lord 65 5 (2m 119y, Wolw, SD, Jan 27)
Samasana (IRE) 59 1 (1m, Souw, SD, Feb 21)
Sandwith 63 3 (5f, Souw, SS, Feb 16)
Sannibel 66 2 (5f, Kemw, SD, Feb 1)
Santefisio 78 2 (7f, Kemw, SD, Feb 1)
Satwa Laird 67 3 (7f, Linw, SD, Jan 4)
Saucy Buck (IRE) 64 3 (7f, Linw, SD, Feb 4)
Scottish Glen 68 1 (7f, Linw, SD, Jan 4)

TOPSPEED'S TOP THREE-YEAR-OLDS AND OLDER HORSES OF 2011

Seek The Fair Land 91 1 (6f, Linw, SD, Jan 21)
Sermons Mount (USA) 75 4 (6f, Linw, SD, Jan 21)
Shabak Hom (IRE) 66 2 (1m 2f, Linw, SD, Jan 14)
Shabora (IRE) 63 3 (1m, Linw, SD, Jan 14)
Shared Moment (IRE) 70 1 (1m, Linw, SD, Jan 13)
Shaunas Spirit (IRE) 62 1 (7f, Kemw, SD, Jan 18)
Shawkantango 70 1 (5f 20y, Wolw, SD, Feb 7)
She Ain't A Saint 66 3 (1m, Kemw, SD, Feb 11)
Sherjawy (IRE) 63 2 (5f, Linw, SD, Jan 6)
Shieldmaiden (USA) 65 1 (1m 4f 50y, Wolw, SD, Jan 5)
Shifting Star (IRE) 80 1 (7f, Linw, SD, Jan 25)
Shisha Threesixty (IRE) 60 1 (1m 2f 150y, Dunw, SD, Jan 27)
Showboating (IRE) 61 3 (6f, Linw, SD, Jan 14)
Silvanus (IRE) 71 2 (5f 20y, Wolw, SD, Feb 24)
Silver Wind 61 9 (6f, Linw, SD, Jan 7)
Sir Geoffrey (IRE) 72 7 (5f, Linw, SD, Feb 11)
Sircozy (IRE) 75 2 (1m 4f, Linw, SD, Feb 3)
Sistine 68 1 (1m 6f, Souw, SD, Jan 31)
Six Wives 72 6 (5f, Linw, SD, Feb 11)
Sleepy Blue Ocean 61 5 (5f, Souw, SD, Jan 1)
Smokey Oakey (IRE) 66 5 (1m 2f, Linw, SD, Feb 11)
Snow Dancer (IRE) 69 (1m 1f 103y, Wolw, SD, Jan 19)
Sole Danser (IRE) 77 2 (6f, Kemw, SD, Feb 11)
Solo Performer (IRE) 63 1 (1m 2f 150y, Dunw, SD, Jan 27)
Somemothersdohavem 71 1 (7f 32y, Wolw, SD, Jan 30)
Sonko (IRE) 74 1 (5f, Linw, SD, Jan 7)
Sonoran Sands (IRE) 65 7 (1m 2f, Linw, SD, Feb 11)
Sonsie Lass 69 2 (6f, Souw, SD, Jan 10)
Soopacal (IRE) 63 2 (5f, Souw, SD, Jan 12)
Sound Amigo (IRE) 59 2 (7f, Souw, SS, Feb 14)
Southern State (USA) 74 3 (1m 4f, Linw, SD, Jan 28)
Speak The Truth (IRE) 70 1 (6f, Linw, SD, Jan 14)
Speedy Yaki (IRE) 69 1 (7f 32y, Wolw, SD, Feb 11)
Spic 'n Span 63 4 (5f, Souw, SS, Feb 16)
Spin Again (IRE) 63 3 (7f 32y, Wolw, SD, Jan 9)
Spin Of A Coin (IRE) 76 1 (1m 2f 150y, Dunw, SD, Feb 10)
Squad 60 5 (1m 4f, Linw, SD, Feb 3)
St Oswald 70 3 (7f, Souw, SS, Feb 14)
Stand Guard 67 1 (1m 4f, Souw, SS, Feb 16)
Standpoint 71 2 (1m 1f 103y, Wolw, SD, Feb 13)
Star Links (USA) 71 4 (1m 141y, Wolw, SD, Feb 2)
Steelcut 75 2 (5f 20y, Wolw, SD, Feb 7)
Stevie Gee (IRE) 79 1 (6f, Kemw, SD, Jan 15)
Strandfield Lady (IRE) 69 4 (1m 4f, Dunw, SD, Jan 27)
Strictly Pink (IRE) 63 8 (6f, Linw, SD, Jan 7)
Striding Edge (IRE) 67 1 (1m 3f, Kemw, SD, Feb 22)
Strike Force 64 7 (1m 4f, Linw, SD, Feb 3)
Striker Torres (IRE) 72 4 (7f 32y, Wolw, SD, Jan 30)
Suddenly Susan (IRE) 74 3 (5f 20y, Wolw, SD, Feb 7)
Sugar Beet 70 4 (5f 216y, Wolw, SD, Feb 3)
Sujet Bellagio 61 3 (6f, Linw, SD, Jan 14)
Sulis Minerva (IRE) 79 2 (5f, Linw, SD, Feb 11)
Sunset Beauty (IRE) 81 3 (1m 2f 150y, Dunw, SD, Feb 10)
Sunset Kitty (USA) 67 1 (1m, Kemw, SD, Jan 12)
Sweet Ovation 69 1 (6f, Linw, SD, Feb 3)
Switzerland (IRE) 73 1 (6f, Linw, SD, Jan 14)
Syrian 62 6 (1m 2f 150y, Dunw, SD, Jan 13)
Taajub (IRE) 84 1 (5f, Linw, SD, Feb 11)
Tadabeer 76 (1m 2f, Linw, SD, Jan 14)
Tamareen (IRE) 83 2 (7f 32y, Wolw, SS, Feb 4)
Tappanappa (IRE) 62 1 (1m 4f, Linw, SD, Jan 25)
Tarooq (USA) 82 2 (1m, Linw, SD, Jan 21)
Tarrsille (IRE) 63 9 (1m, Dunw, SD, Feb 10)
Tartan Trip 74 3 (1m 2f, Linw, SD, Feb 11)
Tenbridge 70 2 (7f, Kemw, SD, Feb 1)
Tevez 78 3 (1m, Linw, SD, Jan 28)
Tewin Wood 68 1 (7f, Souw, SD, Jan 2)
The Dancing Lord 63 2 (6f, Linw, SD, Jan 21)

The Happy Hammer (IRE) 63 5 (7f, Kemw, SD, Jan 12)
The Lock Master (IRE) 67 2 (1m 4f, Souw, SD, Jan 24)
The Mongoose 72 3 (1m 1f 103y, Wolw, SD, Jan 19)
The Rectifier (USA) 83 1 (7f, Kemw, SD, Jan 4)
The Strig 75 2 (6f, Linw, SD, Jan 21)
The Wee Chief (IRE) 74 1 (6f, Linw, SD, Feb 4)
Thunderball 72 9 (6f, Linw, SD, Jan 21)
Thundering Home 65 1 (1m 4f 50y, Wolw, SD, Feb 24)
Thunderstruck 80 (1m 2f, Linw, SD, Jan 14)
Tiablo (IRE) 64 1 (5f 216y, Wolw, SD, Jan 30)
Tinshu (IRE) 94 4 (1m 2f, Linw, SD, Jan 14)
Tiradito (USA) 63 3 (1m, Linw, SD, Feb 18)
Tislaam (IRE) 67 3 (5f 216y, Wolw, SD, Jan 13)
Titan Triumph 74 2 (1m, Linw, SD, Jan 28)
Titus Gent 70 4 (5f, Kemw, SD, Jan 11)
Tombi (USA) 72 3 (5f 216y, Wolw, SD, Feb 13)
Tornado Force (IRE) 82 2 (1m 2f, Linw, SD, Feb 11)
Torres Del Paine 67 1 (6f, Kemw, SD, Jan 22)
Total Reality (IRE) 69 5 (1m, Dunw, SD, Feb 24)
Toufan Express 63 6 (1m, Dunw, SD, Feb 10)
Trans Sonic 61 4 (7f, Souw, SS, Feb 14)
Treadwell (IRE) 62 8 (7f, Kemw, SD, Jan 4)
Tribes And Banner (IRE) 73 1 (1m 4f, Dunw, SD, Jan 27)
Tricksofthetrade (IRE) 66 2 (1m 4f, Souw, SS, Feb 16)
Trip Switch 67 1 (1m 2f, Linw, SD, Jan 20)
Triple Dream 82 1 (5f, Kemw, SD, Feb 15)
Trojan Rocket (IRE) 71 3 (7f, Kemw, SD, Jan 22)
True To Form (IRE) 72 1 (7f, Souw, SS, Feb 14)
Turjuman (USA) 62 4 (1m 4f, Linw, SD, Feb 3)
Tuxedo 60 2 (1m, Linw, SD, Feb 4)
Twice Red 60 4 (5f 20y, Wolw, SD, Feb 24)
Twinkled 65 1 (1m, Linw, SD, Feb 24)
Un Hinged (IRE) 69 7 (1m 2f 150y, Dunw, SD, Feb 10)
Uphold 79 2 (1m 4f, Kemw, SD, Feb 23)
Upper Lambourn (IRE) 72 2 (6f, Souw, SW, Feb 7)
Valmina 74 3 (6f, Linw, SD, Feb 18)
Vanilla Rum 66 1 (1m 1f 103y, Wolw, SD, Feb 20)
Verbeeck 80 1 (6f, Souw, SD, Jan 8)
Veroon (IRE) 68 2 (1m 1f 103y, Wolw, SS, Feb 4)
Vertueux (FR) 62 3 (1m 5f, Linw, SD, Jan 25)
Vhujon (IRE) 63 3 (7f, Kemw, SD, Feb 11)
Viva Ronaldo (IRE) 71 4 (1m, Kemw, SD, Feb 11)
Waabel 68 3 (6f, Linw, SD, Jan 7)
Waseem Faris (IRE) 77 3 (6f, Kemw, SD, Jan 25)
Waterloo Dock 73 1 (6f, Linw, SD, Feb 18)
Welease Bwian (IRE) 66 2 (5f, Linw, SD, Jan 27)
Welsh Inlet (IRE) 61 3 (5f, Linw, SD, Jan 6)
West Coast Dream 77 2 (5f, Kemw, SD, Jan 11)
West End Lad 81 2 (1m 1f 103y, Wolw, SD, Jan 19)
Whaileyy (IRE) 76 1 (6f, Kemw, SD, Jan 26)
What About You (IRE) 68 6 (5f, Souw, SD, Jan 1)
Where's Reiley (USA) 80 5 (5f, Linw, SD, Feb 11)
Whipless (IRE) 71 5 (1m, Dunw, SD, Jan 27)
White Fusion 62 2 (1m 4f, Souw, SD, Jan 2)
Wigram's Turn (USA) 72 2 (7f 32y, Wolw, SD, Jan 30)
Wild Desert (FR) 68 3 (2m 119y, Wolw, SD, Jan 5)
Wild Sauce 65 1 (5f 20y, Wolw, SD, Feb 17)
William Haigh (IRE) 84 1 (1m, Souw, SD, Jan 1)
Woolfall Sovereign (IRE) 75 1 (5f 216y, Wolw, SD, Jan 13)
Worth 62 4 (6f, Kemw, SD, Jan 25)
Yajber (USA) 62 5 (1m, Linw, SD, Feb 11)
Young Dottie 64 5 (1m, Linw, SD, Jan 28)
Yourinthewill (USA) 70 3 (1m 2f, Linw, SD, Jan 14)
Za'lan (USA) 65 2 (1m 4f, Linw, SD, Feb 25)
Zacynthus (IRE) 77 7 (1m, Linw, SD, Jan 21)
Zarzal (IRE) 61 2 (1m 5f, Linw, SD, Feb 15)
Zomerlust 67 3 (7f 32y, Wolw, SD, Feb 6)

totetentofollow

totepool & *RACING P ST*

WIN BIG

IN THE BIGGEST AND MOST SUCCESSFUL HORSERACING COMPETITION

BIG-MONEY DIVIDENDS FOR THE TEN HIGHEST SCORING OVERALL ENTRIES – PLUS MONTHLY AND ROYAL ASCOT MEETING PRIZES

▶▶PLUS – Add two free horses during the bonus horse window

MAKE YOUR SELECTIONS NOW FROM THE LIST OF 250 HORSES STARTING ON PAGE 113

HOW TO ENTER

From the list of 250 horses starting on page 113, select ten to follow in Flat races during the competition – Friday, May 4 to Saturday, October 20, 2012 inclusive.

▶▶**Postal entries cost £12 or €15**
▶▶**OR ENTER ONLINE AND SAVE**
▶▶Online entries cost only £10
    You may enter as many lists as you wish

online ttf.totesport.com
Online entries will be accepted up to 12.00 noon Friday, May 4

We recommend that you place your entry before the closing date to avoid the inevitable late rush which can result in online processing delays and possible disappointment. Entries are not accepted by telephone.

post PO Box 116, Wigan, WN3 4WW
Postal entries must be received by 12.00 noon Friday, May 4

If you place an entry from outside the UK, it is your responsibility to ensure that you comply with any laws applicable to online gambling in the country from where the entry is placed. Totepool does not accept responsibility for any action resulting from use of its online betting operation from jurisdictions where betting may be illegal. It is also your responsibility to ensure that your credit card or debit card issuer allows their card to be used for gambling purposes. Totepool does not accept responsibility for any action taken by a card issuer for use of a card to obtain gambling services.

BONUS HORSES

During the bonus horse window you can add two FREE selections to your original list and then the highest scoring 10 horses from your 12 selections will count*. The Bonus Horse Window opens from Sunday, July 8 until 6pm Friday, July 13.

Points scored by bonus selections qualify for points from Saturday, July 21 (Ascot King George Day)

ONLINE ENTRANTS Add your bonus horse selections online at **ttf.totesport.com**

POSTAL ENTRANTS Will be sent a form to add their bonus horse selections, which must be returned to arrive by no later than 6pm on Friday, July 13. Postal entrants **cannot** add bonus selections online.

MINI-LEAGUES

Online entrants can set-up their own private mini-league for friends, families or a pub or club, where in addition to entering the Tote Ten to Follow competition, you will also be able to view your own online leader board listing the scores of all entries in your mini-league.

To set up a mini-league you need to appoint a member of your group as the organiser, who when placing their online entry, will need to register a name for the mini-league.

After completing an entry and registering the mini-league name, the organiser will be issued with a unique PIN which will enable access to the mini-league. **Other members of the mini-league will need to input this PIN to join the mini-league at the time of making each online entry. Please note that you cannot join a mini-league after your entry has been placed.**

The leader board will be published in the Racing Post each Tuesday & Friday of the competition and also at
ttf.totesport.com

SCORING AND PRIZE-MONEY

Selections winning Flat races under the Rules of Racing (excluding NH Flat races) in Great Britain or Ireland or Group races in France, Germany or Italy during the period of the competition will be awarded points as follows:

▶▶**25 points** Group 1
▶▶**20 points** Group 2 race
▶▶**15 points** Group 3 race
▶▶**12 points** Listed race
▶▶**10 points** Other race

In the event of a dead-heat, points will be divided by the number of horses dead-heating with fractions rounded down. No points for a walkover. The official result on the day will be used for the calculation of points with any subsequent disqualifications disregarded.

BONUS POINTS

Bonus points according to the official Tote / Pari-Mutuel win dividend odds, including a £1 unit stake, will be awarded to winning selections as follows:

▶▶£4 to £7............................**4 points**
▶▶Over £7 up to £11 ....**7 points**
▶▶Over £11 up to £16.........**11 points**
▶▶Over £16 up to £22.........**16 points**
▶▶Over £22 up to £29.........**22 points**
▶▶Over £29 up to £37.........**29 points**
▶▶Over £37 ....**37 points**

In the event of no Tote win dividend being declared, the starting price will determine any bonus points. Should neither a Tote win dividend nor a starting price be returned, bonus points will not apply.

BONUS RACES

An additional **25 points** will also be awarded to the winner and **12 points** to the runner-up in each of these races:

▶▶2,000 Guineas (Newmarket, May 5)
▶▶1,000 Guineas (Newmarket, May 6)
▶▶Oaks (Epsom Downs, June 1)
▶▶Derby (Epsom Downs, June 2)
▶▶Queen Anne Stakes (Royal Ascot, June 19)
▶▶St James's Palace Stakes (Royal Ascot, June 19)
▶▶Prince of Wales's Stakes (Royal Ascot, June 20)

▶▶Ascot Gold Cup (Royal Ascot, June 21)
▶▶Coronation Stakes (Royal Ascot, June 22)
▶▶Golden Jubilee Stakes (Royal Ascot, June 23)
▶▶Irish Derby (Curragh, June 30)
▶▶Eclipse Stakes (Sandown Park, July 7)
▶▶July Cup (Newmarket, July 14)
▶▶King George VI & Queen Elizabeth Stakes (Ascot, July 21)
▶▶Sussex Stakes (Goodwood, August 1)
▶▶International Stakes (York, August 22)
▶▶Nunthorpe Stakes (York, August 24)
▶▶Irish Champion Stakes (Leopardstown, September 1)
▶▶St Leger Stakes (Doncaster, September 15)
▶▶Prix de l'Arc de Triomphe (Longchamp, October 7)
▶▶Champion Stakes (Ascot, October 20)
▶▶Queen Elizabeth II Stakes (Ascot, October 20)

Any of the above races re-scheduled to take place outside the dates of the competition will not count.

PRIZE-MONEY

The Ten to Follow competition is operated as a pool by Totepool. Entry forms are available from Totepool, Betfred and Racing Post publications and online at ttf.totesport.com. All stake money will be aggregated and paid out in dividends after a 30% deduction to cover administration / expenses etc. An amount of £70,000 will be allocated for the monthly and Royal Ascot dividends with the balance divided as follows to the overall winners:

▶▶WINNER 70%
▶▶2nd 10%
▶▶3rd 5%
▶▶4th 4.5%
▶▶5th 3%
▶▶6th 2.5%
▶▶7th 2%
▶▶8th 1.5%
▶▶9th 1%
▶▶10th 0.5%

Seven dividends of £10,000 each, will be paid for scoring most points during:

1) May (4-31)
2) Royal Ascot (June 19-23)
3) June
4) July
5) August
6) September
7) October (1-20)

In the event of a tie for any places the dividends for the places concerned will be shared.

THE RULES

▶▶You must be aged 18 or over to enter and may be required to provide proof of age before receiving payment of any winnings.

▶▶Entries are accepted subject to independent age verification checks and by placing an entry you authorise Totepool to undertake any such age verification as may be required to confirm that you are aged 18 or over. If age cannot be verified the entry will be void.

▶▶The Tote Ten to Follow is operated by Totepool, whose Head Office is: Westgate House, Chapel Lane, Wigan, WN3 4HS.

▶▶Selections cannot be changed or cancelled after an entry has been placed.

▶▶Members of staff (or their immediate families) of Totepool, Betfred or the Racing Post are not eligible to enter.

▶▶The names of winners / leaders will be published in the Racing Post and at ttf.totesport.com Any disagreement with the published list must be made in writing and received within five days of the publication date at: Tote Ten to Follow, PO Box 116, Wigan WN3 4WW OR by e-mail at: totetentofollow@totesport.com Claims received after the five-day period or telephone enquiries will not be considered.

▶▶Totepool reserves the right to refuse to accept or disqualify any entries which, in its sole opinion, do not comply with any of the information stated herein. In all cases the decision of Totepool is final.

▶▶Once accepted, entries are non-refundable.

▶▶Totepool/Betfred betting rules apply to any point not covered above.

POSTAL ENTRIES

▶▶Write the reference numbers – not the horse names – clearly on the entry form using a ballpoint pen. Only horses contained in the list are eligible and must be entered by their reference numbers. Postal entries cannot be viewed online.

▶▶Should a selection be duplicated, points will only be awarded once with the duplication disregarded. Where a selection number is illegible, capable of dual interpretation or is not contained in the prescribed list, the selection will be void and the remaining selections count. Entries containing less than ten selections count for the number of selections made. Where more than ten selections are stated in one line, the first ten selections count with the remainder disregarded.

▶▶You can enter as many lists as you wish, each entry must be made on an official entry form although photocopy entry forms are accepted for multiple entries.

▶▶Each entry form must contain the name, address, date of birth and telephone number of the entrant. Entries in the name of a syndicate must also contain the name and address etc of the organiser.

▶▶Completed entry forms must be accompanied by cheque / postal order payable to: **Totepool** for the amount staked in Sterling or Euro. Payment is not accepted in other currencies. Cash should only be sent by guaranteed delivery. Where the remittance is insufficient to cover the number of entries required, the amount received will be allocated to entries in the order of processing with any remaining entries void.

▶▶Totepool, Betfred or the publishers of the Racing Post do not accept any responsibility for non-receipt of entries. Proof of posting will not be taken as proof of delivery.

If you require help with your entry, call the
Tote Ten to Follow Helpline on:
0800 666 160

ENTRY FORM

EACH SELECTION REQUIRES A FOUR-DIGIT NUMBER. NUMBERS ARE LISTED FROM PAGE 113	EXAMPLE			
1	1	0	8	9
2	1	2	2	4

ENTRY ONE	ENTRY TWO	ENTRY THREE	ENTRY FOUR
1	1	1	1
2	2	2	2
3	3	3	3
4	4	4	4
5	5	5	5
6	6	6	6
7	7	7	7
8	8	8	8
9	9	9	9
10	10	10	10

ENTRY FIVE	ENTRY SIX	ENTRY SEVEN	ENTRY EIGHT
1	1	1	1
2	2	2	2
3	3	3	3
4	4	4	4
5	5	5	5
6	6	6	6
7	7	7	7
8	8	8	8
9	9	9	9
10	10	10	10

Title_____ Surname_____ Forename (s)_____

Syndicate Name (max 20 characters)_____

Address_____

Post Code_____ Phone (day)_____ Phone (evening)_____

I am 18 or over – tick box ❑   Date of Birth_____ DD/MM/YYYY

Number of Entries (each entry costs £12 or €15)_____ I enclose Cheque/Postal Order

payable to: Totepool – Value: £_____ or €_____

Post completed entry form together with your remittance

to: Tote Ten to Follow, PO Box 116, WIGAN WN3 4WW to

arrive by no later than 12.00 noon on Friday, May 4

You must be aged 18 or over to enter and may be required to provide proof of age before receiving payment of any winnings **Bet responsibly and have fun: www.gambleaware.co.uk**

By entering this competition you agree to Totepool notifying you of future Ten to Follow competitions and also forwarding reminders for the Bonus Horse Window. You can opt out at any time by letting us know in writing. Tick this box if you do NOT want to be informed of other Totepool/Betfred betting offers ❑

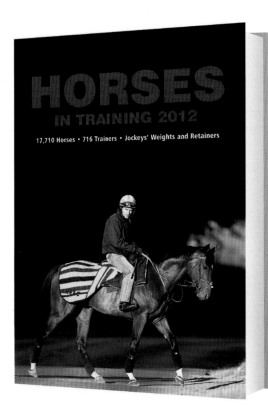

How to read the profiles of the 250 horses in this year's Ten to Follow competition

The number to put on your entry form

Age, colour, sex, sire, dam, dam's sire

Trainer

Career form figures to February 25, 2012

1036 Camelot

3 b c Montjeu - Tarfah (Kingmambo)

Aidan O'Brien (Ir)   Derrick Smith

PLACINGS: 11-   **RPR 119+**

Starts	1st	2nd	3rd	4th	Win & Pl
2	2	-	-	-	£141,679

10/11	Donc	1m Cls1 Gp1 2yo good	£131,567
7/11	Leop	1m Mdn 2yo good	£10,112

Brilliant winner of last season's Racing Post Trophy, coming from last to first under a hugely confident ride on only his second start; could have the speed for the 2,000 Guineas but pedigree suggests he will come into his own over the 1m4f of the Derby; a potential superstar

Owner

Current Racing Post Rating

Career wins

Profile of the horse, including significant going and distance information and, where appropriate, its prospects for the coming season

1000 Abtaal (USA)

3 b c Rock Hard Ten - Appealing Storm (Valid Appeal)

Jean-Claude Rouget (Fr)   Hamdan Al Maktoum

PLACINGS: 211-   RPR **111+**

Starts	1st	2nd	3rd	4th	Win & Pl
3	2	1	-	-	£48,965
	10/11	StCl	1m Gp3 2yo gd-sft		£34,483
	9/11	Fntb	7f 2yo v soft		£10,345

Got close to high-class Sofast and looked highly impressive when winning next two starts by three lengths, including when slamming subsequent Group 1 winner French Fifteen at Saint-Cloud; bypassed later top-level races to wait for this season; potential Classic colt.

1001 Akeed Mofeed

3 b c Dubawi - Wonder Why (Tiger Hill)

John Oxx (Ir)   Jaber Abdullah

PLACINGS: 412-   RPR **114+**

Starts	1st	2nd	3rd	4th	Win & Pl
3	1	1	-	1	£26,258
	9/11	Leop	7f Mdn 2yo good		£10,112

Sent off just 5-6 for Group 2 Beresford Stakes on final start but unable to reel in David Livingston having been left with too much to do (reportedly struggled on heavy ground); had twice made big impression in maidens, winning by five lengths at Leopardstown after catching the eye on his debut.

1002 Al Kazeem *(below, winning)*

4 b c Dubawi - Kazeem (Darshaan)

Roger Charlton   D J Deer

PLACINGS: 51/21222-   RPR **115**

Starts	1st	2nd	3rd	4th	Win & Pl
7	2	4	-	-	£80,725
95	5/11	Newb	1m2f Cls2 77-95 3yo Hcap gd-fm		£18,693
	10/10	Newb	1m Cls4 Mdn 2yo gd-sft		£4,209

Progressed out of handicaps to post three rock-solid efforts in Pattern company, doing best when running Green Destiny to half a length at Newbury and coming up against another smart rival in Beaten Up in St Simon Stakes on final start; more than good enough to win a Group race.

1003 Alainmaar (Fr)

6 b g Johar - Lady Elgar (Sadler's Wells)

Roger Varian   Hamdan Al Maktoum

PLACINGS: 211/11/1-   RPR **117**

Starts	1st	2nd	3rd	4th	Win & Pl
6	5	1	-	-	£77,889
	5/11	Asct	1m4f Cls1 List gd-fm		£17,031
	5/10	Ling	1m2f Cls2 gd-fm		£12,462
102	4/10	Epsm	1m2f Cls2 76-102 Hcap good		£31,155
97	10/09	NmkR	1m2f Cls2 83-97 3yo Hcap gd-fm		£12,462
	9/09	Pont	1m2f Cls5 Mdn gd-fm		£3,238

Restricted to just three runs since start of 2010 but has won all of them in manner of high-class middle-distance horse, most recently when bouncing back from a year's absence to win Listed race at Ascot by six lengths; injured again when being trained for Hardwicke Stakes.

1004 Alanza (Ire)

4 ch f Dubai Destination - Alasha (Barathea)

John Oxx (Ir) H H Aga Khan

PLACINGS: 1/331116- RPR **112+**

Starts	1st	2nd	3rd	4th	Win & Pl
7	4	-	2	-	£103,970
9/11	Donc	7f Cls1 Gp3 good			£29,600
8/11	Tipp	7¹/₂f List gd-fm			£33,621
7/11	Cork	1m List gd-fm			£22,414
9/10	List	6¹/₂f Mdn 2yo yield			£9,465

Beaten favourite on first two starts over 6f last season but relished step up to 1m when landing Listed race at Cork; did well to cope with drop to 7f when winning twice more, most notably in Group 3 at Doncaster, and didn't get good run when sixth in Sun Chariot Stakes; worth another chance at Group 1 level.

1005 Aljamaaheer (Ire)

3 ch c Dubawi - Kelly Nicole (Rainbow Quest)

Roger Varian Hamdan Al Maktoum

PLACINGS: 1- RPR **86+**

Starts	1st	2nd	3rd	4th	Win & Pl
1	1	-	-	-	£3,150
10/11	Yarm	6f Cls5 Mdn 2yo good			£3,151

Well-bred colt who made debut last October having been slow to come to hand but made an immediate mark when quickening clear at Yarmouth despite being slowly away; holds a Derby entry but likely to do best over slightly shorter; should have a bright future.

1006 Alkimos (Ire)

4 b c High Chaparral - Bali Breeze (Common Grounds)

Saeed Bin Suroor Godolphin

PLACINGS: 4112-63 RPR **110**

Starts	1st	2nd	3rd	4th	Win & Pl
6	2	1	1	1	£43,522
6/11	Donc	1m2¹/₂f Cls2 good-fm			£13,017
5/11	Wind	1m2f Cls5 Auct Mdn 3-5yo good			£2,267

Made rapid progress for Luca Cumani last season, winning twice before chasing home Pisco Sour in Group 3 at Royal Ascot; moved to Godolphin with promise of much better to come but deliberately kept off track before making debut for new connections in Dubai this spring.

1007 Alla Speranza

3 gr f Sir Percy - Alvarita (Selkirk)

Jim Bolger (Ir) Miss K Rausing

PLACINGS: 12- RPR **97+**

Starts	1st	2nd	3rd	4th	Win & Pl
2	1	1	-	-	£12,685
10/11	Cork	1m¹/₂f Mdn 2yo soft			£6,543

Just outstayed by Call To Battle in Listed race at Leopardstown last November over 1m1f but pulled nicely clear of rest and enhanced reputation built when easily landing Cork maiden on her debut; half-sister to winner over 1m4f and should appreciate step up to middle distances.

1008 American Devil (Fr)

3 b c American Post - Alcestes Selection (Selkirk)

John Van Handenhove (Fr) Ecurie Haras De Quetieville

PLACINGS: 1135- RPR **111**

Starts	1st	2nd	3rd	4th	Win & Pl
4	2	-	1	-	£54,232
7/11	Lonc	7f List 2yo gd-sft			£23,707
5/11	Chan	6f 2yo good			£14,655

Hugely impressive winner of first two starts last season, including Listed event at Longchamp, but slightly disappointing subsequently; beaten favourite in Group 3 and then only fifth to Dabirsim in Prix Jean-Luc Lagardere; should have more to offer, particularly over middle distances.

1009 Amour Propre *(opposite left)*

6 ch g Paris House - Miss Prim (Case Law)

Henry Candy Simon Broke & Partners

PLACINGS: 7111/105/980/221- RPR **114**

Starts	1st	2nd	3rd	4th	Win & Pl
13	5	2	-	-	£136,881
8/11	Curr	5f Gp3 good			£32,220
5/09	NmkR	5f Cls1 Gp3 gd-fm			£36,901
10/08	Asct	5f Cls1 Gp3 2yo gd-sft			£28,385
7/08	Bath	5f Cls2 2yo firm			£4,857
6/08	Wwck	5f Cls5 Mdn Auct 2yo gd-fm			£3,071

Spent a couple of years in the doldrums after terrific juvenile campaign in 2008 but bounced back last season, deservedly landing first win for more than two years in Group 3 at the Curragh after two near misses; lightly raced and remains fragile but high-class sprinter on his day.

1010 Anam Allta (Ire)

4 b f Invincible Spirit - Kiltubber (Sadler's Wells)

Dermot Weld (Ir)   Ballylinch Stud

PLACINGS: 51/3121-   **RPR 115**

Starts		1st	2nd	3rd	4th	Win & Pl
6		3	1	1	-	£81,591
	10/11 Tipp	7¹/₂f Gp3 heavy				£36,422
89	7/11 Gway	7f 72-93 Hcap good				£19,612
	8/10 Curr	6f Mdn 2yo good				£10,686

Highly progressive filly last season, showing marked improvement with every run; won at second attempt in a handicap at Galway and followed up terrific second to Alanza on good to firm ground by running away with Group 3 at Tipperary by six lengths, relishing much more testing conditions.

1011 Angels Will Fall (Ire)

3 b f Acclamation - Coconut Squeak (Bahamian Bounty)

Charles Hills   Mrs E O'Leary

PLACINGS: 11773-   **RPR 107+**

Starts		1st	2nd	3rd	4th	Win & Pl
5		2		1	-	£49,379
	7/11 Asct	6f Cls1 Gp3 2yo gd-sft				£28,355
	5/11 Wind	5f Cls4 Mdn 2yo good				£3,432

Did well to win Princess Margaret Stakes on second start and gave herself little chance by pulling too hard in subsequent races; still managed to finish fine third in Cheveley Park Stakes and seems capable of much better if learning to settle; unlikely to stay 1m.

1012 Apollo (Ire)

3 b c Galileo - Golden Coral (Slew O'Gold)

Aidan O'Brien (Ir)   Derrick Smith

PLACINGS: 1-   **RPR 98+**

Starts		1st	2nd	3rd	4th	Win & Pl
1		1	-	-	-	£10,112
	7/11 Curr	7f Mdn 2yo yield				£10,112

Missed second half of last season but had made big impression when landing a decent Curragh maiden on his debut, galloping clear having raced prominently throughout; expected to be even better on quicker ground and should do best over middle distances.

1013 Arctic Cosmos (USA)

5 b h North Light - Fifth Avenue Doll (Marquetry)

John Gosden   Rachel Hood & Rjh Geffen

PLACINGS: 44/131231/24-   **RPR 113**

Starts		1st	2nd	3rd	4th	Win & Pl
10		3	2	2	3	£393,182
	9/10 Donc	1m6¹/₂f Cls1 Gp1 3yo good				£283,850
78	6/10 Kemp	1m4f Cls4 68-81 3yo Hcap stand				£4,209
	4/10 Wolv	1m1¹/₂f Cls6 Auct Mdn 3yo stand				£1,774

Off the track for more than a year following win in 2010 St Leger having injured a cannon bone; returned with highly promising second in Cumberland Lodge Stakes but failed to build on that when fourth in Group 1 in Canada; may benefit from return to racing beyond 1m4f.

1014 Artistic Jewel (Ire)

3 ch f Excellent Art - Danish Gem (Danehill)

Ed McMahon   R L Bedding

PLACINGS: 15311-   **RPR 98 +**

Starts	1st	2nd	3rd	4th	Win & Pl
5	3		1	-	£24,195

10/11	NmkR	6f Cls1 List 2yo good	£12,193
9/11	Sals	6f Cls2 2yo soft	£7,763
7/11	Wind	5f Cls5 Mdn 2yo good	£2,264

Smart sprinting filly who took time to build on promising debut win (beaten favourite in Listed race next time) but came good on final two starts; won at Salisbury despite looking unsuited by soft ground and did much better on quicker surface when easily landing Listed contest.

1015 Astrology (Ire)

3 b c Galileo - Ask For The Moon (Dr Fong)

Aidan O'Brien (Ir)   Derrick Smith

PLACINGS: 133-   **RPR 108**

Starts	1st	2nd	3rd	4th	Win & Pl
3	1	-	2	-	£21,141

8/11	Leop	1m Mdn 2yo good	£10,112

Made impressive winning debut over 1m and possibly not seen in best light when beaten twice subsequently, finding drop to 7f against him in red-hot Futurity Stakes and struggling to cope with Newmarket's undulations in Autumn Stakes; smart middle-distance prospect.

1016 Await The Dawn (USA) *(below)*

5 b h Giant's Causeway - Valentine Band (Dixieland Band)

Aidan O'Brien (Ir)

Michael Tabor, Mrs John Magnier & Derrick Smith

PLACINGS: 17/11/1137-   **RPR 125 +**

Starts	1st	2nd	3rd	4th	Win & Pl
8	5		1	-	£220,656

6/11	Asct	1m4f Cls1 Gp2 soft	£61,964
5/11	Ches	1m2½f Cls1 Gp3 gd-fm	£28,385
9/10	Leop	1m2f Gp3 good	£34,513
8/10	Cork	1m2f gd-fm	£10,075
7/09	Naas	1m Mdn 2yo soft	£10,399

Hugely impressive on first two starts last season, most notably when stepping up to 1m4f for first time to win Hardwicke Stakes at Royal Ascot; found to be suffering from travel sickness when third in Juddmonte International and again below par in Breeders' Cup Turf; acts on any going.

1017 Balty Boys (Ire)

3 b c Cape Cross - Chatham Islands (Elusive Quality)

Charles Hills   Sir A Ferguson, Cavendish Invltd & J Hanson

PLACINGS: 719344-   **RPR 110**

Starts	1st	2nd	3rd	4th	Win & Pl
6	1	-		2	£32,887

7/11	Newb	6f Cls4 Mdn 2yo good	£4,464

Hard to judge his level last season having run best race when racing alone on far side in Middle Park Stakes, eventually not beaten far in fourth; poor ninth in Acomb

Stakes on only previous run in Pattern company but twice ran fairly well in sales races; something to prove.

1018 Bapak Chinta (USA)

3 gr/ro c Speightstown - Suena Cay (Maria's Mon)

Kevin Ryan   T A Rahman

PLACINGS: 110-   **RPR 106+**

Starts	1st	2nd	3rd	4th	Win & Pl
3	-	-	-	-	£45,815
	6/11 Asct	5f Cls1 Gp2 2yo gd-sft			£42,578
	5/11 Haml	5f Cls5 Mdn 2yo good			£3,238

Looked sure to figure among leading juvenile sprinters in Britain last season when winning Norfolk Stakes at Royal Ascot, although form failed to work out; suffered setback when being trained for Nunthorpe Stakes and seen only once since when tailed off in Middle Park Stakes.

1019 Baraan (Fr)

4 gr c Dalakhani - Brusca (Grindstone)

Jean-Claude Rouget (Fr)   H H Aga Khan

PLACINGS: 4/113-   **RPR 120+**

Starts	1st	2nd	3rd	4th	Win & Pl
4	2	-	1	1	£193,868
	4/11 Lonc	1m2¹/₂f Gp3 3yo good			£34,483
	3/11 Deau	1m1¹/₂f 3yo stand			£10,345

Did remarkably well to finish third in Prix du Jockey Club last season having lost ten lengths at the start; had been sent off joint-favourite after beating Pour Moi to win Group 3 at Longchamp but off the track after Chantilly; could be a big force in top middle-distance races.

1020 Barbican

4 b g Hurricane Run - The Faraway Tree (Suave Dancer)

Alan Bailey   John Stocker

PLACINGS: 1142511131-   **RPR 116+aw**

Starts	1st	2nd	3rd	4th	Win & Pl
10	6	1	1	1	£161,495
	11/11 Kemp	1m4f Cls1 List stand			£17,013
	9/11 Asct	1m6f Cls1 List 3yo good			£19,849
100	9/11 Asct	1m4f Cls2 86-100 3yo Hcap good			£97,035
	8/11 NmkJ	1m2f Cls3 3yo good			£7,159
79	4/11 Donc	1m2¹/₂f Cls3 77-85 3yo Hcap good			£5,828
	2/11 Wolv	1m¹/₂f Cls5 Mdn 3yo stand			£2,008

Hugely progressive when stepped up in trip in second half of last season, springing 16-1 surprise in valuable Ascot handicap and just following up with win over Highland Castle in Listed race at same track; well beaten by Beaten Up and Al Kazeem when dropped to 1m4f next time.

1021 Bated Breath

5 b h Dansili - Tantina (Distant View)

Roger Charlton   K Abdulla

PLACINGS: 11134/011529228-   **RPR 122**

Starts	1st	2nd	3rd	4th	Win & Pl
14	5	3	1	1	£271,742
	5/11 Wind	6f Cls1 List gd-fm			£17,031
	5/11 Hayd	6f Cls2 good			£12,462
95	7/10 Hayd	6f Cls2 83-95 3yo Hcap gd-fm			£12,952
90	6/10 Pont	6f Cls3 71-90 3yo Hcap good			£9,714
	4/10 Pont	6f Cls5 Mdn good			£3,238

Among leading sprinters last season when unlucky to finish close second three times in Group 1 races, most notably when beaten a nose by Dream Ahead in Haydock Sprint Cup; struggled on only start over 5f in Nunthorpe Stakes; should be a big player in top sprints.

1022 Be Fabulous (Ger)

5 b m Samum - Bandeira (Law Society)

Mahmood Al Zarooni   Godolphin Snc

PLACINGS: 7/24111-   **RPR 111**

Starts	1st	2nd	3rd	4th	Win & Pl
6	3	1	-	1	£164,870
	10/11 Lonc	1m7¹/₂f Gp1 good			£123,147
	10/11 StCl	1m6f List gd-sft			£22,414
	6/11 MsnL	1m5f 4yo gd-sft			£12,069

Highly progressive stayer for Andre Fabre last season when winning last three starts, showing a potent turn of foot on each occasion; gained biggest win when stepped up to 1m7¹/₂f to easily land Prix Royal-Oak at Longchamp; may well have more to offer for new trainer.

1023 Beaten Up

4 b g Beat Hollow - Frog (Akarad)

William Haggas   B Haggas, B Mathieson & R Smith

PLACINGS: 111-   **RPR 123+**

Starts	1st	2nd	3rd	4th	Win & Pl
3	3	-	-	-	£39,426
	10/11 Newb	1m4f Cls1 Gp3 gd-fm			£28,355
	9/11 Donc	1m2¹/₂f Cls3 good			£8,093
	4/11 Ripn	1m2f Cls5 Mdn 3yo gd-fm			£2,979

Missed much of last season after winning debut in April but made big impression during the autumn; easily landed classified stakes at Doncaster and followed up with devastating win in St Simon Stakes despite pulling hard on step up to 1m4f; looks sure to go on to bigger things.

1024 Best Terms

3 b f Exceed And Excel - Sharp Terms (Kris)

Richard Hannon   R Barnett

PLACINGS: 11115-   **RPR** 114+

Starts	1st	2nd	3rd	4th	Win & Pl
5	4	-	-	-	£115,417
	8/11	York	6f Cls1 Gp2 2yo gd-sft		£61,380
	6/11	Asct	5f Cls1 Gp2 2yo good		£42,578
	5/11	Newb	5f Cls3 2yo gd-fm		£4,673
	4/11	Wind	5f Cls5 Mdn 2yo gd-fm		£2,388

Produced arguably the best performance by a juvenile filly in Britain last season when making all in Lowther Stakes at York, following up narrow victory in Queen Mary; sent off warm favourite for Cheveley Park Stakes but unable to dominate and well beaten in fifth; not certain to train on.

1025 Bible Belt (Ire)

4 br f Big Bad Bob - Shine Silently (Bering)

Jessica Harrington (Ir)   Anamoine Limited

PLACINGS: 413/11172-   **RPR** 114

Starts	1st	2nd	3rd	4th	Win & Pl
8	4	1	1	1	£151,304
	8/11	Curr	1m1f Gp3 good		£37,823
	8/11	Gowr	1m1½f List good		£28,017
102	7/11	Leop	1m1f 76-102 Hcap good		£19,612
	9/10	Rosc	7f Mdn 2yo sft-hvy		£7,022

Rattled up a hat-trick last season over 1m1f, culminating in Group 3 at the Curragh, before flopping on softer ground; bounced back with fine second to Dancing

Rain at Ascot, proving even more effective over 1m4f; should continue to excel over middle distances.

1026 Black Caviar (Aus) *(above)*

6 br m Bel Esprit - Helsinge (Desert Sun)

Peter Moody (Aus)   G J Wilkie, Mrs K J Wilkie Et Al

PLACINGS: 11/1111/11111111-111   **RPR** 133+

Starts	1st	2nd	3rd	4th	Win & Pl
19	19	-	-	-	£3,251,782
	2/12	Flem	5f Gp1 good		£297,697
	2/12	Caul	7f Gp1 gd-sft		£159,211
	1/12	Moon	6f Gp2 good		£82,895
	11/11	Flem	6f Gp1 good		£393,791
	10/11	Moon	6f Gp2 gd-sft		£119,281
	10/11	Caul	6f Gp2 gd-sft		£79,085
	5/11	Doom	5f Gp2 gd-sft		£170,915
	4/11	Rand	6f Gp1 gd-sft		£394,314
	3/11	Moon	6f Gp1 good		£202,614
	3/11	Flem	6f Gd1 Hcap good		£395,425
	2/11	Flem	5f Gp1 gd-sft		£295,752
	11/10	Flem	6f Gp1 gd-sft		£251,389
	10/10	Moon	6f Gp2 gd-sft		£102,778
	10/10	Caul	5f Gp2 good		£67,222
	1/10	Moon	6f Gp2 good		£68,056
	9/09	Flem	6f Gp2 3yo good		£73,544
	8/09	Moon	6f List 3yo good		£33,010
	5/09	Caul	6f List good		£32,403
	4/09	Flem	5f Hcap gd-sft		£32,403

Record-breaking sprinter who has swept all before her in Australia; took step up to 7f in her stride in February when landing 18th of her 19 successive wins, setting up possibility of clash with Frankel at some stage; likely to come to Royal Ascot with Diamond Jubilee Stakes another possibility.

1027 Bogart

3 ch c Bahamian Bounty - Lauren Louise (Tagula)

Kevin Ryan   Mrs Angie Bailey

PLACINGS: 171618-   **RPR 107**

Starts	1st	2nd	3rd	4th	Win & Pl
6	3	-	-	-	£269,491

	10/11	Rdcr	6f Cls1 List 2yo gd-fm	£117,787
	8/11	York	6f Cls2 2yo gd-sft	£136,868
	5/11	Ayr	6f Cls4 Mdn 2yo gd-sft	£4,468

Inconsistent last season but smart on his day, landing red-hot sales race at York and running away with Redcar Two-Year-Old Trophy; well-beaten favourite in Group 2 at Maisons-Laffitte on final start; raced too freely to stay trip on only run beyond 6f.

1028 Bohemian Melody

5 b g Desert Sun - Chamonis (Affirmed)

Marco Botti   Mrs L Botti

PLACINGS: 21224124/59031-53   **RPR 108+**

Starts	1st	2nd	3rd	4th	Win & Pl
15	3	4	2	2	£46,043

91	10/11	Donc	6f Cls2 89-105 Hcap good	£11,450
85	7/10	Kemp	6f Cls3 82-91 3yo Hcap stand	£6,044
	3/10	Kemp	7f Cls5 Mdn 3yo stand	£2,590

Had become frustrating until dropped to 6f on final two starts last season, finishing fine third at Ripon when drawn on wrong side and making amends with runaway win in competitive handicap at Doncaster; benefited from first-time blinkers that day but has Group potential if progressing.

1029 Bonfire

3 b c Manduro - Night Frolic (Night Shift)

Andrew Balding   Highclere Thoroughbred Racing-Pocahontas

PLACINGS: 13-   **RPR 113+**

Starts	1st	2nd	3rd	4th	Win & Pl
2	1	-	-	-	£29,323

| | 9/11 | Sals | 1m Cls4 Mdn 2yo soft | £4,690 |

Pitched into Group 1 company after winning Salisbury maiden and looked unlucky not to win Criterium International at Saint-Cloud, finishing strongly in third having had no room; exciting.

1030 Born To Sea (Ire)

3 b c Invincible Spirit - Urban Sea (Miswaki)

John Oxx (Ir)   Christopher Tsui

PLACINGS: 12-   **RPR 106+**

Starts	1st	2nd	3rd	4th	Win & Pl
2	1	1	-	-	£30,193

| | 9/11 | Curr | 6f List 2yo yld-sft | £22,414 |

Subject of much fanfare prior to debut

being a half-brother to Sea The Stars and appeared to justify hype when winning Listed race at the Curragh, challenging for favouritism in 2,000 Guineas and Derby; beaten at odds-on by Nephrite next time but found to be lame.

1031 Brigantin (USA)

5 ch h Cozzene - Banyu Dewi (Poliglote)

Andre Fabre (Fr)   Team Valor

PLACINGS: 21/72211d16/94133738-   **RPR 114**

Starts	1st	2nd	3rd	4th	Win & Pl
18	5	3	3	1	£238,850

	5/11	Lonc	1m7¹/₂f Gp2 good	£63,879
	9/10	Lonc	1m7f Gp3 3yo good	£35,398
	6/10	Frau	1m4f 3yo good	£28,743
	11/09	StCl	1m2f 2yo heavy	£16,505
	9/09	Fntb	1m 2yo soft	£5,825

Gained biggest win in Group 2 at Longchamp last May but went on to impress most when faced with severe stamina test, finishing third to Fame And Glory in Ascot Gold Cup and filling same spot in Prix du Cadran; lacks speed over shorter trips but should again do well over extreme distances.

1032 Bronterre

3 b c Oasis Dream - Wondrous Story (Royal Academy)

Richard Hannon   Michael Pescod

PLACINGS: 114-   **RPR 115**

Starts	1st	2nd	3rd	4th	Win & Pl
3	2	-	-	1	£33,712

| | 9/11 | Gdwd | 7f Cls1 List 2yo gd-sft | £12,193 |
| | 7/11 | Sals | 7f Cls4 Mdn 2yo gd-fm | £4,528 |

Spectacular five-length winner of Listed race at Goodwood last season on good to soft ground and probably capable of better than fourth in Dewhurst Stakes (still beaten only just over a length) having hung right; won maiden on good to firm but may rely on cut in ground to show best form.

1033 Brown Panther

4 b c Shirocco - Treble Heights (Unfuwain)

Tom Dascombe   Owen Promotions Limited

PLACINGS: 1/4111522-   **RPR 119**

Starts	1st	2nd	3rd	4th	Win & Pl
8	4	2	-	1	£187,598

91	6/11	Asct	1m4f Cls2 85-99 3yo Hcap gd-sft	£31,155
81	5/11	Hayd	1m4f Cls3 76-90 3yo Hcap good	£9,970
73	5/11	Ches	1m4¹/₂f Cls3 73-85 3yo Hcap gd-fm	£9,066
	11/10	Sthl	7f Cls6 Mdn Auct 2yo stand	£1,619

Completed hat-trick of handicap wins with six-length romp at Royal Ascot last season;

disappointed in German Derby but proved he can shine at the highest level with terrific second in St Leger, relishing step up in trip despite possibly finding ground too quick.

1034 Burwaaz

3 b c Exceed And Excel - Nidhaal (Observatory)

Ed Dunlop   Hamdan Al Maktoum

PLACINGS: 21422320-   **RPR 110**

Starts	1st	2nd	3rd	4th	Win & Pl
8	1	4	1	1	£48,323
	5/11	Leic	5f Cls6 Auct Mdn 2yo good		£1,706

Showed all his best form over 5f last season, finishing best of those on stands side in Norfolk Stakes before chasing home Requinto in Molecomb Stakes and Flying Childers Stakes (beaten only a short head); not as convincing in three runs at 6f, although still third in Gimcrack.

1035 Call To Battle (Ire)

3 b c King's Best - Dance The Classics (Sadler's Wells)

John Oxx (Ir)   Neil Jones

PLACINGS: 611-   **RPR 101+**

Starts	1st	2nd	3rd	4th	Win & Pl
3	2	-	-	-	£29,935
	11/11	Leop	1m1f List 2yo yield		£21,013
	10/11	Curr	1m Mdn 2yo yld-sft		£8,922

Has a staying pedigree and did remarkably well to land slowly run Eyrefield Stakes at Leopardstown last November, keeping on dourly with the first two pulling nicely clear; seems sure to improve when stepped up to middle distances and could even develop into St Leger type.

1036 Camelot

3 b c Montjeu - Tarfah (Kingmambo)

Aidan O'Brien (Ir)   Derrick Smith

PLACINGS: 11-   **RPR 119+**

Starts	1st	2nd	3rd	4th	Win & Pl
2	2	-	-	-	£141,679
	10/11	Donc	1m Cls1 Gp1 2yo good		£131,567
	7/11	Leop	1m Mdn 2yo good		£10,112

Brilliant winner of last season's Racing Post Trophy, coming from last to first under a hugely confident ride on only his second start; could have the speed for the 2,000 Guineas but pedigree suggests he will come into his own over the 1m4f of the Derby; potential superstar.

1037 Carlton House (USA)

4 b c Street Cry - Talented (Bustino)

Sir Michael Stoute   The Queen

PLACINGS: 21/134-   **RPR 121+**

Starts	1st	2nd	3rd	4th	Win & Pl
5	2	1	1	1	£257,665
	5/11	York	1m2½f Cls1 Gp2 3yo good		£85,155
	10/10	Newb	1m Cls4 Mdn 2yo gd-sft		£4,209

Made Derby favourite after impressive win in Dante Stakes but finished only third at Epsom, making up lots of ground before run petered out; below that form when only fourth in Irish Derby; not ready for planned return in Champion Stakes; may prove best at 1m2f.

1038 Casamento (Ire)

4 ch c Shamardal - Wedding Gift (Always Fair)

Mahmood Al Zarooni   Godolphin

PLACINGS: 1211/0910-   **RPR 111+**

Starts	1st	2nd	3rd	4th	Win & Pl
8	4	1	-	-	£274,666
	9/11	Lonc	1m2f Gp3 3yo good		£34,483
	10/10	Donc	1m Cls1 Gp1 2yo good		£140,790
	9/10	Curr	1m Gp2 2yo yld-sft		£57,522
	8/10	Tipp	7½f Mdn 2yo gd-fm		£8,243

Won Racing Post Trophy for Michael Halford in 2010 before move to Godolphin; paid price for trying to chase Frankel in 2,000 Guineas, finishing tailed off, and still not right when ninth in Prix du Jockey Club; given long break before winning Group 3 at Longchamp but flopped again in Champion Stakes.

1039 Caspar Netscher

3 b c Dutch Art - Bella Cantata (Singspiel)

Alan McCabe   Charles Wentworth

PLACINGS: 1243231158-   **RPR 114+**

Starts	1st	2nd	3rd	4th	Win & Pl
10	3	2	2	1	£143,398
	9/11	Newb	6f Cls1 Gp2 2yo good		£34,026
	8/11	York	6f Cls1 Gp2 2yo gd-sft		£82,880
	5/11	Bevl	5f Cls5 Mdn 2yo gd-fm		£2,423

Thrived with racing last season, steadily improving to emerge as one of Britain's leading juveniles over 6f; won Gimcrack and Mill Reef Stakes before unlucky-in-running fifth when favourite for Middle Park; didn't appear to stay 1m in Breeders' Cup Juvenile Turf.

1040 Cavaleiro (Ire)

3 ch c Sir Percy - Khibraat (Alhaarth)

Marcus Tregoning   Guy Brook

PLACINGS: 33211-   **RPR 93+**

Starts	1st	2nd	3rd	4th	Win & Pl
5	2	1	2	-	£14,108
9/11	Newb	1m Cls2 2yo gd-sft			£9,338
8/11	Chep	1m Cls5 Mdn 2yo gd-fm			£2,264

Slow to come to hand last season, needing four attempts to break maiden tag, but then followed up by claiming decent scalp of Harvard N Yale in good conditions event at Newbury; likely to improve again according to connections and could benefit from step up to middle distances.

1041 Census (Ire)

4 b g Cacique - Slieve (Selkirk)

Richard Hannon   Highclere Thoroughbred Racing (Beeswing)

PLACINGS: 721/12215-   **RPR 118**

Starts	1st	2nd	3rd	4th	Win & Pl
8	3	3	-	-	£70,204
	8/11	Newb	1m5½f Cls1 Gp3 good		£28,355
85	5/11	Newb	1m3f Cls4 72-85 3yo Hcap gd-fm		£3,886
	10/10	Bath	1m Cls5 Mdn 2yo good		£2,008

Well-beaten second behind Brown Panther at Royal Ascot but made great strides subsequently, reversing form with that rival at Newbury having run Masked Marvel to a head at Newmarket; below that form when only fifth in St Leger, possibly finding trip too far.

1042 Chachamaidee (Ire)

5 b m Footstepsinthesand - Canterbury Lace (Danehill)

Sir Henry Cecil   R A H Evans

PLACINGS: 1365/1025/3121322-   **RPR 116**

Starts	1st	2nd	3rd	4th	Win & Pl
15	4	4	3	-	£170,047
7/11	Gdwd	7f Cls1 Gp3 gd-fm			£28,355
5/11	York	7f Cls3 good			£8,419
5/10	York	1m Cls1 List 3yo gd-fm			£22,708
6/09	Ling	6f Cls5 Mdn 2yo gd-fm			£3,562

Progressed into high-class filly last season, gaining most notable win in Group 3 at Goodwood; did most of her racing at 7f but looked equally good over 1m when second to Sahpresa in Group 1 Sun Chariot Stakes at Newmarket on penultimate start; has never run on ground softer than good.

1043 Chandlery (Ire)

3 b c Choisir - Masai Queen (Mujadil)

Richard Hannon   Mrs J Wood

PLACINGS: 1021-   **RPR 110**

Starts	1st	2nd	3rd	4th	Win & Pl
4	2	1	-	-	£50,164
7/11	Gdwd	7f Cls1 Gp2 2yo good			£34,026
6/11	Gdwd	6f Cls5 Mdn 2yo gd-fm			£3,238

Missed second half of last season but had already shown himself to be a smart juvenile when winning Vintage Stakes at Goodwood; had just lost out to Red Duke in Superlative Stakes and benefited from shrewd tactical ride when reversing form; may struggle with Group 2 penalty.

1044 Cirrus Des Aigles (Fr)

6 b g Even Top - Taille De Guepe (Septieme Ciel)

Corine Barande-Barbe (Fr)

Jean-Claude-Alain Dupouy & Xavier Niel

PLACINGS: 4311297/23212111215-   **RPR 130**

Starts	1st	2nd	3rd	4th	Win & Pl
39	13	15	5	2	£1,641,232
10/11	Asct	1m2f Cls1 Gp1 good			£737,230
8/11	Deau	1m4½f Gp2 v soft			£98,276
8/11	Deau	1m2f Gp3 heavy			£34,483
7/11	Vich	1m2f Gp3 v soft			£34,483
6/11	Lonc	1m2f Gp3 gd-sft			£34,483
10/10	Lonc	1m2f Gp2 v soft			£65,575
9/10	Lonc	1m2f List good			£23,009
9/09	Lonc	1m2f Gp3 3yo good			£38,835
8/09	Le L	1m2f List 3yo gd-sft			£26,699
5/09	Lonc	1m2½f 3yo soft			£27,760
5/09	Lonc	1m2f 3yo good			£14,078
1/09	Cagn	1m 3yo stand			£9,709

Failed to win on first six Group 1 attempts but improved throughout last season and gained confidence at lower level before landing thrilling win in Champion Stakes at Ascot; barred from Arc as a gelding but sure to have other top middle-distance races on agenda.

1045 Cityscape

6 ch h Selkirk - Tantina (Distant View)

Roger Charlton   K Abdulla

PLACINGS: 212/20/4211/2381212-   **RPR 123**

Starts	1st	2nd	3rd	4th	Win & Pl
16	5	7	1	1	£641,447
10/11	StCl	1m Gp3 v soft			£34,483
9/11	Curr	1m Gp3 yield			£32,220
10/10	NmkR	1m Cls1 Gp3 gd-sft			£34,062
9/10	Hayd	1m Cls1 List good			£22,708
9/08	Sals	1m Cls4 2yo good			£4,695

High-class miler who has won trio of Group 3 races with cut in ground but proved equally effective on quicker going when doing well at Group 1 level last season, finishing second in Italy and Hong Kong; connections are determined to claim elusive Group 1.

1046 Colombian (Ire)

4 b c Azamour - Clodora (Linamix)

John Gosden   H R H Princess Haya Of Jordan

PLACINGS: 3/31434421-   **RPR 117**

Starts	1st	2nd	3rd	4th	Win & Pl
9	2	1	3	3	£150,784
11/11	Cros	1m2½f List 3yo v soft			£23,707
5/11	Ches	1m2½f Cls4 Mdn 3yo gd-fm			£6,152

Campaigned almost exclusively in France after winning maiden at Chester last season, showing much improved form when fourth in Prix du Jockey Club and Prix Niel; below par when second at 4-6 returned to quicker surface at Leicester before bouncing back to make Listed breakthrough.

1047 Colour Vision (Fr)

4 gr g Rainbow Quest - Give Me Five (Monsun)

Saeed Bin Suroor   Sheikh Hamdan Bin Mohammed Al Maktoum

PLACINGS: 0108/397112485133-   **RPR 113+**

Starts	1st	2nd	3rd	4th	Win & Pl
16	4	1	3	1	£68,504
10/11	Pont	2m2f Cls3 gd-fm			£6,412
7/11	Hayd	1m6f Cls4 72-88 3yo Hcap gd-fm			£5,822
7/11	Ches	2m Cls4 66-84 Hcap good			£5,175
8/10	Thsk	1m Cls4 Mdn 2yo gd-fm			£4,339

(88, 82 marginal figures)

Showed smart form for Mark Johnston last season, winning handicap at Haydock by ten lengths and finally building on that when stepped up to extreme distances to finish third off lofty mark of 105 in Cesarewitch and get within a length of Fame And Glory at Ascot; top staying prospect.

1048 Coquet

3 b f Sir Percy - One So Marvellous (Nashwan)

Hughie Morrison   Hon Mary Morrison & Partners

PLACINGS: 411-   **RPR 95**

Starts	1st	2nd	3rd	4th	Win & Pl
3	2	-	-	1	£14,508
10/11	NmkR	1m Cls1 List 2yo good			£12,193
10/11	Wolv	1m½f Cls6 Auct Mdn 2yo stand			£2,070

Won Wolverhampton maiden over 1m½f and put stamina to good use when outstaying more fancied rivals at 20-1 in Listed race at Newmarket; bare form looked moderate for the grade but seems sure to stay at least 1m4f and connections are keen

to aim her at the Oaks.

1049 Coral Wave (Ire)

3 b f Rock Of Gibraltar - Common Knowledge (Rainbow Quest)

Patrick Prendergast (Ir)   Richard Barnes

PLACINGS: 4211-   **RPR 105**

Starts	1st	2nd	3rd	4th	Win & Pl
4	2	1	-	1	£69,939
9/11	Curr	7f Gp3 2yo heavy			£30,819
9/11	Curr	1m List 2yo soft			£33,621

Beaten twice on good ground but showed much-improved form when encountering testing conditions to win twice at a higher level at the Curragh, most notably in strong Group 3 on final start; regarded as an Oaks filly by her trainer but not certain to stay 1m4f on pedigree.

1050 Coupe De Ville (Ire)

3 b c Clodovil - Fantastic Account (Fantastic Light)

Richard Hannon   Macdonald, Wright, Creed, Smith & Jiggins

PLACINGS: 211151-   **RPR 104+**

Starts	1st	2nd	3rd	4th	Win & Pl
6	4	1	-	-	£297,532
10/11	NmkR	7f Cls2 2yo gd-fm			£270,550
8/11	Sals	1m Cls1 List 2yo gd-sft			£12,193
7/11	Newb	7f Cls4 2yo good			£4,669
6/11	NmkJ	7f Cls5 Mdn 2yo gd-sft			£3,238

Maintained yard's phenomenal record in major sales race in Tattersalls Millions Trophy on final start, beating subsequent Horris Hill winner Tell Dad and proving ability to cope with big fields; has also won over 1m and could stay slightly further; seems effective on any going.

1051 Crius (Ire)

3 b c Heliostatic - Fearless Flyer (Brave Act)

Richard Hannon   Titan Assets

PLACINGS: 11221-   **RPR 110**

Starts	1st	2nd	3rd	4th	Win & Pl
5	3	2	-	-	£33,648
9/11	NmkR	7f Cls1 Gp3 2yo gd-fm			£19,281
7/11	NmkJ	7f Cls4 2yo gd-fm			£3,881
7/11	Wwck	7f Cls5 Auct Mdn 2yo good			£2,976

Showed fair form early last season before taking big leap forward with comfortable win in Somerville Tattersall Stakes, beating three horses who were all at least placed at the top level on their next start; likely comeback in Greenham Stakes could determine Guineas prospects.

1052 Crusade (USA)

3 b/br c Mr Greeley - La Traviata (Johannesburg)

Aidan O'Brien (Ir)   M Tabor, D Smith & Mrs John Magnier

PLACINGS: 81416-   **RPR 114**

Starts	1st	2nd	3rd	4th	Win & Pl
5	2	-	-	1	£104,655
10/11	NmkR	6f Cls1 Gp1 2yo good			£92,721
8/11	Curr	6f Mdn 2yo good			£10,112

Had mixed record last season but proved among leading sprint juveniles when springing 25-1 surprise in Middle Park Stakes; well beaten on all three attempts beyond 6f, doing best when fourth in Somerville Tattersall Stakes; could try 1m again but likely to do best sprinting.

1053 Cry Fury

4 b g Beat Hollow - Cantanta (Top Ville)

Roger Charlton   K Abdulla

PLACINGS: 0/15180-   **RPR 101 +**

Starts	1st	2nd	3rd	4th	Win & Pl
88	2	-	-	-	£8,913
8/11	Gdwd	1m2f Cls3 80-88 Hcap good			£6,792
4/11	Kemp	1m3f Cls6 Auct Mdn 3yo stand			£1,748

Laid out for the Cambridgeshire after hugely impressive win at Goodwood last season, then warming up over an inadequate 7f, but let down his backers at Newmarket when finishing well down the field; still held in highest regard and could exploit handicap mark before tackling bigger tasks.

1054 Dabirsim (Fr) *(above)*

3 b c Hat Trick - Rumored (Royal Academy)

Christophe Ferland (Fr)   Simon Springer

PLACINGS: 11111-   **RPR 120 +**

Starts	1st	2nd	3rd	4th	Win & Pl
5	5	-	-	-	£396,965
10/11	Lonc	7f Gp1 2yo good			£172,405
8/11	Deau	6f Gp1 2yo good			£172,405
7/11	Deau	6f Gp3 2yo good			£34,483
7/11	Buch	6f 2yo gd-sft			£11,638
6/11	Buch	6f 2yo gd-sft			£6,034

Arguably the outstanding juvenile in Europe last season, easily winning the Prix Morny at Deauville by three lengths and coming from last to first with a devastating turn of foot to follow up in Prix Jean-Luc Lagardere; likely to run in French 2,000 Guineas rather than Newmarket version.

1055 Daddy Long Legs (USA)

3 ch c Scat Daddy - Dreamy Maiden (Meadowlake)

Aidan O'Brien (Ir)   M Tabor, D Smith & Mrs John Magnier

PLACINGS: 1410-   RPR 114+

Starts	1st	2nd	3rd	4th	Win & Pl
4	2	-	-	1	£69,652
9/11	NmkR	1m Cls1 Gp2 2yo gd-fm			£56,710
8/11	Gowr	7f Mdn 2yo gd-fm			£8,922

Strong galloper who showed vast improvement when stepped up to 1m in Royal Lodge Stakes, making all the running for clear-cut win; bred for dirt but didn't seem to enjoy surface when disappointing in Breeders' Cup Juvenile; style of running suggests he could stay 1m2f.

1056 Dance And Dance (Ire)

6 b g Royal Applause - Caldy Dancer (Soviet Star)

Ed Vaughan   Mohammed Rashid

PLACINGS: 3/12061/203125265-60   RPR 116+

Starts	1st	2nd	3rd	4th	Win & Pl
29	5	8	3	-	£113,023
97	6/11	Epsm	1m1/2f Cls2 82-100 Hcap good		£15,578
90	9/10	NmkR	1m Cls3 81-93 Hcap soft		£8,723
85	5/10	Ches	7f Cls4 81-85 Hcap gd-sft		£7,124
79	10/09	Kemp	7f Cls4 66-80 Hcap stand		£4,727
	2/09	Ling	7f Cls5 Mdn stand		£2,730

Smart miler who proved one of the most unlucky horses in training last season, often finding trouble in running as he failed to follow up impressive handicap win at Epsom in June; ambitiously campaigned in Group 1 races abroad having finished third in Group 3 at Salisbury.

1057 Dancing Rain (Ire)

4 ch f Danehill Dancer - Rain Flower (Indian Ridge)

William Haggas   M J & L A Taylor

PLACINGS: 2/1215110-   RPR 118

Starts	1st	2nd	3rd	4th	Win & Pl
8	4	2	-	-	£543,719
10/11	Asct	1m4f Cls1 Gp2 good			£141,775
8/11	Duss	1m3f Gp1 3yo soft			£198,276
6/11	Epsm	1m4f Cls1 Gp1 3yo good			£184,503
4/11	Newb	1m2f Cls4 Mdn 3yo gd-fm			£4,533

Top-class filly who made all the running to win Oaks at Epsom and proved that was no fluke with runaway victory in German Oaks and further triumph at Ascot on Champions Day; not ridden forcefully enough according to jockey when only fifth in Irish Oaks.

1058 Danedream (Ger) *(below)*

4 b f Lomitas - Danedrop (Danehill)

Peter Schiergen (Ger)   Gestut Burg Eberstein & T Yoshida

PLACINGS: 131d63/43151116-   RPR 128+

Starts	1st	2nd	3rd	4th	Win & Pl
13	5	-	4	1	£2,475,258
10/11	Lonc	1m4f Gp1 good			£1,970,345
9/11	Badn	1m4f Gp1 v soft			£129,310
7/11	Hopp	1m4f Gd1 good			£86,207
5/11	Siro	1m3f Gp2 3yo good			£172,414
6/10	Wiss	6f 2yo good			£5,310

Inconsistent early last season but found her feet with easy wins in two Group 1s in Germany and produced sensational repeat performance to land Arc by five lengths; possibly flattered by winning margin but no

doubt she was the best in the race; given too much to do when sixth in Japan Cup.

1059 David Livingston (Ire)

3 b c Galileo - Mora Bai (Indian Ridge)

Aidan O'Brien (Ir) D Smith, Mrs J Magnier & M Tabor

PLACINGS: 51431- **RPR 115**

Starts	1st	2nd	3rd	4th	Win & Pl
5	2	-	1	1	£82,508
9/11	Curr	1m Gp2 2yo heavy			£53,233
6/11	Curr	7f Mdn 2yo yld-sft			£11,302

Largely came up short in Pattern races last season but did well to hold his own over 7f, particularly when third in National Stakes, given he looked all about stamina when grinding out Group 2 win on heavy ground over 1m on final start; may be more to come when stepped up to middle distances.

1060 Deacon Blues

5 b g Compton Place - Persario (Bishop Of Cashel)

James Fanshawe Jan & Peter Hopper & Michelle Morris

PLACINGS: 51/32182230/211111- **RPR 125**

Starts	1st	2nd	3rd	4th	Win & Pl
16	7	4	2	-	£326,170
10/11	Asct	6f Cls1 Gp2 good			£141,775
9/11	Newb	5f Cls1 Gp3 good			£28,355
8/11	Curr	6f Gp3 gd-yld			£35,022
7/11	Newb	6f Cls1 Gp3 good			£28,355
98 6/11	Asct	6f Cls2 96-109 Hcap soft			£62,310
81 6/10	Yarm	6f Cls4 69-85 Hcap good			£4,163
10/09	Leic	6f Cls4 Mdn 2yo gd-fm			£5,181

Won last five starts, steadily climbing in grade to win Champions Sprint at Ascot having looked equally effective over 5f prior to that; began year with fourth defeat on good to firm (twice as favourite) since maiden win; should be a leading contender for Group 1 sprints. **Ruled out for the whole season after sustaining a tendon injury as book went to print.**

1061 Delegator

6 b h Dansili - Indian Love Bird (Efisio)

Saeed Bin Suroor Godolphin

PLACINGS: 5/12821d35/148/1590-1 **RPR 117+**

Starts	1st	2nd	3rd	4th	Win & Pl
18	5	3	1	1	£425,890
111 2/12	Meyd	7f 105-116 Hcap good			£67,742
5/11	York	6f Cls1 Gp2 good			£56,770
9/10	Newb	7f Cls1 List good			£19,870
4/09	NmkR	1m Cls1 Gp3 3yo gd-fm			£36,901
8/08	NmkJ	7f Cls4 Mdn 2yo good			£5,181

Top-class miler for Brian Meehan in 2009, chasing home Sea The Stars in 2,000

Guineas, but has failed to show best form in last two seasons for Godolphin; did well when dropped to 6f to win Duke of York Stakes on return last season but disappointing again after; made winning return at Meydan.

1062 Desert Law (Ire)

4 b c Oasis Dream - Speed Cop (Cadeaux Genereux)

Andrew Balding J C Smith

PLACINGS: 271/2042160- **RPR 109**

Starts	1st	2nd	3rd	4th	Win & Pl
10	2	3	-	1	£39,300
8/11	Bath	5½f Cls2 gd-fm			£14,426
10/10	NmkR	6f Cls4 Mdn 2yo good			£5,181

Unlucky to miss out on major targets last season, twice finishing second in valuable handicaps and gaining sole win in impressive fashion in conditions event at Bath (only start on preferred good to firm ground); disappointing on last two starts but looks a potential improver.

1063 Diala (Ire)

3 b f Iffraaj - Quaich (Danehill)

William Haggas Abdulla Al Khalifa

PLACINGS: 21- **RPR 87+**

Starts	1st	2nd	3rd	4th	Win & Pl
2	1	1	-	-	£4,582
10/11	NmkR	7f Cls5 Mdn Auct 2yo good			£3,235

Did well to push Lyric Of Light close on her debut, particularly having been caught short of room when making her effort, and built on that with wide-margin success at Newmarket next time; declared a non-runner when well fancied for Listed race after; should make mark at that level.

1064 Discourse (USA)

3 b/br f Street Cry - Divine Dixie (Dixieland Band)

Mahmood Al Zarooni Godolphin

PLACINGS: 11- **RPR 113+**

Starts	1st	2nd	3rd	4th	Win & Pl
2	2	-	-	-	£30,052
8/11	NmkJ	7f Cls1 Gp3 2yo good			£25,520
6/11	NmkJ	6f Cls4 Mdn 2yo gd-fm			£4,533

Yet to be tried at high level (missed late-season targets after a setback) but made big impression when winning both starts last season; overcame market weakness to win strong maiden on her debut and eased to wide-margin win in Group 3 at Newmarket; major 1,000 Guineas contender.

1065 Dragon Pulse (Ire)

3 ch c Kyllachy - Poetical (Croco Rouge)

Jessica Harrington (Ir)   Tan Kai Chah

PLACINGS: 2112-   **RPR 117**

Starts	1st	2nd	3rd	4th	Win & Pl
4	2	2	-	-	£95,077

	8/11	Curr	7f Gp2 2yo good	£49,267
	7/11	Leop	6f Mdn 2yo soft	£10,707

Impressive winner of strong Futurity Stakes last season (Dewhurst winner in second) but just outbattled by Power when second in National Stakes; seems likely to improve with experience (still looked green that day) and looks a leading Classic contender; may not be as effective on quick ground.

1066 Dubai Prince (Ire)

4 b c Shamardal - Desert Frolic (Persian Bold)

Mahmood Al Zarooni   Godolphin

PLACINGS: 11/10-7   **RPR 114+**

Starts	1st	2nd	3rd	4th	Win & Pl
5	3	-	-	-	£42,503

	9/11	Newb	1m1f Cls3 gd-sft	£7,159
	10/10	Leop	7f Gp3 2yo gd-fm	£28,761
	9/10	Gowr	1m Mdn 2yo yield	£6,584

High-class juvenile for Dermot Weld in 2010 but has become very fragile since move to Godolphin, suffering hairline fracture of pelvis last spring and again going wrong in Champion Stakes at Ascot; suggested he still possesses plenty of talent when winning at Newbury in September.

1067 Dubawi Gold

4 b c Dubawi - Savannah Belle (Green Desert)

Richard Hannon   Andrew Tinkler

PLACINGS: 1200419/1122641444-   **RPR 121**

Starts	1st	2nd	3rd	4th	Win & Pl
17	5	3	-	5	£415,598

	8/11	Gdwd	1m Cls1 Gp2 gd-sft	£56,710
	4/11	Ling	1m Cls1 List 3yo stand	£17,031
	3/11	Ling	7f Cls1 List 3yo stand	£17,031
	10/10	Asct	7f Cls2 2yo gd-sft	£6,916
	5/10	Ayr	6f Cls4 Mdn 2yo gd-fm	£4,533

Hugely consistent miler last season, winning Celebration Mile at Goodwood and running a string of good races in Group 1 company; came closest to major victory when fast-finishing second in Irish 2,000 Guineas and beaten just a length when fourth in Hong Kong Mile on final start.

1068 Dunaden (Fr)

6 b h Nicobar - La Marlia (Kaldounevees)

Mikel Delzangles   Pearl Bloodstock Ltd

PLACINGS: 48233622112/3129111-   **RPR 121**

Starts	1st	2nd	3rd	4th	Win & Pl
21	7	6	3	2	£3,422,289

	12/11	ShTn	1m4f Gp1 gd-fm	£658,960
0	11/11	Flem	2m Gd1 Hcap good	£2,483,660
0	10/11	Geel	1m4f Gd3 Hcap gd-sft	£98,039
	4/11	Lonc	1m7¹/₂f Gp3 good	£34,483
	11/10	Pari	1m4f List soft	£23,009
0	10/11	Lonc	1m4f Hcap soft	£19,965
	1/10	Cagn	1m3f 4yo v soft	£8,850

Late developer who really came good when sent abroad at the end of last year, just pipping Red Cadeaux to win the Melbourne Cup and successfully dropping to 1m4f to add the Hong Kong Vase; potent turn of foot may well make him a factor in top championship races in France.

1069 Ecliptic (USA)

4 ch c Kingmambo - Indy Five Hundred (A.P. Indy)

Mahmood Al Zarooni   Abdulla Al Mansoori

PLACINGS: 212/14-7   **RPR 111+**

Starts	1st	2nd	3rd	4th	Win & Pl
6	2	2	-	1	£29,733

	10/11	Sals	7f Cls3 good	£6,663
	6/10	Sand	7f Cls4 Mdn 2yo good	£4,857

High-class juvenile in 2010, winning maiden by eight lengths and going close in Group 2 Superlative Stakes, but then missed more than a year with injury; returned with impressive win in conditions race at Salisbury before disappointing when odds-on at Newmarket; full of potential.

1070 Ektihaam (Ire)

3 b c Invincible Spirit - Liscune (King's Best)

Roger Varian   Hamdan Al Maktoum

PLACINGS: 119-   **RPR 98+**

Starts	1st	2nd	3rd	4th	Win & Pl
3	2	-	-	-	£15,130

	9/11	Donc	7f Cls2 2yo good	£10,894
	7/11	Newb	7f Cls4 Mdn 2yo gd-fm	£4,237

Impressive winner of first two starts, most notably when landing conditions race at Doncaster by four lengths; faced sharp step up in class in Dewhurst Stakes and finished last but not given hard race after pulling hard in early stages; seems sure to prove much better.

1071 Elusive Kate (USA) *(above)*

3 b f Elusive Quality - Gout De Terroir (Lemon Drop Kid)

John Gosden   Magnolia Racing Llc & Teruya Yoshida

PLACINGS: 411118-   RPR **115**

Starts	1st	2nd	3rd	4th	Win & Pl
6	4	-	-	1	£209,593
10/11	Lonc	1m Gp1 2yo good			£147,776
8/11	Deau	7f Gp3 2yo good			£34,483
7/11	Deau	7f List 2yo gd-sft			£23,707
6/11	Kemp	7f Cls5 Mdn 2yo stand			£3,238

Did particularly well when sent to France last season, completing a hat-trick when landing weak renewal of Prix Marcel Boussac; disappointing eighth in Breeders' Cup Juvenile Fillies Turf on final start; likely to have French 1,000 Guineas as main early-season target.

1072 Elusivity (Ire)

4 b g Elusive City - Tough Chic (Indian Ridge)

Brian Meehan   Mrs P Good

PLACINGS: 76553/12222244122-   RPR **102+**

Starts	1st	2nd	3rd	4th	Win & Pl
16	2	7	1	2	£23,078
85	8/11	NmkJ	6f Cls4 74-85 Hcap soft		£4,528
	4/11	Kemp	7f Cls5 3yo stand		£2,418

Found it hard to win last season when second seven times and beaten favourite on five occasions but did little wrong towards end of season when winning at Newmarket and then running into handicap blots in

Sirius Prospect and Bohemian Melody; potential Group sprinter.

1073 Elzaam (Aus)

4 b c Redoute's Choice - Mambo In Freeport (Kingmambo)

Roger Varian   Hamdan Al Maktoum

PLACINGS: 1233/514854-   RPR **117**

Starts	1st	2nd	3rd	4th	Win & Pl
10	3	2	2	2	£89,634
5/11	Newb	6f Cls1 List 3yo gd-fm			£17,031
5/10	York	6f Cls3 Mdn 2yo gd-fm			£7,124

Earned step up to top level with six-length win in Listed sprint at Newbury in May and generally acquitted himself well when beaten no more than four lengths in three Group 1 races, doing best when fourth in Golden Jubilee Stakes; more to offer in Group 1 sprints.

1074 Emulous

5 b m Dansili - Aspiring Diva (Distant View)

Dermot Weld (Ir)   K Abdulla

PLACINGS: 1/22311/6111-   RPR **120+**

Starts	1st	2nd	3rd	4th	Win & Pl
10	6	2	1	-	£283,765
9/11	Leop	1m Gp1 good			£106,466
6/11	Fair	7f Gp3 good			£43,427
5/11	Curr	1m Gp3 gd-fm			£33,621
10/10	Naas	1m List good			£35,951
10/10	Tipp	7¹/₂f Gp3 good			£40,265
10/09	Curr	7f Mdn 2yo soft			£8,721

Maintained sharp upward curve when

coming from last to first to win Group 1 Matron Stakes at Leopardstown last season; likely to face much tougher tasks at top level but had clearly been on the upgrade when impressively winning pair of Group 3 races before that.

1075 Encke (USA)

3 b c Kingmambo - Shawanda (Sinndar)

Mahmood Al Zarooni   Godolphin

PLACINGS: 21-   **RPR 89+**

Starts	1st	2nd	3rd	4th	Win & Pl
2	1	1	-	-	£7,388
	10/11	NmkR	1m Cls4 Mdn 2yo gd-fm		£5,175

Just beaten in useful maiden at Doncaster on his debut and put that right with hugely impressive win at Newmarket, easily drawing clear under gentle handling; well fancied for Racing Post Trophy on that evidence but missed race after late setback; could be a Derby contender.

1076 Entifaadha

3 b c Dansili - Model Queen (Kingmambo)

William Haggas   Hamdan Al Maktoum

PLACINGS: 1135-   **RPR 107**

Starts	1st	2nd	3rd	4th	Win & Pl
4	2	-	1	-	£54,498
	8/11	York	7f Cls1 Gp3 2yo gd-sft		£29,600
	7/11	NmkJ	7f Cls4 Mdn 2yo good		£4,528

Stepped up on maiden win to land Acomb Stakes at York last season but beaten favourite twice after that, fading into third having been forced to make running into a headwind in Champagne Stakes and possibly finding good to firm ground too quick both times; should stay further.

1077 Eton Forever (Ire)

5 b g Oratorio - True Joy (Zilzal)

Roger Varian   H R H Sultan Ahmad Shah

PLACINGS: 6125/1452-   **RPR 110+**

Starts	1st	2nd	3rd	4th	Win & Pl
8	2	2	-	1	£39,288
92	4/11	Donc	1m Cls2 87-93 Hcap good		£24,924
	5/10	Kemp	1m Cls4 Mdn 3yo stand		£3,886

Hugely impressive winner of Spring Mile at Doncaster at start of last season and slightly disappointing not to win again on that form; still ran well in top handicaps at Ascot and Doncaster off 11lb higher mark and may be capable of better, especially if dropped to 7f.

1078 Eton Rifles (Ire)

7 b g Pivotal - Maritsa (Danehill)

Stuart Williams   The Eton Riflemen

PLACINGS: 31/4806222/54132141-   **RPR 113**

Starts	1st	2nd	3rd	4th	Win & Pl
24	6	6	4	3	£192,360
	11/11	Fntb	6f List v soft		£22,414
	10/11	Curr	6f List soft		£22,414
97	8/11	Gdwd	7f Cls2 93-103 Hcap gd-sft		£62,250
	9/09	Haml	6f Cls2 good		£12,462
80	5/09	Hayd	6f Cls4 68-81 Hcap heavy		£6,476
	9/08	Catt	7f Cls5 Mdn 3-4yo gd-sft		£2,590

Changed hands for 105,000gns last October having made tremendous progress following switch to David Elsworth earlier in season, finishing second in Ayr Gold Cup and winning Listed race at the Curragh; disappointing fourth at Doncaster on debut for new yard.

1079 Excelebration (Ire)

4 b c Exceed And Excel - Sun Shower (Indian Ridge)

Aidan O'Brien (Ir)   Manfredini, Tabor, Smith & Magnier

PLACINGS: 411/213112-   **RPR 129**

Starts	1st	2nd	3rd	4th	Win & Pl
9	5	2	1	1	£617,197
	9/11	Lonc	1m Gp1 v soft		£221,664
	8/11	Newb	7f Cls1 Gp2 good		£45,368
	5/11	Colo	1m Gp2 3yo sft		£86,207
	7/10	NmkJ	6f Cls3 2yo gd-fm		£7,771
	6/10	Donc	6f Cls5 Mdn Auct 2yo gd-fm		£3,238

Progressed throughout last season for Marco Botti and proved himself a truly top-class miler when winning Prix du Moulin and comfortably beating all bar Frankel in Queen Elizabeth II Stakes; flattered to get closer to Frankel when third in St James's Palace Stakes; sure to win more good races.

1080 Fallen For You

3 b f Dansili - Fallen Star (Brief Truce)

John Gosden   Normandie Stud Ltd

PLACINGS: 125-   **RPR 111**

Starts	1st	2nd	3rd	4th	Win & Pl
3	1	1	-	-	£23,976
	7/11	NmkJ	7f Cls4 Mdn 2yo gd-fm		£4,528

Looked a smart filly when winning maiden at Newmarket and lost no caste in defeat when just beaten by Lyric Of Light in May Hill Stakes despite looking green; pulled too hard in Fillies' Mile but still travelled well until final furlong before fading into fifth; looks sure to progress.

1081 Fame And Glory (above, leading)

6 b h Montjeu - Gryada (Shirley Heights)

Aidan O'Brien (Ir)

Mrs F Hay, D Smith, Mrs J Magnier & M Tabor

PLACINGS: 21266/311115/111241-   **RPR 121+**

Starts	1st	2nd	3rd	4th	Win & Pl
21	13	3	1	1	£2,285,405

10/11	Asct	2m Cls1 Gp3 good		£113,420
6/11	Asct	2m4f Cls1 Gp1 gd-sft		£154,698
5/11	Leop	1m6f List gd-fm		£26,616
4/11	Navn	1m5f List yield		£22,414
8/10	Curr	1m2f Gp2 good		£53,097
6/10	Epsm	1m4f Cls1 Gp1 good		£127,733
5/10	Curr	1m2¹/₂f Gp1 gd-fm		£123,451
5/10	Curr	1m2f Gp3 good		£43,142
6/09	Curr	1m4f Gp1 3yo gd-yld		£818,447
5/09	Leop	1m2f Gp2 3yo good		£75,728
4/09	Leop	1m2f Gp3 3yo gd-yld		£41,083
11/08	StCl	1m2f Gp1 2yo heavy		£105,037
10/08	Navn	1m Mdn 2yo heavy		£6,097

Top-class middle-distance performer in 2009 and 2010 who benefited from step up to staying trips last season, easily winning Ascot Gold Cup and following up in Long Distance Cup; twice beaten over 1m6f in between; sets the standard in top staying races again.

S. Rock S. Moon Sole Power

1082 Famous Name

7 b h Dansili - Fame At Last (Quest For Fame)

Dermot Weld (Ir)   K Abdulla

PLACINGS: 123/111671/11311234-   **RPR 123**

Starts	1st	2nd	3rd	4th	Win & Pl
29	14	7	4	1	£1,001,866

7/11	Leop	1m1f Gp3 soft		£32,220
6/11	Curr	1m2f Gp3 soft		£33,642
5/11	Leop	1m Gp3 good		£32,220
4/11	Leop	1m List gd-fm		£22,414
10/10	Leop	1m2f gd-fm		£24,447
7/10	Leop	1m1f Gp3 yield		£34,513
5/10	Leop	1m Gp3 gd-fm		£34,513
4/10	Leop	1m List gd-fm		£24,447
8/09	Curr	1m Gp3 sft-hvy		£39,126
7/09	Curr	1m2f Gp3 soft		£44,175
6/09	Curr	1m List gd-yld		£39,502
10/08	Curr	1m2f List yld-sft		£23,934
4/08	Leop	1m Gp3 3yo yield		£33,507
7/07	Naas	6f Mdn 2yo soft		£7,937

Prolific winner in Ireland (including eight times at Group 3 level) but has failed to triumph in higher grade and was again frustrated in search for elusive Group 1 victory last season, including when second at odds-on in Germany; equally effective on any going from 1m to 1m2f.

1083 Fanunalter

6 b g Falbrav - Step Danzer (Desert Prince)

Marco Botti   Scuderia Rencati Srl

PLACINGS: 93/21448771/231254-0   **RPR 118**

Starts	1st	2nd	3rd	4th	Win & Pl
21	5	4	2	3	£169,320
6/11	Epsm	1m¹/₂f Cls1 Gp3 gd-fm			£28,385
11/10	Kemp	1m Cls1 List stand............................			£14,484
4/10	Donc	1m Cls1 List gd-fm			£23,704
8/09	Kemp	1m Cls5 Mdn stand............................			£2,590

Surprise 16-1 winner of Diomed Stakes at Epsom last June and proved that was no fluke with even better performances in defeat later in season, most notably when close second in Summer Mile at Ascot; should find plenty more opportunities in Group races over a mile.

1084 Farraaj (Ire)

3 b c Dubai Destination - Pastorale (Nureyev)

Roger Varian   Sheikh Ahmed Al Maktoum

PLACINGS: 21123-   **RPR 110**

Starts	1st	2nd	3rd	4th	Win & Pl
5	2	2	1	-	£78,460
9/11	Sand	7f Cls4 2yo good			£3,558
8/11	Wwck	7f Cls5 Mdn 2yo good			£2,976

Gained a big reputation with five-length victory over Group 3 winner Tell Dad at Sandown; just fell short of expectations

when second to Crius next time but produced another solid display when third in Breeders' Cup Juvenile Turf; highly unlikely to stay beyond 1m.

1085 Fencing (USA)

3 ch c Street Cry - Latice (Inchinor)

John Gosden   George Strawbridge

PLACINGS: 313-   **RPR 111**

Starts	1st	2nd	3rd	4th	Win & Pl
3	1	-	2	-	£37,829
8/11	Newb	7f Cls1 List 2yo good			£12,193

Looked a smart prospect when easily winning Listed contest at Newbury on second start but made to look one-paced by Camelot in Racing Post Trophy, not helped by racing keenly; always regarded as type to do better at three and could improve over middle distances.

1086 Fiorente (Ire)

4 br c Monsun - Desert Bloom (Pilsudski)

Sir Michael Stoute   Ballymacoll Stud

PLACINGS: 5122-   **RPR 111+**

Starts	1st	2nd	3rd	4th	Win & Pl
4	1	2	-	-	£48,491
5/11	Newb	1m2f Cls4 Mdn 3yo gd-fm			£4,857

Did well when faced with sharp step up in

class last season, chasing home top-class Nathaniel in King Edward VII Stakes before just getting touched off by Namibian in Gordon Stakes; picked up an injury there and trainer decided against backend campaign to aim for bigger prizes this year.

1087 Firdaws (USA)

3 b f Mr Greeley - Eswarah (Unfuwain)

Roger Varian   Hamdan Al Maktoum

PLACINGS: 213-   **RPR 98**

Starts	1st	2nd	3rd	4th	Win & Pl
3	1	1	1	-	£25,293
	9/11	Sals	7f Cls3 Mdn 2yo good		£6,469

Smart middle-distance prospect who shaped with great promise in two good maidens before just about holding her own on sharp rise in class in Fillies' Mile, lacking speed of principals in third; likely to improve over much longer distances and could develop into Oaks contender.

1088 Fire Lily (Ire) *(opposite)*

3 b f Dansili - Beauty Is Truth (Pivotal)

David Wachman (Ir)   M Tabor, D Smith & Mrs John Magnier

PLACINGS: 1341222-   **RPR 109+**

Starts	1st	2nd	3rd	4th	Win & Pl
7	2	3	1	1	£165,056
	7/11	Curr	6¹/₂f Gp3 2yo yld-sft		£29,138
	4/11	Navn	5f Mdn 2yo gd-yld		£8,922

Unlucky not to add to impressive Group 3 win in Anglesey Stakes, chasing home Best Terms in Lowther before twice finishing second at Group 1 level, most recently behind Elusive Kate at Longchamp; trainer still sees her as a Classic filly and could run her in French 1,000 Guineas.

1089 Firebeam

4 b g Cadeaux Genereux - Firebelly (Nicolotte)

William Haggas   Highclere Thoroughbred Racing-Blue Peter

PLACINGS: 231131-   **RPR 109+**

Starts	1st	2nd	3rd	4th	Win & Pl
6	3	1	2	-	£20,946
	9/11	Hayd	7f Cls3 gd-sft		£6,663
85	7/11	York	7f Cls3 76-87 3yo Hcap good		£7,439
	6/11	Ling	6f Cls5 Mdn soft		£3,071

Took three attempts to break maiden last season but made rapid progress after that, winning two of next three starts with only defeat coming when unsuited by drop to 6f; impressive when making all to win conditions event at Haydock; ready for step up in class.

1090 Fox Hunt (Ire)

5 ch g Dubawi - Kiltubber (Sadler's Wells)

Mahmood Al Zarooni
     Sheikh Hamdan Bin Mohammed Al Maktoum

PLACINGS: 1442/221641124617-1   **RPR 118+**

Starts	1st	2nd	3rd	4th	Win & Pl
17	6	4	-	4	£255,401
110	2/12	Meyd	1m6f 95-110 Hcap good		£58,065
	9/11	Dort	1m6f Gp3 soft		£27,586
99	6/11	Asct	1m4f Cls2 91-101 Hcap soft		£31,155
95	6/11	Epsm	1m4f Cls2 78-97 Hcap gd-fm		£12,462
	3/11	Deau	1m4f 4yo stand		£12,069
	8/10	Wind	1m2f Cls5 Mdn 3-4yo gd-fm		£2,457

Made rapid progress for Mark Johnston last season, winning handicaps at Epsom and Ascot before coping well with step up in class to finish close fourth in Goodwood Cup; went on to win Group 3 in Germany before seventh in Melbourne Cup; won on Godolphin debut at Meydan.

1091 Frankel

4 b c Galileo - Kind (Danehill)

Sir Henry Cecil   K Abdulla

PLACINGS: 1111/11111-   **RPR 139+**

Starts	1st	2nd	3rd	4th	Win & Pl
9	9	-	-	-	£1,372,709
	10/11	Asct	1m Cls1 Gp1 good	*Excel*	£567,100
	7/11	Gdwd	1m Cls1 Gp1 good	*C C*	£170,130
	6/11	Asct	1m Cls1 Gp1 3yo good		£141,925
	4/11	NmkR	1m Cls1 Gp1 3yo gd-fm	*D G*	£198,695
	4/11	Newb	7f Cls1 Gp3 3yo gd-fm		£28,385
	10/10	NmkR	1m Cls1 Gp1 2yo gd-sft		£180,074
	9/10	Asct	1m Cls1 Gp2 2yo gd-sft		£70,963
	9/10	Donc	7f Cls2 2yo good		£10,904
	8/10	NmkJ	1m Cls4 Mdn 2yo soft		£4,533

Reigned supreme over 1m last season when taking unbeaten record to nine, including four more Group 1 wins; blasted rivals into submission in 2,000 Guineas and proved he could settle with equally sensational performances in Sussex Stakes and Queen Elizabeth II Stakes; may step up to 1m2f.

1092 French Fifteen (Fr)

3 ch c Turtle Bowl - Spring Morning (Ashkalani)

Nicolas Clement (Fr)   Raymond Tooth

PLACINGS: 511121-   **RPR 114**

Starts	1st	2nd	3rd	4th	Win & Pl
6	4	1	-	-	£178,706
	10/11	StCl	1m Gp1 2yo v soft		£123,147
	9/11	Crao	1m List 2yo gd-sft		£23,707
	8/11	Le L	7f 2yo soft		£10,776
	7/11	Chat	5¹/₂f 2yo soft		£5,819

Won four out of six starts last season, culminating in Group 1 win at Saint-Cloud after a powerful late burst of speed, but may have benefited from very soft ground (flopped on debut on only start on good); had been progressive at lower level before being well beaten by Abtaal in Group 3; likely to run in 2,000 Guineas.

1093 French Navy

4 b c Shamardal - First Fleet (Woodman)

Mahmood Al Zarooni   Godolphin

PLACINGS: 1115/1196-   **RPR 115+**

Starts	1st	2nd	3rd	4th	Win & Pl
8	5	-	-	-	£108,869
9/11	Gdwd	1m2f Cls1 Gp3 gd-sft			£28,355
8/11	Nmkj	1m2f Cls2 good			£12,450
9/10	Lonc	1m Gp3 2yo gd-sft			£35,398
8/10	Deau	1m 2yo gd-sft			£15,044
8/10	Deau	1m 2yo good			£10,619

Missed first half of last season following switch to Godolphin but looked full of promise when easily landing first two starts, most notably in Group 3 at Goodwood; well below that level next twice, including when tried on good to firm for first time; may have more to offer at 1m4f.

1094 Furner's Green (Ire)

3 b c Dylan Thomas - Lady Icarus (Rainbow Quest)

Aidan O'Brien (Ir)   Michael Tabor

PLACINGS: 1744-   **RPR 113**

Starts	1st	2nd	3rd	4th	Win & Pl
4	1	-	-	2	£15,362
7/11	Tipp	7½f Mdn 2yo yield			£7,733

Largely disappointing following impressive maiden win at Tipperary but encountered slower conditions every time and may well do better on quicker ground; looked a smart colt in the making when staying on into close fourth in National Stakes; should benefit from step up to middle distances.

1095 Fury

4 gb g Invincible Spirit - Courting (Pursuit Of Love)

William Haggas   Cheveley Park Stud

PLACINGS: 11/52547-   **RPR 109**

Starts	1st	2nd	3rd	4th	Win & Pl
7	2	1	-	1	£300,094
10/10	NmkR	7f Cls2 2yo soft			£278,898
9/10	Newb	7f Cls4 Mdn 2yo gd-fm			£4,533

Won Tattersalls Millions at Newmarket as a juvenile in 2010 and began last season well, including fair fifth in 2,000 Guineas; form tailed off disastrously after that when finishing last on final three starts, including

twice at odds-on; remains highly capable if bouncing back.

1096 Galikova (Fr)

4 b f Galileo - Born Gold (Blushing Groom)

Freddy Head (Fr)   Wertheimer & Frere

PLACINGS: 15/112119-   **RPR 121+**

Starts	1st	2nd	3rd	4th	Win & Pl
8	5	1	-	-	£603,815
9/11	Lonc	1m4f Gp1 v soft			£172,405
8/11	Deau	1m2f Gp2 3yo gd-sft			£196,552
5/11	StCl	1m2½f Gp3 3yo gd-sft			£34,483
4/11	StCl	1m2f 3yo gd-sft			£14,655
9/10	Lonc	1m 2yo gd-sft			£10,619

Beaten only by Golden Lilac (when found to be in season) in first five starts last season; showed improved form when stepped up to 1m4f for first time in Prix Vermeille, getting well on top in closing stages to win comfortably; failed to run to form when disappointing ninth in the Arc.

1097 Gamilati

3 b f Bernardini - Illustrious Miss (Kingmambo)

Saeed Bin Suroor   Godolphin

PLACINGS: 2210-11   **RPR 114+aw**

Starts	1st	2nd	3rd	4th	Win & Pl
6	3	2	-	-	£152,852
2/12	Meyd	1m List 3yo stand			£96,774
1/12	Meyd	7f 3yo stand			£19,355
7/11	NmkJ	6f Cls1 Gp2 2yo good			£34,026

Unlucky to be beaten twice in maidens, losing out in photos to subsequent Group winners including smart stablemate Discourse; atoned for those near misses with impressive victory in Cherry Hinton Stakes before struggling on bad ground in Lowther; won UAE 1,000 Guineas at Meydan this spring.

1098 Genki (Ire)

8 ch g Shinko Forest - Emma's Star (Darshaan)

Roger Charlton   Ms Gillian Khosla

PLACINGS: 3/4610342/178164458-   **RPR 117**

Starts	1st	2nd	3rd	4th	Win & Pl
34	8	6	2	6	£294,426
6/11	Newc	6f Cls1 Gp3 gd-sft			£28,385
4/11	NmkR	6f Cls1 List gd-fm			£17,031
7/10	Hayd	6f Cls2 gd-fm			£14,020
96	8/09	Gdwd	6f Cls2 93-106 Hcap soft		£62,310
94	9/07	Asct	6f Cls2 85-97 3yo Hcap good		£12,464
86	8/07	Asct	6f Cls2 86-100 3yo Hcap gd-fm		£17,234
80	5/07	NmkR	6f Cls2 72-95 3yo Hcap gd-fm		£24,928
	4/07	Folk	6f Cls5 Auct Mdn 3yo good		£2,915

Former high-class sprint handicapper (won Stewards' Cup in 2009) who got better and better in top company last season, producing career-best to finish close fourth to Dream Ahead in Haydock Sprint Cup having won first Group race at Newcastle; could improve again.

1099 Golden Lilac (Ire)

4 b f Galileo - Grey Lilas (Danehill)

Andre Fabre (Fr)　　　　　　　　　Gestut Ammerland

PLACINGS: 11/1113-　　　　　　　　　**RPR 116**

Starts	1st	2nd	3rd	4th	Win & Pl
6	5	-	1	-	£736,715
	6/11	Chan	1m2¹/₂f Gp1 3yo gd-sft		£418,698
	5/11	Lonc	1m Gp1 3yo good		£221,664
	4/11	Lonc	1m Gp3 3yo good		£34,483
	10/10	StCl	1m 2yo v soft		£15,044
	9/10	StCl	1m 2yo gd-sft		£10,619

Enjoyed sensational first half to last season when landing Classic double, looking particularly impressive in Prix de Diane; lost unbeaten record when third behind Galikova next time and missed rest of campaign having been struck down by virus; has option of stepping up to 1m4f.

1100 Gray Pearl

3 gr f Excellent Art - Divine Grace (Definite Article)

Charles Hills　　　　　　　　　　　H R Mould

PLACINGS: 13-　　　　　　　　　　**RPR 109**

Starts	1st	2nd	3rd	4th	Win & Pl
2	1	-	1	-	£10,531
	8/11	Newb	6f Cls4 Mdn 2yo good		£4,075

Won decent Newbury maiden on debut and outran odds of 20-1 when fine third in Rockfel Stakes behind Wading, making most of the running before just being left behind in final furlong; big filly who seems sure to progress again over further.

1101 Hamish McGonagall

7 b g Namid - Anatase (Danehill)

Tim Easterby　　　　　　　　　Reality Partnerships I

PLACINGS: 113461444/318842323-　　**RPR 117**

Starts	1st	2nd	3rd	4th	Win & Pl
47	8	9	7	10	£300,785
	4/11	Muss	5f Cls2 gd-sft		£12,462
104	8/10	York	5¹/₂f Cls2 85-108 Hcap good		£25,904
99	6/10	Muss	5f Cls2 82-99 Hcap gd-fm		£31,155
92	5/10	York	5f Cls2 80-101 Hcap gd-fm		£25,904
95	10/08	Muss	5f Cls2 92-104 Hcap gd-sft		£37,386
91	7/08	Ches	5f Cls3 80-95 3yo Hcap gd-sft		£9,462
84	5/08	York	5f Cls3 71-90 3yo Hcap gd-fm		£9,714
	11/07	Muss	5f Cls5 Mdn 2yo good		£3,239

Remained progressive last season when running a succession of good races in Group company, most notably when second in Nunthorpe Stakes at 28-1; may well have

been favoured by the draw that day but capable of winning good sprints in slightly lower grade.

1102 Harbour Watch (Ire)

3 b c Acclamation - Gorband (Woodman)

Richard Hannon　　　　　　　　　H Robin Heffer

PLACINGS: 111-　　　　　　　　　**RPR 117+**

Starts	1st	2nd	3rd	4th	Win & Pl
3	3	-	-	-	£50,531
	7/11	Gdwd	6f Cls1 Gp2 2yo gd-fm		£34,026
	7/11	NmkJ	6f Cls3 2yo good		£7,763
	6/11	Sals	6f Cls2 Mdn 2yo soft		£8,743

Won all three starts last season, producing best performance when overcoming trouble in running to easily land strong Richmond Stakes at Goodwood; made 2,000 Guineas favourite after that but missed Dewhurst owing to small setback; yet to race beyond 6f but likely to step up to 7f in the Greenham.

1103 Harris Tweed

5 b g Hernando - Frog (Akarad)

William Haggas　　　　　　　　　B Haggas

PLACINGS: 75/1212711/32243-　　**RPR 118**

Starts	1st	2nd	3rd	4th	Win & Pl
14	4	4	2	1	£164,291
	9/10	NmkR	1m6f Cls1 List 3yo soft		£19,870
	9/10	Ches	1m4¹/₂f Cls1 List soft		£21,926
86	6/10	Muss	1m4¹/₂f Cls2 81-104 3yo Hcap gd-fm		£49,848
	4/10	Ripn	1m2f Cls5 Mdn 3yo gd-fm		£2,914

Dual Listed winner in 2010 but largely struggled in Group races last season, coming closest when touched off by a head in Group 3 at Glorious Goodwood; stays 1m6f well but disappointed on only attempt at 2m when fading into fourth in Lonsdale Cup at York.

1104 Harvard N Yale (USA)

3 ch c Smart Strike - Compete (El Prado)

Jeremy Noseda　　　　　　The Honorable Earle I Mack

PLACINGS: 2122-　　　　　　　　　**RPR 92+**

Starts	1st	2nd	3rd	4th	Win & Pl
4	1	3	-	-	£9,258
	8/11	NmkJ	1m Cls4 Mdn 2yo good		£4,528

Failed to justify big reputation last season, looking workmanlike in justifying odds of 8-15 in Newmarket maiden before getting turned over at odds-on in conditions race at Newbury and Wolverhampton; may still have lots more to offer and could find improvement over middle distances.

1105 Helmet (Aus)

4 ch c Exceed And Excel - Accessories (Singspiel)

Peter Snowden (Aus)   Sheikh Mohammed

PLACINGS: 3/111133118-5   **RPR 121**

Starts	1st	2nd	3rd	4th	Win & Pl
11		3	-		£1,023,738
10/11	Caul	1m Gp1 3yo gd-sft			£397,386
9/11	Caul	7f Gp3 3yo good			£69,118
4/11	Rand	1m Gp1 2yo heavy			£159,020
4/11	Rand	7f Gp1 2yo gd-sft			£198,235
2/11	Rose	6f 2yo Hcap good			£27,451
2/11	Rose	6f 2yo Hcap good			£27,451

Multiple Group 1 winner for Godolphin in Australia last year over 7f and 1m; disappointing eighth when favourite for Cox Plate in October on first run at 1m2f, fading close home having made the running; due to be switched to Europe having stayed with current trainer for stint in Dubai.

1106 Highland Castle

4 b g Halling - Reciprocal (Night Shift)

David Elsworth   J Wotherspoon & W Harrison-Allan

PLACINGS: 3115812-   **RPR 113+**

Starts	1st	2nd	3rd	4th	Win & Pl
7	3	1	1	-	£29,843
9/11	Sals	1m6f Cls2 good			£9,960
7/11	Hayd	1m4f Cls3 76-90 3yo Hcap gd-fm			£8,410
6/11	Wind	1m2f Cls5 Mdn good			£2,267

Made debut only last June but made rapid progress to land Haydock handicap on third start and showed he could mix it in better company when easily winning conditions event at Salisbury and just losing out to Barbican in Listed race at Ascot; raced too keenly on only try at 2m.

1107 Hitchens (Ire)

7 b g Acclamation - Royal Fizz (Royal Academy)

David Barron   Laurence O'Kane & Paul Murphy

PLACINGS: 0613221/554410396-21   **RPR 117**

Starts	1st	2nd	3rd	4th	Win & Pl
41	8	4	5	3	£502,158
2/12	Meyd	6f Gp3 stand			£77,419
5/11	Curr	6f Gp3 gd-fm			£35,022
11/10	Ling	6f Cls1 List stand			£19,870
9/10	York	6f Cls2 86-98 Hcap gd-fm			£11,657
9/09	Hayd	6f Cls2 85-99 Hcap gd-fm			£12,952
4/09	Thsk	6f Cls3 firm			£7,851
6/08	Wind	6f Cls2 95-104 Hcap gd-fm			£31,155
8/07	Folk	6f Cls5 Mdn 2yo gd-fm			£2,817

Much-improved sprinter last season, following up excellent Group 3 win at the Curragh by finishing close third to Dream Ahead in July Cup; given a break after that run and not at his best subsequently but

1108 Holberg (UAE)

6 b h Halling - Sweet Willa (Assert)

Saeed Bin Suroor   Sheikh Hamdan Bin Mohammed Al Maktoum

PLACINGS: 64511/131/15216/30-0   **RPR 107**

Starts	1st	2nd	3rd	4th	Win & Pl
16	6	1	2	1	£200,124
9/10	Gdwd	1m2f Cls1 List gd-fm			£19,870
6/10	Gdwd	1m4f Cls1 List gd-fm			£23,704
6/09	Asct	2m Cls1 Gp3 3yo gd-fm			£39,739
85	4/09	Leic	1m4f Cls3 78-85 3yo Hcap gd-fm		£9,347
79	12/08	Kemp	1m Cls4 59-79 2yo Hcap stand		£4,094
11/08	Sthl	7f Cls5 Auct Mdn 2yo stand			£3,562

Progressed into a high-class middle-distance performer in 2010; disappointing when returned to staying trips last season (had won Queen's Vase over 2m for Mark Johnston in 2009) but should do better on quicker ground given all turf wins have come on good to firm.

1109 Homecoming Queen (Ire)

3 b f Holy Roman Emperor - Lagrion (Diesis)

Aidan O'Brien (Ir)   Mrs John Magnier

PLACINGS: 63965431210-   **RPR 104**

Starts	1st	2nd	3rd	4th	Win & Pl
11	2	1	2	1	£39,465
10/11	Curr	1m List 2yo yld-sft			£22,414
72	9/11	Fair	7f 63-80 2yo Hcap yld-sft		£5,948

Looked moderate for much of last season but made rapid strides once encountering longer trips and more testing conditions towards end of year, getting close to Coral Wave in Group 3 before running away with Listed contest over 1m; failed to handle dirt at Breeders' Cup.

1110 Hoof It

5 b g Monsieur Bond - Forever Bond (Danetime)

Mick Easterby   A Chandler & L Westwood

PLACINGS: 1/8111057021/171163-   **RPR 124**

Starts	1st	2nd	3rd	4th	Win & Pl
19	8	1	1	2	£190,317
111	7/11	Gdwd	6f Cls2 94-111 Hcap gd-fm		£62,250
105	7/11	York	6f Cls2 87-105 Hcap good		£32,345
99	5/11	York	6f Cls2 89-105 Hcap gd-fm		£12,952
94	10/10	Donc	5f Cls2 87-99 Hcap good		£31,155
81	5/10	Hayd	5f Cls3 73-81 3yo Hcap gd-fm		£5,181
72	5/10	York	5f Cls4 66-79 3yo Hcap gd-fm		£6,541
66	5/10	Bevl	5f Cls5 63-75 3yo Hcap good		£2,396
8/09	Newc	5f Cls5 Auct Mdn 2yo gd-fm			£2,590

Won four of last five starts in handicaps, culminating in easy win off top-weight in Stewards' Cup; did fairly well in two runs at Group 1 level, finishing sixth despite bad draw in Nunthorpe Stakes and close third in Haydock Sprint Cup; seems slightly better over 6f.

1111 I'm A Dreamer (Ire)

5 b m Noverre - Summer Dreams (Sadler's Wells)

David Simcock — St Albans Bloodstock Llp

PLACINGS: 11153/15642- **RPR 115**

Starts	1st	2nd	3rd	4th	Win & Pl
10	4	1	1	1	£190,273
5/11	NmkR	1m1f Cls1 Gp3 gd-fm			£28,385
81 6/10	NmkJ	1m Cls4 75-82 Hcap gd-fm			£6,476
77 5/10	Gdwd	1m Cls4 72-85 3yo Hcap good			£4,209
4/10	Yarm	1m Cls5 Mdn Auct 3-5yo good			£3,497

Looked a much-improved filly when running away with Group 3 at Newmarket on first start last season but struggled to build on that; showed much more promise when only just denied in Group 1 in Canada on final start when stepped up to 1m2f for first time; acts on any going.

1112 Immortal Verse (Ire)

4 b f Pivotal - Side Of Paradise (Sadler's Wells)

Robert Collet (Fr) — R C Strauss

PLACINGS: 12/4011137- **RPR 123+**

Starts	1st	2nd	3rd	4th	Win & Pl
9	4	1	1	1	£641,090
8/11	Deau	1m Gp1 gd-sft			£295,552
6/11	Asct	1m Cls1 Gp1 3yo gd-sft			£141,925
6/11	Chan	1m Gp2 3yo soft			£63,879
8/10	Deau	6½f 2yo gd-sft			£15,044

Made rapid progress last season after slow start to career; landed best win when beating Goldikova and Sahpresa in Prix Jacques le Marois and best of rest behind Frankel and Excelebration in Queen Elizabeth II Stakes; should get plenty of opportunities in fillies' races.

1113 Imperial Monarch (Ire)

3 b c Galileo - Ionian Sea (Slip Anchor)

Aidan O'Brien (Ir) — Mrs John Magnier

PLACINGS: 1- **RPR 90+**

Starts	1st	2nd	3rd	4th	Win & Pl
1	1	-	-	-	£8,922
9/11	Curr	1m Mdn 2yo yld-sft			£8,922

Ran away with decent Curragh maiden last September, defying market drift to pull well clear; clearly handles cut in the ground but should be equally effective on quicker going; related to 2003 Derby runner-up The Great Gatsby and could well develop into Epsom contender.

1114 Inxile (Ire)

7 b g Fayruz - Grandel (Owington)

David Nicholls — Mrs Jackie Love & David Nicholls

PLACINGS: 655/257611131410-72 **RPR 118+**

Starts	1st	2nd	3rd	4th	Win & Pl
36	10	5	7	2	£358,016
8/11	Tipp	5f List gd-fm			£22,414
6/11	Cork	5f List good			£25,216
5/11	Lonc	5f Gp3 good			£34,483
4/11	Cork	6f List good			£22,414
4/11	Naas	5f List yld-sft			£22,414
3/10	Donc	6f Cls5 List soft			£22,708
6/09	Naas	5f List gd-fm			£26,862
4/09	Naas	5f List yield			£28,442
8/08	Deau	5f List soft			£19,118
9/07	Hayd	5f Cls5 Mdn 2yo gd-fm			£3,239

Globetrotting sprinter who did all his racing abroad last season apart from poor effort on final start in Nunthorpe Stakes; won four times at Listed level (eight-time winner in that grade overall) and added Group 3 at Longchamp; takes his racing well and should remain prolific.

1115 Jet Away

5 b h Cape Cross - Kalima (Kahyasi)

Sir Henry Cecil — K Abdulla

PLACINGS: 51126/129214- **RPR 116**

Starts	1st	2nd	3rd	4th	Win & Pl
11	4	3	-	1	£38,868
10/11	York	1m2¹/₂f Cls3 good			£7,763
5/11	Ling	1m2f Cls3 gd-fm			£9,066
86 8/10	Sand	1m2f Cls3 74-90 3yo Hcap gd-fm			£7,124
7/10	Ling	1m1f Cls5 Mdn 3-4yo firm			£2,388

Inconsistent last season but twice looked full of promise when running away with conditions events at Lingfield and York by combined total of more than 12 lengths; below form both starts on ground softer than good and looked uneasy on undulations at Newmarket last time.

1116 Joshua Tree (Ire)

5 b h Montjeu - Madeira Mist (Grand Lodge)

Marco Botti — K K Al Nabooda & K Albahou

PLACINGS: 121/3510/4124232-7 **RPR 117**

Starts	1st	2nd	3rd	4th	Win & Pl
15	4	4	2	2	£1,141,271
2/11	Dohr	1m4f good			£50,532
10/10	Wood	1m4f Gd1 good			£705,882
9/09	Asct	1m Cls1 Gp2 2yo good			£86,188
8/09	Gowr	7f Mdn 2yo soft			£10,399

Group 1 winner for Aidan O'Brien in 2010 and returned to Europe last autumn after disappointing stint in Qatar; placed on both starts in Europe before attempting a repeat win in Canadian International on final start last year, finishing second to Sarah Lynx.

1117 Jukebox Jury (Ire) *(above, grey)*

6 gr h Montjeu - Mare Aux Fees (Kenmare)

Mark Johnston   A D Spence & Bamford/Ryan Partnership

PLACINGS: 7614112/01794/13110-   RPR **119**

Starts	1st	2nd	3rd	4th	Win & Pl
22	9	2	2	3	£857,187
9/11	Curr	1m6f Gp1 yld-sft			£73,017
8/11	Deau	1m7f Gp2 good			£63,879
6/11	NmkJ	1m4f Cls1 List gd-sft			£17,031
5/10	NmkR	1m4f Cls1 Gp2 gd-fm			£56,770
9/09	Colo	1m4f Gp1 good			£97,087
8/09	Deau	1m4½f Gp2 good			£110,680
8/09	Hayd	1m2½f Cls1 Gp3 good			£36,901
9/08	Asct	1m Cls1 Gp2 2yo good			£76,038
8/08	Gdwd	7f Cls2 Mdn 2yo gd-fm			£12,952

High-class middle-distance performer who took tally of Group wins to seven when looking better than ever last season; easily landed Prix Kergorlay at Deauville before dead-heating with Duncan in Irish St Leger; due to be aimed at Ascot Gold Cup but finished lame when disappointing in Melbourne Cup.

1118 King Torus (Ire)

4 b c Oratorio - Dipterous (Mujadil)

Richard Hannon   Sir Robert Ogden

PLACINGS: 14117/41701-   RPR **113+**

Starts	1st	2nd	3rd	4th	Win & Pl
10	5	-	-	2	£118,033
11/11	Nott	1m½f Cls3 soft			£6,412
9/11	Hayd	1m Cls1 List gd-fm			£17,013
7/10	Gdwd	7f Cls1 Gp2 2yo gd-fm			£45,416
7/10	NmkJ	7f Cls1 Gp2 2yo gd-fm			£39,739
5/10	Leic	6f Cls4 Mdn 2yo gd-fm			£4,533

Dual Group 2 winner as a juvenile in 2010;

missed first half of last season and produced mixed results on return, doing best when landing Listed race at Haydock on second start; won again in moderate soft-ground contest at Nottingham but has done all other winning on good to firm.

1119 Kinglet (USA)

3 br c Kingmambo - Karen's Caper (War Chant)

Mahmood Al Zarooni   Godolphin

PLACINGS: 1331-21   RPR **103aw**

Starts	1st	2nd	3rd	4th	Win & Pl
6	3	1	2	-	£111,091
2/12	Meyd	1m Gp3 3yo stand			£96,774
10/11	Kemp	1m Cls4 2yo stand			£3,429
8/11	NmkJ	7f Cls5 Mdn 2yo good			£3,235

Showed fair form as a juvenile last season when landing good win at Kempton having twice been third in novice events; looked much improved at Meydan this spring when winning UAE 2,000 Guineas over 1m and may do even better when stepped up in trip.

1120 Kirthill (Ire)

4 b c Danehill Dancer - Kirtle (Hector Protector)

Luca Cumani   Leonidas Marinopoulos

PLACINGS: 2/8125291-   RPR **104+**

Starts	1st	2nd	3rd	4th	Win & Pl
8	2	3	-	-	£40,355
94					
10/11	Newb	1m2f Cls2 87-105 Hcap gd-fm			£31,125
6/11	NmkJ	1m Cls5 Mdn 3yo gd-sft			£2,914

Knocking on the door in good 1m2f

handicaps last season until landing valuable contest at Newbury on final start; had been kept to easy surfaces until then but looked much better on good to firm ground and could develop into a smart performer over middle distances.

1121 Kissed (Ire)

3 b f Galileo - Gwynn (Darshaan)

Aidan O'Brien (Ir)   Derrick Smith

PLACINGS: 1-   **RPR 92+**

Starts	1st	2nd	3rd	4th	Win & Pl
1	1	-	-	-	£8,922
	10/11	Navn	1m Mdn 2yo soft		.....£8,922

Beautifully bred filly (half-sister to Pour Moi by Galileo) who made a big impression on her debut at Navan in October, justifying a major plunge when ridden with great confidence to win well; has much more to come having raced greenly; top-class middle-distance prospect.

1122 La Collina (Ire)

3 ch f Strategic Prince - Starfish (Galileo)

Kevin Prendergast (Ir)   Joerg Vasicek

PLACINGS: 1213-   **RPR 114+**

Starts	1st	2nd	3rd	4th	Win & Pl
4	2	1	1	-	£127,969
	8/11	Curr	6f Gp1 2yo gd-yld		.....£95,000
	6/11	Limk	7f Mdn Auct 2yo good		.....£7,733

Confirmed strength of Ireland's juvenile fillies when upsetting the top colts at 33-1 in Phoenix Stakes last season, coming from last to first to pip Power on only start at 6f; perhaps not quite as effective over 7f, running Maybe close once but below par when third behind same rival in Moyglare Stud Stakes.

1123 Lacily (USA)

3 b f Elusive Quality - Lailani (Unfuwain)

Mahmood Al Zarooni   Godolphin

PLACINGS: 1-   **RPR 80+**

Starts	1st	2nd	3rd	4th	Win & Pl
1	1	-	-	-	£2,975
	10/11	Donc	1m Cls5 Mdn 2yo good		.....£2,976

Beautifully bred filly who made an impeccable debut at Doncaster, always travelling well in a slowly run race and staying on strongly; possesses plenty of speed but looks likely to stay 1m4f and may

well add to stable's considerable firepower for Epsom Oaks.

1124 Lay Time

4 b f Galileo - Time Saved (Green Desert)

Andrew Balding   R Barnett

PLACINGS: 5/1241-   **RPR 111+**

Starts	1st	2nd	3rd	4th	Win & Pl
5	2	1	-	1	£25,389
	9/11	Sand	1m Cls1 List good		.....£17,013
	7/11	NmkJ	7f Cls5 Mdn 3yo gd-sft		.....£3,881

Beaten favourite twice after easily winning maiden at Newmarket, once when not appearing comfortable on good to firm ground, but confirmed potential when running away with Listed contest at Sandown on final start; expected by trainer to stay beyond 1m.

1125 Learn (Ire)

3 b c Galileo - Kentucky Warbler (Spinning World)

Aidan O'Brien (Ir)   M Tabor, D Smith & Mrs John Magnier

PLACINGS: 32144-   **RPR 110**

Starts	1st	2nd	3rd	4th	Win & Pl
5	1	1	1	2	£38,344
	8/11	Leop	7f Mdn 2yo good		.....£10,112

Twice placed in strong maidens before winning by five lengths at Leopardstown; thrown in at deep end when twice fourth at Group 1 level, setting pace for Camelot in Racing Post Trophy and again swamped by fast finishers at Saint-Cloud; could still be useful over middle distances.

1126 Libranno

4 b c Librettist - Annabelle Ja (Singspiel)

Richard Hannon   Mcdowell Racing

PLACINGS: 11165/24314401730-   **RPR 117**

Starts	1st	2nd	3rd	4th	Win & Pl
16	5	1	2	3	£220,297
	8/11	Gdwd	7f Cls1 Gp3 good		.....£28,355
	6/11	NmkJ	7f Cls1 Gp3 gd-sft		.....£28,385
	7/10	Gdwd	6f Cls1 Gp2 2yo good		.....£45,416
	7/10	NmkJ	6f Cls1 Gp2 2yo gd-fm		.....£39,739
	5/10	NmkR	6f Cls4 Mdn 2yo good		.....£5,181

Dual Group 2 winner as a juvenile who trained on well last season, gaining both wins in 7f Group 3 races but proving equally adept at 6f when fourth in July Cup and third in Champions Sprint at Ascot; takes his racing well and sure to find plenty of good opportunities again.

1127 Lightening Pearl (Ire)

3 b f Marju - Jioconda (Rossini)

Ger Lyons (Ir)   Pearl Bloodstock Ltd

PLACINGS: 21311-   **RPR 111+**

Starts	1st	2nd	3rd	4th	Win & Pl
5	3	1	1	-	£137,845

9/11	NmkR	6f Cls1 Gp1 2yo gd-fm	£92,721
8/11	Curr	6f Gp3 2yo good	£29,418
7/11	Rosc	7f Mdn 2yo gd-fm	£6,543

Well held by Maybe when third in Debutante Stakes and may not have had to improve much to win twice subsequently, even when landing weak Cheveley Park Stakes; should stay 1m; yet to race on ground softer than good to yielding and well suited by quicker going.

1128 Loi (Ire)

3 b c Lawman - Lockup (Inchinor)

Jean-Marie Beguigne (Fr)   E Ciampi & L Disaro

PLACINGS: 311-   **RPR 106**

Starts	1st	2nd	3rd	4th	Win & Pl
3	2	-	1	-	£52,241

10/11	Lonc	1m1f Gp3 2yo good	£34,483
9/11	StCl	1m 2yo gd-sft	£14,655

Stepped up on Saint-Cloud maiden win when cosily landing Group 3 at Longchamp over 1m1f despite failing to settle in early stages; regarded as a Classic prospect by connections and already earmarked as a possible for Epsom Derby given strong-galloping style.

1129 Lost In The Moment (Ire)

5 b h Danehill Dancer - Streetcar (In The Wings)

Saeed Bin Suroor   Godolphin

PLACINGS: /9711421/1892232746-   **RPR 115**

Starts	1st	2nd	3rd	4th	Win & Pl
18	4	4	1	2	£219,119

97	1/11	Meyd	1m3f 95-109 Hcap stand	£57,692
91	10/10	Newb	1m2f Cls2 86-97 Hcap gd-sft	£9,347
80	8/10	Wind	1m¹/₂f Cls4 67-81 Hcap gd-fm	£4,533
73	6/10	Newb	1m Cls5 68-74 3yo Hcap gd-fm	£3,238

Progressive handicapper for Jeremy Noseda before switch to Godolphin last season; failed to follow up debut win at Meydan but maintained upward curve in defeat, particularly when stepped up to 2m, finishing second in Goodwood Cup and sixth in Melbourne Cup.

1130 Lyric Of Light *(below)*

3 b f Street Cry - Suez (Green Desert)

Mahmood Al Zarooni   Godolphin

PLACINGS: 111-   **RPR 113+**

Starts	1st	2nd	3rd	4th	Win & Pl
3	3	-	-	-	£136,946

9/11	NmkR	1m Cls1 Gp1 2yo gd-fm	£92,721
9/11	Donc	1m Cls1 Gp2 2yo good	£39,697
8/11	NmkJ	7f Cls4 Mdn 2yo gd-sft	£4,528

Regarded as just below Discourse at her yard but stepped into the breach to win May Hill and Fillies' Mile last season, taking unbeaten record to three; showed impressive turn of foot on final outing,

pouncing late having struggled slightly to get going; potentially a high-class miler.

1131 Main Sequence (USA)

3 ch c Aldebaran - Ikat (Pivotal)

David Lanigan   Niarchos Family

PLACINGS: 11-   **RPR 92 +**

Starts	1st	2nd	3rd	4th	Win & Pl
2		2			£7,346
79	10/11	NmkR	1m1f Cls4 75-84 2yo Hcap good		£3,881
	9/11	Yarm	1m Cls5 Mdn 2yo good		£3,466

Unbeaten in two starts last season, following up York maiden win with wide-margin victory in Newmarket nursery off 79; produced tremendous finishing burst on both occasions and looks sure to make mark in much higher grade; seems likely to stay at least 1m4f.

1132 Majestic Myles (Ire)

4 b g Majestic Missile - Gala Style (Elnadim)

Richard Fahey   James Gaffney

PLACINGS: 141125/157172027-   **RPR 114**

Starts	1st	2nd	3rd	4th	Win & Pl
15	5	3	-	1	£84,930
93	7/11	Ches	7f Cls1 List good		£17,013
84	5/11	NmkR	6f Cls2 78-95 3yo Hcap good		£27,416
77	7/10	Pont	6f Cls4 67-84 2yo Hcap good		£3,886
	7/10	Rdcr	6f Cls4 57-80 2yo Hcap gd-fm		£4,533
	4/10	Muss	5f Cls4 Mdn 2yo gd-fm		£5,828

Developed into smart Listed performer over 7f last season, winning at that level at Chester and twice losing out in close finishes; had also won good handicap over 6f; disappointing in Ayr Gold Cup on soft ground (all other starts on good or quicker).

1133 Mandaean

3 b c Manduro - Summertime Legacy (Darshaan)

Mahmood Al Zarooni   Godolphin Snc

PLACINGS: 11-   **RPR 114 +**

Starts	1st	2nd	3rd	4th	Win & Pl
2	2	-	-	-	£133,491
	11/11	StCl	1m2f Gp1 2yo heavy		£123,147
	10/11	Lonc	1m1f 2yo good		£10,345

Won both starts for Andre Fabre last season, culminating in Group 1 at Saint-Cloud when overcoming clear signs of greenness (drifted both ways in final quarter-mile) to win well; form looks moderate for top grade but clearly stays well and handles different going; fair Derby prospect.

1134 Margot Did (Ire)

4 b f Exceed And Excel - Special Dancer (Shareef Dancer)

Michael Bell   T Redman & P Philipps

PLACINGS: 1122235/3411410-   **RPR 118**

Starts	1st	2nd	3rd	4th	Win & Pl
14	5	3	2	2	£263,183
	8/11	York	5f Cls1 Gp1 gd-sft		£156,066
	6/11	Ayr	5f Cls1 List soft		£22,708
	6/11	Sand	5f Cls1 List 3yo soft		£17,031
	6/10	Yarm	6f Cls5 2yo gd-fm		£3,532
	5/10	Newb	6f Cls5 Mdn 2yo gd-fm		£3,886

Had found it hard to win at Pattern level before being revitalised by drop to 5f and switch to front-running tactics last summer, gaining biggest win when strongly favoured by the draw in Nunthorpe Stakes at York; flopped in Prix de l'Abbaye at Longchamp when yard was affected by virus.

1135 Masamah (Ire)

6 gr g Exceed And Excel - Bethesda (Distant Relative)

Kevin Ryan   Dr Marwan Koukash

PLACINGS: 140411700/318118020-   **RPR 118**

Starts	1st	2nd	3rd	4th	Win & Pl
24	8	2	1	2	£181,596
	7/11	Gdwd	5f Cls1 Gp2 gd-fm		£48,204
	7/11	York	5f Cls1 List good		£17,760
100	5/11	York	5f Cls2 84-101 Hcap good		£28,494
	8/10	Ches	6f Cls1 List gd-sft		£21,005
96	7/10	Asct	5f Cls2 79-105 Hcap gd-fm		£20,251
90	5/10	Ches	5f Cls2 86-105 Hcap good		£13,878
	8/08	Ling	5f Cls5 2yo stand		£3,886
	5/08	York	5f Cls3 2yo gd-fm		£8,419

Made rapid progress out of handicap company in first half of last season when winning three times, most notably in Group 2 at Glorious Goodwood; went off the boil after that but remains highly capable given a fast 5f; has struggled over 6f since Chester win in 2010.

1136 Masked Marvel

4 b c Montjeu - Waldmark (Mark Of Esteem)

John Gosden   B E Nielsen

PLACINGS: 16/518110-   **RPR 124 +**

Starts	1st	2nd	3rd	4th	Win & Pl
8	4	-	-	-	£357,742
	9/11	Donc	1m6½f Cls1 Gp1 3yo gd-fm		£306,262
	7/11	NmkJ	1m5f Cls1 Gp3 3yo good		£28,355
	5/11	Gdwd	1m3f Cls1 List 3yo good		£17,031
	9/10	Sand	1m Cls4 Mdn 2yo good		£4,209

Inconsistent last season and well below par in both Derby and Arc (only runs in double-figure fields) but proved a high-class colt on his day with impressive win in St Leger as well as landing good races at Goodwood and Newmarket; may be more to come.

1137 Maybe (Ire)

3 b f Galileo - Sumora (Danehill)

Aidan O'Brien (Ir)　　M Tabor, D Smith & Mrs John Magnier

PLACINGS: 11111-　　　　**RPR 114+**

Starts	1st	2nd	3rd	4th	Win & Pl
5	5	-	-	-	£229,656
8/11	Curr	7f Gp1 2yo good			£112,500
8/11	Curr	7f Gp2 2yo gd-yld			£53,233
7/11	Leop	7f Gp3 2yo good			£26,616
6/11	Asct	7f Cls1 List 2yo soft			£28,385
5/11	Naas	6f Mdn 2yo gd-fm			£8,922

Best of a strong bunch of Irish juvenile fillies last season when unbeaten in five races, coping with step up in grade every time and finishing campaign with terrific win in Moyglare Stud Stakes; sure to stay 1m and may well stay further; seems equally effective on all going; looks hard to beat in 1,000 Guineas.

1138 Meandre (Fr)

4 gr c Slickly - Penne (Sevres Rose)

Andre Fabre (Fr)　　　　Rothschild Family

PLACINGS: 634d5/2211126-　　**RPR 123+**

Starts	1st	2nd	3rd	4th	Win & Pl
11	3	3	1	-	£373,038
7/11	Lonc	1m4f Gp1 3yo gd-sft			£295,552
5/11	Lonc	1m4f List 3yo good			£23,707
4/11	MsnL	1m2½f 3yo good			£14,655

Moderate juvenile who went from strength to strength in first half of last season, winning Group 1 Grand Prix de Paris when too quick for Seville; beaten favourite when second to Reliable Man in Prix Niel but did best of three-year-old colts when sixth to Danedream in the Arc.

1139 Medicean Man *(above)*

6 ch g Medicean - Kalindi (Efisio)

Jeremy Gask　　　　Stuart Dobb & Miss Kate Dobb

PLACINGS: 9105205/28732112380-　　**RPR 113+**

Starts	1st	2nd	3rd	4th	Win & Pl
28	7	4	3	3	£89,088
101	7/11	Asct	5f Cls2 76-101 Hcap good		£24,900
96	7/11	Asct	5f Cls2 85-100 Hcap good		£12,450
89	5/10	Asct	6f Cls3 81-95 Hcap good		£7,124
83	3/10	Wolv	5f Cls3 82-95 Hcap stand		£6,939
78	8/09	Ripn	6f Cls4 76-85 3yo Hcap good		£4,857
74	7/09	Hayd	6f Cls4 67-78 3yo Hcap gd-sft		£5,505
	6/09	Donc	6f Cls5 Mdn good		£3,238

Seems to reserve best form for Ascot (scene of last three wins) and took form to another level there last season when winning pair of handicaps over 5f and only just being denied hat-trick off 10lb higher mark; fair third at Doncaster on next start when denied clear run.

1140 Meeznah (USA)

5 b m Dynaformer - String Quartet (Sadler's Wells)

Mahmood Al Zarooni　　　　Godolphin

PLACINGS: 33/12d4437/321715P-　　**RPR 115**

Starts	1st	2nd	3rd	4th	Win & Pl
15	3	1	4	2	£137,495
9/11	Donc	1m6½f Cls1 Gp2 good			£45,368
7/11	Gdwd	1m6f Cls1 Gp3 gd-fm			£28,355
5/10	NmkR	1m4f Cls4 Mdn 3yo gd-fm			£5,181

Trained by David Lanigan when bouncing back to form to win pair of Group contests last season (had been second past post in 2010 Oaks); still below that level on several other starts; failed to cope with dirt when pulled up in Breeders' Cup Marathon.

1141 Memphis Tennessee (Ire)

4 b c Hurricane Run - Hit The Sky (Cozzene)

Aidan O'Brien (Ir)   Mrs John Magnier, M Tabor & D Smith

PLACINGS: 51/243-   **RPR 119**

Starts	1st	2nd	3rd	4th	Win & Pl
5	1	1	1	1	£185,402
	11/10	Dund	1m Mdn 2yo stand		.£5,735

Surprise package among trainer's middle-distance team last season, running terrific races to finish close fourth in Epsom Derby and third in Irish Derby; remains lightly raced after just five starts and should continue to pay his way in top races at 1m4f and possibly further.

1142 Mighty Ambition (USA)

3 b c Street Cry - New Morning (Sadler's Wells)

Mahmood Al Zarooni   Godolphin

PLACINGS: 1-   **RPR 81+**

Starts	1st	2nd	3rd	4th	Win & Pl
1	1	-	-	-	£4,722
	9/11	Newb	7f Cls4 Mdn 2yo good		.£4,722

Won sole start last September at Newbury, finding less than expected having travelled well but doing enough to land fair maiden; slow pace may have been against him given middle-distance pedigree and likely to leave form behind when stepped up in trip.

1143 Modun (Ire)

5 br g King's Best - Olympienne (Sadler's Wells)

Saeed Bin Suroor   Godolphin

PLACINGS: 12/1022410-   **RPR 113+aw**

Starts	1st	2nd	3rd	4th	Win & Pl
9				1	£84,374
	9/11	Kemp	1m4f Cls1 Gp3 stand		.£28,355
84	4/11	Newb	1m2f Cls4 71-85 Hcap gd-fm		.£5,181
	9/10	Folk	1m1½f Cls5 Mdn gd-fm		.£2,730

Unlucky not to land a major handicap for Sir Michael Stoute last season, twice finishing second after impressive win at Newbury and failing to see out 1m6f when fourth in the Ebor having travelled strongly; not a factor in Melbourne Cup on debut for Godolphin.

1144 Mojave (Ire)

3 b c Dubawi - Desert Frolic (Persian Bold)

Mahmood Al Zarooni   Godolphin

PLACINGS: 911-   **RPR 96**

Starts	1st	2nd	3rd	4th	Win & Pl
3	2	-	-	-	£11,169
	10/11	NmkR	1m2f Cls3 2yo good		.£7,159
	10/11	Leic	1m1½f Cls4 2yo good		.£4,011

Won Leicester maiden by six lengths on second start and progressed again when stepped up to 1m2f in Zetland Stakes at Newmarket, winning well with first two six lengths clear of rest; could be a smart middle-distance performer and likely to have Derby credentials tested in a major trial.

1145 Monsieur Chevalier (Ire)

5 b h Chevalier - Blue Holly (Blues Traveller)

PJ O'Gorman   Mrs Valerie Hubbard & Ian Higginson

PLACINGS: 1111511338/402051-   **RPR 117**

Starts	1st	2nd	3rd	4th	Win & Pl
16	7	1	2	1	£302,022
	9/11	Gdwd	6f Cls1 List gd-sft		.£17,013
	7/09	Gdwd	5f Cls1 Gp3 2yo good		.£34,062
	7/09	Newb	5f Cls2 2yo gd-sft		.£98,480
	5/09	Sand	5f Cls1 List 2yo good		.£17,031
	5/09	Wind	5f Cls2 2yo good		.£11,657
	4/09	NmkR	5f Cls3 2yo gd-fm		.£9,066
	4/09	Folk	5f Cls6 Auct Mdn 2yo gd-fm		.£2,730

Changed hands for 210,000gns last October after doing well on return from long-term injury for Richard Hannon last season; finished half-length second to Society Rock in Golden Jubilee Stakes and earned overdue victory in Listed event at Goodwood by a nose.

1146 Monterosso

5 b h Dubawi - Porto Roca (Barathea)

Mahmood Al Zarooni   Godolphin

PLACINGS: 5/2111211475/13-   **RPR 118aw**

Starts	1st	2nd	3rd	4th	Win & Pl
13	6	2	1	1	£896,368
	3/11	Meyd	1m4½f Gp2 good		.£96,054
	6/10	Asct	1m4f Cls1 Gp2 3yo gd-fm		.£92,947
94	5/10	NmkR	1m2f Cls3 84-94 3yo Hcap good		.£11,657
83	4/10	Ripn	1m Cls3 76-95 3yo Hcap good		.£7,477
78	2/10	Ling	1m Cls4 70-78 3yo Hcap stand		.£4,209
	1/10	Ling	1m Cls5 Mdn 3yo stand		.£2,457

Smart middle-distance three-year-old for Mark Johnston in 2010, winning King Edward VII Stakes; made excellent start for Godolphin last spring, finishing third in

Dubai World Cup over seemingly inadequate 1m2f; missed rest of season but returned at Meydan in March.

1147 Moonlight Cloud

4 b f Invincible Spirit - Ventura (Spectrum)

Freddy Head (Fr)   George Strawbridge

PLACINGS: 114/172115-   **RPR 122+**

Starts	1st	2nd	3rd	4th	Win & Pl
9	5	1		1	£255,979
	8/11	Deau	6½f Gp1 soft		£123,147
	7/11	Lonc	7f Gp3 good		£34,483
	4/11	MsnL	7f Gp3 3yo good		£34,483
	9/10	Lonc	7f 2yo soft		£15,044
	8/10	Deau	6½f 2yo stand		£10,619

Failed to stay 1m when sent off favourite for 1,000 Guineas last season (only run on good to firm) but benefited from drop in trip with four-length win in Prix Maurice de Gheest; unlucky in running when fast-finishing fifth in Champions Sprint at Ascot.

1148 Most Improved (Ire)

3 b c Lawman - Tonnara (Linamix)

Brian Meehan   Iraj Parvizi

PLACINGS: 213-   **RPR 116**

Starts	1st	2nd	3rd	4th	Win & Pl
3	1	1	1	-	£39,600
	8/11	NmkJ	7f Cls4 Mdn 2yo gd-sft		£4,528

Made big impression when landing maiden at second attempt by five lengths at Newmarket and did well on step up into Group 1 company with close third in Dewhurst Stakes; likely to improve on that form having taken keen early hold and may well be good enough to make his mark in top races.

1149 Nahrain

4 ch f Selkirk - Bahr (Generous)

Roger Varian   Sheikh Ahmed Al Maktoum

PLACINGS: 11112-   **RPR 118+**

Starts	1st	2nd	3rd	4th	Win & Pl
5	4	1	-	-	£429,577
	10/11	Lonc	1m2f Gp1 good		£172,405
	7/11	Sand	1m Cls1 List 3yo good		£17,013
87	6/11	Hayd	1m Cls3 71-89 3yo Hcap gd-sft		£7,124
	5/11	Wind	1m½f Cls5 Mdn gd-fm		£2,267

Made rapid progress through the ranks after making her debut only last May, completing brilliant four-timer when landing Prix de l'Opera by a nose at Longchamp; lost nothing in defeat when second in Breeders' Cup Filly & Mare Turf,

just lacking pace of winner.

1150 Naqshabban (USA)

4 b g Street Cry - Reem Three (Mark Of Esteem)

Mahmood Al Zarooni   Godolphin

PLACINGS: 1/16623-1   **RPR 111**

Starts	1st	2nd	3rd	4th	Win & Pl
7	3	1	1	-	£73,000
102	1/12	Meyd	1m4f 99-105 Hcap good		£42,581
	4/11	Sand	1m Cls3 3yo good		£7,166
	10/10	Leic	7f Cls4 Mdn 2yo gd-sft		£4,209

Had mixed season for Luca Cumani last season; looked a tricky ride sometimes and twice proved bitterly disappointing but looked back on upward curve when placed in two major handicaps at Newbury; moved to Godolphin in the winter and won first start at Meydan.

1151 Nathaniel (Ire)

4 b c Galileo - Magnificient Style (Silver Hawk)

John Gosden   Lady Rothschild

PLACINGS: 22/12115-   **RPR 126**

Starts	1st	2nd	3rd	4th	Win & Pl
7	3	3	-	-	£749,890
	7/11	Asct	1m4f Cls1 Gp1 gd-sft		£611,124
	6/11	Asct	1m4f Cls1 Gp2 3yo gd-sft		£86,750
	4/11	Hayd	1m4f Cls5 Mdn 3yo gd-fm		£2,914

Benefited from much softer surface when bouncing back from Chester Vase defeat to easily land King Edward VII Stakes and land slowly run and sub-standard King George; withdrawn from Arc because of quicker ground and found 1m2f too sharp when fifth in Champion Stakes.

1152 Native Khan (Fr)

4 gr c Azamour - Viva Maria (Kendor)

John Oxx (Ir)   V I Araci

PLACINGS: 114/1357-   **RPR 118**

Starts	1st	2nd	3rd	4th	Win & Pl
7	3	-	1	1	£144,025
	4/11	NmkR	1m Cls1 Gp3 3yo gd-fm		£28,385
	8/10	Sand	7f Cls1 Gp3 2yo gd-fm		£21,289
	7/10	NmkJ	7f Cls2 Mdn 2yo gd-fm		£9,714

Did well over 1m last season, winning the Craven Stakes and finishing third in the 2,000 Guineas, given he always looked a middle-distance prospect; good fifth in the Derby before running well below that form at the Curragh; given a break and should progress again; has left Ed Dunlop's yard.

1153 Nephrite *(below)*

3 ch c Pivotal - Cape Merino (Clantime)

Aidan O'Brien (Ir)   Michael Tabor

PLACINGS: 11-   **RPR 110+**

Starts	1st	2nd	3rd	4th	Win & Pl
2	2	-	-	-	£36,728

10/11	Leop	7f Gp3 2yo yield		£26,616
9/11	Curr	6f Mdn 2yo soft		£10,112

Put himself in the frame for the 2,000 Guineas with easy win over much-hyped Born To Sea in Group 3 at Leopardstown having run away with a maiden on his debut; seems sure to stay 1m and expected to improve on quicker ground; could be a leading miler.

1154 Noble Mission

3 b c Galileo - Kind (Danehill)

Sir Henry Cecil   K Abdulla

PLACINGS: 2-   **RPR 73+**

Starts	1st	2nd	3rd	4th	Win & Pl
1	-	1	-	-	£866

Brother to Frankel and hinted at above-average ability when second to Swedish Sailor on only start at Yarmouth last October, staying on well having looked very green; expected to stay further than his brother and could prove best at 1m4f.

1155 Nocturnal Affair (SAF)

6 b g Victory Moon - Aretha (Centenary)

David Marnane (Ir)   Emma Bifova

PLACINGS: 3250/15916/792151-25   **RPR 111+**

Starts	1st	2nd	3rd	4th	Win & Pl
24	6	5	3	-	£118,343

	10/11	Dund	5f List stand	£22,414
101	9/11	Donc	5¹/₂f Cls2 92-106 Hcap gd-fm	£37,350
	6/10	Scot	7f good	£4,446
	4/10	Scot	7f Gd3 3yo yield	£10,460
	9/09	Keni	6f 2yo holding	£3,339
	5/09	Keni	6f Gd3 2yo Hcap good	£7,054

Bought out of South Africa after unsuccessful stint at Meydan last spring and soon took advantage of lenient handicap mark when winning Portland Handicap at Doncaster; only fifth at York next time but looked good when easily landing Listed event at Dundalk after that.

1156 Ocean War

4 gr g Dalakhani - Atlantic Destiny (Royal Academy)

Mahmood Al Zarooni   Godolphin

PLACINGS: 5/110-   **RPR 108+**

Starts	1st	2nd	3rd	4th	Win & Pl
4	2	-	-	-	£27,241

4/11	NmkR	1m2f List Cls1 3yo gd-fm	£22,708
4/11	NmkR	1m2f Cls4 Mdn 3yo gd-fm	£4,533

Emerged as surprise Derby candidate last season, impressively winning Listed contest

at Newmarket less than three weeks after landing maiden; failed to handle track when only 11th at Epsom and not seen again but reported to be back in full training this spring.

1157 Opinion Poll (Ire) *(below)*

6 b h Halling - Ahead (Shirley Heights)

Mahmood Al Zarooni   Godolphin

PLACINGS: 1/1313143/223421122-   **RPR 120**

Starts	1st	2nd	3rd	4th	Win & Pl
22	8	5	5	2	£552,136
	8/11	York	2m¹/₂f Cls1 Gp2 good		£79,394
	7/11	Gdwd	2m Cls1 Gp2 gd-fm		£56,710
	8/10	York	2m¹/₂f Cls1 Gp2 good		£79,478
	6/10	Chan	1m7f List gd-sft		£23,009
	4/10	Nott	1m6f Cls1 List soft		£22,708
95	10/09	Asct	1m4f Cls2 89-102 Hcap gd-sft		£46,733
88	5/09	Hayd	1m4f Cls2 79-98 3yo Hcap heavy		£12,462
	10/08	Leic	1m¹/₂f Cls4 Mdn 2yo good		£5,181

Progressed well following switch to Godolphin last season, winning Goodwood Cup and Lonsdale Cup over 2m as well as twice finding only Fame And Glory too

good; again due to start campaign in Dubai this spring; should continue to pay his way in top staying contests.

1158 Our Jonathan

5 b g Invincible Spirit - Sheik'n Swing (Celtic Swing)

Kevin Ryan   Dr Marwan Koukash

PLACINGS: 1/670507/3312856210-   **RPR 117**

Starts	1st	2nd	3rd	4th	Win & Pl
22	6	2	3	-	£286,004
105	9/11	Ayr	6f Cls2 97-111 Hcap soft		£74,700
95	5/11	Ches	7f Cls2 93-102 Hcap good		£12,952
	11/09	MsnL	6f Gp2 2yo holding		£105,146
	10/09	Asct	5f Cls1 Gp3 2yo gd-sft		£31,224
	8/09	Dund	5f List 2yo stand		£30,022
	8/09	Pont	5f Cls4 Mdn 2yo gd-fm		£5,828

Dual Group winner as a juvenile who bounced back from a spell in the doldrums last season when winning good Chester handicap; beaten favourite next three times but took form to another level again with clear-cut win in Ayr Gold Cup; equally effective at 6f and 7f.

1159 Overdose

7 b h Starborough - Our Poppet (Warning)

Jozef Roscival (Hun)   Miko Racing & Trading Kft

PLACINGS: 1:/111111/1/117/1741-   **RPR 119**

Starts	1st	2nd	3rd	4th	Win & Pl
19	16	-	-	1	£206,213

11/11	Capa	6f Gp3 gd-sft		£34,483
4/11	Hopp	5f good		£4,310
8/10	KcPk	5f good		£7,087
7/10	Brat	5f soft		£4,425
4/09	KcPk	5f good		£13,818
11/08	Capa	6f Gp3 heavy		£26,801
8/08	Badn	6f Gp2 good		£30,882
7/08	Hamb	6f Gp3 soft		£29,418
6/08	Brat	6f good		£9,290
5/08	Badn	6f List 3yo good		£11,029
4/08	MagR	5½f fast		£2,316
10/07	MagR	6½f 2yo good		£6,081
9/07	KcPk	7f good		£3,484
9/07	Freu	6f good		£5,068
7/07	Brat	6f good		£1,075
6/07	KcPk	5f good		£536

High-class Hungarian sprinter who raced in Britain for first time last season, finding good to firm ground too quick in the Temple Stakes before good fourth in the King's Stand; connections remain keen to win a Group 1 in Britain.

1160 Parish Hall (Ire)

3 b c Teofilo - Halla Siamsa (Montjeu)

Jim Bolger (Ir)   Mrs J S Bolger

PLACINGS: 12821-   **RPR 118**

Starts	1st	2nd	3rd	4th	Win & Pl
5	2	2	-	-	£213,223

10/11	NmkR	7f Cls1 Gp1 2yo good		£179,771
4/11	Leop	6f Mdn 2yo gd-fm		£10,112

Sprang 20-1 surprise in Dewhurst Stakes last season, making much of the running to hold off Power in tight finish; had been beaten three times before that but reportedly unsuited by cut in ground twice and second to Dragon Pulse worked out well; seen as a Derby horse by his trainer.

1161 Pastoral Player

5 b g Pastoral Pursuits - Copy-Cat (Lion Cavern)

Hughie Morrison   The Pursuits Partnership

PLACINGS: 7/2040091/138566451-   **RPR 114**

Starts	1st	2nd	3rd	4th	Win & Pl
19	4	1	1	2	£159,512

101	10/11	Asct	7f Cls2 95-110 Hcap good	£93,375
96	5/11	NmkR	6f Cls2 82-105 Hcap gd-fm	£24,924
92	10/10	Ffos	6f Cls3 82-95 Hcap good	£7,771
	9/09	Newb	6f Cls4 Mdn 2yo gd-fm	£5,505

Knocking on the door in major handicaps last season before finally landing valuable prize in decisive fashion over 7f at Ascot

(had previously shown best form over 6f); capable of winning again off 6lb higher mark but connections more likely to look at Pattern races.

1162 Perennial

3 ch c Motivator - Arum Lily (Woodman)

Charles Hills   K Abdulla

PLACINGS: 12-   **RPR 101**

Starts	1st	2nd	3rd	4th	Win & Pl
2	1	1	-	-	£14,749

9/11	Donc	1m Cls3 Mdn 2yo good		£7,439

Did well to beat Encke on his debut at Doncaster but still looked slightly green when stepped up in class at Newmarket next time, running on late into second in Autumn Stakes; seems likely to prove much better than that and should be most effective over middle distances.

1163 Peter Martins (USA)

4 ch c Johannesburg - Pretty Meadow (Meadowlake)

Jeremy Noseda   The Honorable Earle I Mack

PLACINGS: 1/

Starts	1st	2nd	3rd	4th	Win & Pl
1	1	-	-	-	£6,476

7/10	NmkJ	7f Cls4 2yo gd-fm		£6,476

Kept off the track by injury since registering five-length win on his debut in July 2010; well fancied for the 2,000 Guineas last season before being ruled out with a leg problem; reported to be back in training this spring and could still turn out to be a smart miler.

1164 Pimpernel (Ire)

3 b f Invincible Spirit - Anna Pallida (Sadler's Wells)

Mahmood Al Zarooni   Godolphin

PLACINGS: 1213121-2   **RPR 110**

Starts	1st	2nd	3rd	4th	Win & Pl
8	4	3	1	-	£87,215

	10/11	Newb	7f Cls1 List 2yo gd-fm	£12,193
96	9/11	NmkR	7f Cls2 73-96 2yo Hcap gd-fm	£12,450
90	8/11	NmkJ	7f Cls2 69-90 2yo Hcap good	£10,350
	6/11	Ling	5f Cls5 Mdn 2yo good	£3,412

Steady improver last season, winning twice in nurseries before producing best effort when chasing home Wading in the Rockfel Stakes; easily justified favouritism to land Listed event at Newbury on final start; started three-year-old career in Dubai this spring.

1165 Planteur (Ire)

5 b h Danehill Dancer - Plante Rare (Giant's Causeway)

Marco Botti   Ecurie Wildenstein

PLACINGS: 121/1222dis5/11458-   **RPR 124+**

Starts	1st	2nd	3rd	4th	Win & Pl
14	5	4	-	1	£850,908
	4/11	Lonc	1m2½f Gp1 good		£147,776
	4/11	Lonc	1m2f Gp2 good		£63,879
	4/10	Lonc	1m2½f Gp2 3yo soft		£65,575
	9/09	StCl	1m 2yo gd-sft		£16,505
	8/09	Deau	1m 2yo soft		£11,650

Switched from Elie Lellouche's yard having failed to build on terrific start to last season; showed fine turn of foot to beat Sarafina in Prix Ganay but disappointing fourth in Prince of Wales's Stakes and twice below par when dropped to 1m; had shown smart form over 1m4f in 2010.

1166 Poet

7 b h Pivotal - Hyabella (Shirley Heights)

Clive Cox   H E Sheikh Sultan Bin Khalifa Al Nahyan

PLACINGS: 12/00631342/3268413-   **RPR 118**

Starts	1st	2nd	3rd	4th	Win & Pl
27	6	4	7	4	£279,370
	9/11	Ayr	1m2f Cls1 List soft		£22,684
	8/10	Hayd	1m2½f Cls1 Gp3 soft		£32,359
	9/09	Leop	1m2f Gp3 gd-yld		£39,126
107	8/09	Curr	1m 83-107 Hcap heavy		£58,350
	8/09	Klny	1m1½f List gd-yld		£28,442
	3/08	Curr	1m Mdn 3yo heavy		£9,574

Group 3 winner for Aidan O'Brien in 2009 who has done well at that level in two seasons for Clive Cox, winning and being placed five times as well as landing Listed win last year at Ayr; much better on soft ground and may again travel abroad to find suitable conditions.

1167 Power

3 b c Oasis Dream - Frappe (Inchinor)

Aidan O'Brien (Ir)   Derrick Smith

PLACINGS: 111212-   **RPR 118**

Starts	1st	2nd	3rd	4th	Win & Pl
6	4	2	-	-	£284,538
	9/11	Curr	7f Gp1 2yo yld-sft		£100,000
	6/11	Asct	6f Cls1 Gp2 2yo good		£48,255
	5/11	Curr	5f List 2yo gd-fm		£26,897
	5/11	Curr	6f Mdn 2yo gd-fm		£10,112

Tough and consistent two-year-old last season, winning Coventry Stakes and running well three times at Group 1 level including victory in National Stakes; ran another good race in the Dewhurst when second to Parish Hall having been trapped on rail; potential Guineas colt in open year.

1168 Premio Loco (USA) *(above, winning)*

8 ch g Prized - Crazee Mental (Magic Ring)

Chris Wall   Bernard Westley

PLACINGS: 11/5711328/43765127-   **RPR 117**

Starts	1st	2nd	3rd	4th	Win & Pl
31	12	4	2	1	£507,298
	9/11	Donc	7f Cls1 Gp2 gd-fm		£56,710
	7/10	Asct	1m Cls1 Gp2 gd-fm		£56,770
	6/10	NmkJ	7f Cls1 Gp2 gd-fm		£36,901
	9/09	Colo	1m Gp2 good		£38,835
	9/09	Badn	1m Gp2 good		£38,835
	5/09	Gdwd	1m Cls1 List good		£22,708
	2/09	Kemp	1m Cls1 List stand		£22,708
	1/09	Ling	1m Cls3 stand		£7,771
99	9/08	Kemp	1m Cls2 77-99 Hcap stand		£30,825
92	7/08	Kemp	1m Cls3 82-95 3yo Hcap stand		£7,477
83	9/07	Newb	7f Cls4 75-83 3yo Hcap gd-fm		£4,858
	4/07	Ling	1m Cls5 Auct Mdn 3yo stand		£2,915

Slightly disappointing for much of last season despite having sights lowered following terrific third to Canford Cliffs in Lockinge Stakes; still managed to win Group 2 at Doncaster on only run at 7f since finishing second in same race in 2010; may well win more Group races.

1169 Princess Sinead (Ire)

3 b/br f Jeremy - Princess Atoosa (Gone West)

Jessica Harrington (Ir)   Mrs J Maxwell Moran

PLACINGS: 22153-   **RPR 104**

Starts	1st	2nd	3rd	4th	Win & Pl
5	1	2	1	-	£31,978
	6/11	Curr	7f Mdn 2yo yld-sft £10,707		

Ran into smart fillies on first two starts before winning maiden; well beaten on first attempt at Pattern level but did much better when half-length third in Group 3 at the Curragh last time despite finding heavy ground against her; picked out by her trainer as one to follow.

1170 Prohibit

7 b g Oasis Dream - Well Warned (Warning)

Robert Cowell   Dasmal, Rix, Barr, Morley & Mrs Penney

PLACINGS: 312136/814594321317-   **RPR 121**

Starts	1st	2nd	3rd	4th	Win & Pl
43	9	5	7	5	£495,020
	9/11	Lonc	5f Gp3 gd-sft £34,483		
	6/11	Asct	5f Cls1 Gp1 good £170,310		
108	2/11	Meyd	5f 100-111 Hcap good £67,308		
	9/10	Donc	5f Cls1 List good £23,704		
100	8/10	Asct	5f Cls2 90-100 Hcap gd-fm £14,769		
	3/10	Kemp	6f Cls3 stand £6,543		
	10/08	GrLe	6f Cls3 stand £7,771		
86	4/08	NmkR	6f Cls2 82-96 3yo Hcap good £11,657		
	10/07	Nott	6f Cls5 Mdn 2yo gd-fm £3,886		

Progressed into leading 5f performer last season when winning King's Stand Stakes at Ascot and doing best of those drawn on wrong side to finish third in Nunthorpe Stakes; disappointing seventh when favourite for Prix de l'Abbaye; should continue to do well.

1171 Quest For Peace (Ire)

4 b c Galileo - Play Misty For Me (Danehill Dancer)

Luca Cumani   O T I Racing

PLACINGS: 3/31115-   **RPR 116+**

Starts	1st	2nd	3rd	4th	Win & Pl
6	3	-	2	-	£84,030
	10/11	Asct	1m4f Cls1 Gp3 good £31,191		
	7/11	Rosc	1m4f List gd-fm £22,414		
	4/11	Leop	1m2f Mdn 3yo gd-fm £9,517		

Sold out of Aidan O'Brien's yard after Listed win at Roscommon last July and made winning start for new Australian owners in

Group 3 at Ascot; good fifth in Grade 1 in Canada on final start; likely to stay beyond 1m4f; could be trained for Melbourne Cup.

1172 Questioning (Ire)

4 b c Elusive Quality - Am I (Thunder Gulch)

John Gosden   H R H Princess Haya Of Jordan

PLACINGS: 15/3537203-   **RPR 112**

Starts	1st	2nd	3rd	4th	Win & Pl
9	1	1	3	-	£71,402
	8/10	Ling	1m Cls5 Mdn 2yo stand £2,388		

Slightly disappointing in sales races following debut win but showed far more promise towards end of last season, most notably when just touched off by King Torus in Listed race at Haydock; got no sort of run when unable to take advantage of lenient mark in the Cambridgeshire.

1173 Ransom Note

5 b h Red Ransom - Zacheta (Polish Precedent)

Charles Hills   H R Mould

PLACINGS: 71/1217910/18525188-   **RPR 118**

Starts	1st	2nd	3rd	4th	Win & Pl
19	7	2	-	-	£231,369
	9/11	NmkR	1m Cls1 Gp2 gd-fm £56,710		
	4/11	NmkR	1m1f Cls1 Gp3 gd-fm £28,385		
100	8/10	York	1m Cls2 92-104 Hcap good £32,380		
92	6/10	Asct	1m Cls2 81-103 3yo Hcap gd-fm £62,310		
77	4/10	Donc	1m Cls4 76-81 3yo Hcap good £4,777		
72	10/09	Gdwd	7f Cls4 71-85 2yo Hcap gd-sft £5,505		
	8/09	Ches	7f Cls3 Mdn 2yo gd-fm £7,318		

Hit and miss last season, showing best form when able to dominate small fields from the front at Newmarket, most notably in Group 2 Joel Stakes in September; produced three worst performances when racing abroad; well beaten on all four runs at Group 1 level.

1174 Rebellious Guest

3 b c Cockney Rebel - Marisa (Desert Sun)

George Margarson   John Guest Racing

PLACINGS: 1010-   **RPR 99+**

Starts	1st	2nd	3rd	4th	Win & Pl
4	2	-	-	-	£9,060
	8/11	Wind	6f Cls3 2yo gd-sft £5,822		
	6/11	Wind	6f Cls5 Auct Mdn 2yo gd-sft £3,238		

Highly regarded colt who twice ran out a ready winner on good to soft ground at Windsor last season, most notably when slamming rivals in a decent conditions event; well beaten on both starts in Pattern company, possibly finding ground too quick; could be underrated.

1175 Red Cadeaux

6 ch g Cadeaux Genereux - Artisia (Peintre Celebre)

Ed Dunlop   R J Arculli

PLACINGS: 71842229/2014105323-   RPR **119**

Starts	1st	2nd	3rd	4th	Win & Pl
25	5	6	3	2	£817,053
	6/11	Curr	1m6f Gp3 yld-sft..		£32,328
103	5/11	Haml	1m4f Cls1 List 95-109 Hcap good...................		£26,667
90	4/10	Ling	1m4f Cls2 84-103 Hcap stand........................		£10,362
84	8/09	Donc	1m4f Cls4 72-85 3yo Hcap soft		£4,857
72	6/09	Wolv	1m4f Cls4 61-79 3yo Hcap stand		£5,181

Improved out of all recognition after winning Hamilton handicap last May, getting beaten by a nose in Melbourne Cup before equally creditable third in Hong Kong Vase; again likely to be aimed at the big Australian handicap but could pick up some good races along the way.

1176 Red Duke (USA)

3 ch c Hard Spun - Saudia (Gone West)

John Quinn   Maxilead Limited

PLACINGS: 311328-   RPR **111**

Starts	1st	2nd	3rd	4th	Win & Pl
6	2	1	2	-	£60,518
	7/11	NmkJ	7f Cls1 Gp2 2yo gd-fm...........................		£34,026
	6/11	Rdcr	7f Cls5 Mdn 2yo good.............................		£2,979

Did well to win Group 2 Superlative Stakes at Newmarket and had excuses for next two defeats, getting no room when third in Vintage Stakes and undone only by 3lb penalty in Champagne Stakes; below-par eighth in Dewhurst on final start but could bounce back.

1177 Red Jazz (USA)

5 b h Johannesburg - Now That's Jazz (Sword Dance)

Charles Hills   R J Arculli

PLACINGS: 1173/182228531/3542-   RPR **115**

Starts	1st	2nd	3rd	4th	Win & Pl
17	4	4	3	1	£264,580
	10/10	NmkR	7f Cls1 Gp2 gd-sft..................................		£51,093
107	4/10	NmkR	7f Cls1 List 100-108 3yo Hcap good.........		£22,708
	4/09	Asct	5f Cls3 2yo gd-fm.................................		£6,543
	4/09	Wind	5f Cls5 Mdn 2yo good...........................		£2,730

Bordering on top class over 7f and 1m in 2010 when finishing close third in Queen Elizabeth II Stakes and winning Challenge Stakes at Newmarket; just fell short of that level last season but produced best effort on final start when chasing home Strong Suit at Goodwood.

1178 Redwood

6 b h High Chaparral - Arum Lily (Woodman)

Charles Hills   K Abdulla

PLACINGS: /19/275212132/22470-   RPR **117**

Starts	1st	2nd	3rd	4th	Win & Pl
17	4	6	1	1	£1,422,866
	9/10	Wood	1m4f Gd1 firm.......................................		£229,412
	7/10	Gdwd	1m4f Cls1 Gp3 good-fm..........................		£39,739
	4/09	NmkR	1m1f Cls1 List 3yo gd-fm.......................		£25,547
	10/08	NmkR	1m Cls4 Mdn 2yo gd-fm..........................		£6,476

Much improved over 1m4f in 2010, winning Group 1 in Canada and finishing second in Hong Kong Vase; began last season well when second in Dubai Duty Free but went off the boil later, including when beaten favourite twice; capable of bagging a big prize if recovering his form.

1179 Reliable Man

4 gr c Dalakhani - On Fair Stage (Sadler's Wells)

Alain de Royer-Dupre (Fr) Pride Racing Club

PLACINGS: 111310- RPR **123+**

Starts	1st	2nd	3rd	4th	Win & Pl
6	4	-	1	-	£886,879
9/11	Lonc	1m4f Gp2 3yo gd-sft			£63,879
6/11	Chan	1m2½f Gp1 3yo soft			£738,879
5/11	Chan	1m2f 3yo good			£14,655
4/11	StCl	1m2f 3yo good			£10,345

Relished soft ground when winning Prix du Jockey Club and bounced back from first defeat in Grand Prix de Paris when impressively landing Prix Niel; may well have found ground too firm when disappointing in Arc and left out of Champion Stakes owing to lack of rain.

1180 Remember Alexander

3 b f Teofilo - Nausicaa (Diesis)

Jessica Harrington (Ir) Noel O'Callaghan

PLACINGS: 24155- RPR **105+**

Starts	1st	2nd	3rd	4th	Win & Pl
5	1	1	-	1	£29,547
7/11	Leop	7f Gp3 2yo soft			£26,616

Beat Dewhurst winner Parish Hall by four lengths in Tyros Stakes but defeats in all four other races (three when favourite) raise doubts over validity of that form; looked one-paced on quicker ground but struggled to cope on heavy on final start; could improve over further.

1181 Reply (Ire)

3 b c Oasis Dream - Cap Coz (Indian Ridge)

Aidan O'Brien (Ir) Mrs Magnier, Tabor, Smith & Mordukhovitch

PLACINGS: 315613- RPR **111**

Starts	1st	2nd	3rd	4th	Win & Pl
6	2	-	2	-	£240,420
9/11	Donc	6½f Cls2 2yo good			£207,294
5/11	Curr	6f Mdn 2yo good			£10,707

Looked to have limitations exposed on first two runs in Pattern company but showed improved form to win valuable sales race at York and built on that with fine third in Middle Park Stakes; seems well suited by big fields and strong end-to-end gallop; not certain to stay 1m.

1182 Requinto (Ire) *(above, 3)*

3 b c Dansili - Damson (Entrepreneur)

David Wachman (Ir) M Tabor, D Smith & Mrs John Magnier

PLACINGS: 31511016- RPR **110**

Starts	1st	2nd	3rd	4th	Win & Pl
8	4	-	1	-	£98,428
9/11	Donc	5f Cls1 Gp2 2yo good			£39,697
7/11	Gdwd	5f Cls3 Gp3 2yo good			£22,684
7/11	Tipp	5f List 2yo yield			£23,815
4/11	Cork	5f 2yo good			£11,207

Best juvenile in Europe over 5f last season, edging out Burwaaz in Molecomb Stakes and Flying Childers Stakes before finishing respectable sixth against older sprinters in Prix de l'Abbaye; below par on only run on good to soft in Nunthorpe.

1183 Rio De La Plata (USA)

7 ch h Rahy - Express Way (Ahmad)

Saeed Bin Suroor   Godolphin

PLACINGS: 25/01171211/343222-7   **RPR 119+**

Starts	1st	2nd	3rd	4th	Win & Pl
27	8	7	4	2	£974,559
11/10	Capa	1m2f Gp1 soft			£119,469
10/10	Siro	1m Gp1 soft			£119,469
8/10	York	1m1f Cls1 Gp3 gd-fm			£48,255
7/10	Pont	1m Cls1 List gd-fm			£15,658
6/10	Nott	1m¹/₂f Cls2 gd-fm			£9,970
10/07	Lonc	7f Gp1 2yo gd-sft			£135,128
8/07	Gdwd	7f Cls1 Gp2 2yo good			£39,746
7/07	NmkJ	7f Cls2 Mdn 2yo good			£9,716

Consistent globetrotting performer during last two seasons, gaining Group 1 honours twice at backend of 2010 in Italy; unable to follow up those wins last season but ran well in defeat on several occasions, including when terrific second in Prix du Moulin.

1184 Rite Of Passage

8 ch g Giant's Causeway - Dahlia's Krissy (Kris S)

Dermot Weld (Ir)   Dr R Lambe

PLACINGS: 11/1/3-   **RPR 113+**

Starts	1st	2nd	3rd	4th	Win & Pl
4	3		1	-	£174,659
	6/10	Asct	2m4f Cls1 Gp1 gd-fm		£141,925
88	11/09	Leop	2m 73-97 Hcap heavy		£24,017
	9/09	Baln	1m6f Mdn yld-sft		£5,032

Talented National Hunt performer in bumpers and novice hurdles before making sensational switch to the Flat when landing Ascot Gold Cup in 2010; fair third to Fame And Glory over inadequate 1m6f on return last season before being ruled out for rest of year through injury.

1185 Royal Rock *(above, white face)*

8 b g Sakhee - Vanishing Point (Caller I.D.)

Chris Wall   Ms Aida Fustoq

PLACINGS: 3/16419/60/63093114-   **RPR 117**

Starts	1st	2nd	3rd	4th	Win & Pl
24	8	1	4	2	£144,356
	10/11	Asct	6f Cls1 Gp3 good		£39,697
	9/11	Yarm	6f Cls3 good		£6,490
	10/09	Asct	6f Cls1 Gp3 gd-sft		£36,901
	5/09	Hayd	6f Cls2 good		£12,462
94	4/08	Yarm	6f Cls2 85-94 Hcap gd-fm		£9,970
84	7/07	Wind	6f Cls4 72-85 3yo Hcap soft		£6,477
77	6/07	Kemp	6f Cls4 71-80 3yo Hcap stand		£4,728
	5/07	Ling	7f Cls5 Mdn 3yo good		£2,591

Reserves best form for Ascot and bounced back to form there having been out of sorts for much of last season; followed up soft win at Yarmouth by landing same Group 3 he had won in 2009 before being beaten a length in fourth behind Deacon Blues in Champions Sprint.

1186 Saamidd

4 b c Street Cry - Aryaamm (Galileo)

Saeed Bin Suroor   Godolphin

PLACINGS: 116/0-

Starts	1st	2nd	3rd	4th	Win & Pl
4	2		-	-	£76,525
	9/10	Donc	7f Cls1 Gp2 2yo good		£67,386
	8/10	Newb	7f Cls4 Mdn 2yo gd-fm		£4,857

Exciting juvenile in 2010, cruising to

victory in Champagne Stakes before pulling too hard in Dewhurst; ran only once last season when finishing next to last in 2,000 Guineas but reported to be back in full training this spring; likely to stick to top 1m contests.

1187 Saddler's Rock (Ire)

4 b c Sadler's Wells - Grecian Bride (Groom Dancer)

John Oxx (Ir)   Michael O'Flynn

PLACINGS: 751131-   **RPR 122**

Starts	1st	2nd	3rd	4th	Win & Pl
6	3	-	1	-	£73,494
87	9/11	Donc	2m2f Cls1 Gp2 good		£56,710
	7/11	Leop	1m6f 70-89 Hcap gd-fm		£7,733
	6/11	Tipp	1m4¹/₂f Mdn gd-yld		£5,948

Did not make his debut until last May, taking three runs to win in maiden company, but improved rapidly to win Doncaster Cup on final start, relishing 2m2f trip on good ground; seems likely to progress again and may well become a leading contender for Ascot Gold Cup.

1188 Saigon

3 b c Royal Applause - Luanshya (First Trump)

James Toller   P C J Dalby & R D Schuster

PLACINGS: 1153362-   **RPR 109**

Starts	1st	2nd	3rd	4th	Win & Pl
7	2	1	2	-	£36,676
	7/11	Newb	6f Cls1 List 2yo gd-fm		£12,193
	6/11	Yarm	6f Cls5 Mdn 2yo gd-fm		£3,238

Pounced late to beat Caspar Netscher in Listed race in July and had excuses for all subsequent defeats, appearing to find 6f too sharp and having trouble in running before staying on for second in Horris Hill Stakes on only start at 7f; remains capable of much better.

1189 Samitar

3 b f Rock Of Gibraltar - Aileen's Gift (Rainbow Quest)

Mick Channon   Nick & Olga Dhandsa & John & Zoe Webster

PLACINGS: 312321-   **RPR 109**

Starts	1st	2nd	3rd	4th	Win & Pl
6	2	2	2	-	£264,340
	10/11	NmkR	7f Cls2 2yo gd-fm		£162,330
	6/11	Asct	6f Cls1 Gp3 2yo gd-sft		£34,062

Did remarkably well to win Albany Stakes at Royal Ascot over 6f given her subsequent improvement when stepped up to 1m,

running Lyric Of Light to a head in Fillies' Mile; didn't need to run to anywhere near that form to land valuable sales race at Newmarket next time.

1190 Sapphire (Ire)

4 b f Medicean - Polished Gem (Danehill)

Dermot Weld (Ir)   Moyglare Stud Farm

PLACINGS: 6/151321-   **RPR 113+**

Starts	1st	2nd	3rd	4th	Win & Pl
7	3	1	1	-	£62,577
	10/11	Curr	1m4f List yld-sft		£22,414
	6/11	Naas	1m2f yld-sft		£11,207
	3/11	Curr	1m Mdn 3yo soft		£9,517

Beaten on first three attempts at Pattern level but did much better on final run last season when easily landing Listed race at the Curragh with rivals well strung out, relishing softer surface and step up to 1m4f (blinkers removed for first time all year); may have more to come.

1191 Sea Moon

4 b c Beat Hollow - Eva Luna (Alleged)

Sir Michael Stoute   K Abdulla

PLACINGS: 21/1132-   **RPR 126+**

Starts	1st	2nd	3rd	4th	Win & Pl
6	3	2	1	-	£511,337
	8/11	York	1m4f Cls1 Gp2 3yo gd-sft		£89,872
92	6/11	York	1m2¹/₂f Cls2 73-92 3yo Hcap good		£12,952
	10/10	Yarm	1m Cls5 Mdn 2yo heavy		£2,902

Late developer who was trained for St Leger last season, winning Great Voltigeur Stakes by eight lengths (possibly flattered as rivals toiled on bad ground) only to find trouble in running when third at Doncaster; produced a solid effort when second in Breeders' Cup Turf on final start.

1192 Sea Of Heartbreak (Ire)

5 b m Rock Of Gibraltar - Top Forty (Rainbow Quest)

Roger Charlton   D G Hardisty Bloodstock

PLACINGS: 01/111024/2421315-   **RPR 111**

Starts	1st	2nd	3rd	4th	Win & Pl
15	6	3	1	2	£138,848
	10/11	Lonc	1m4¹/₂f Gp2 good		£63,879
	7/11	Newb	1m4f Cls1 List good		£17,013
85	6/10	Newb	1m2f Cls4 77-85 3yo Hcap gd-fm		£4,209
78	6/10	Sals	1m2f Cls4 67-80 Hcap good		£6,476
	5/10	Sals	1m2f Cls5 3yo gd-fm		£3,238
	11/09	Wolv	7f Cls5 Mdn 2yo stand		£3,238

Progressed throughout last season, breaking through at Listed level at fourth attempt at Newbury before showing brilliant turn of foot to land weak Group 2 at Longchamp; close fifth in Group 1 in Canada on final start; likely to be aimed at Group 1 races for fillies and mares.

1193 Secret Asset (Ire) *(below, grey)*

7 gr g Clodovil - Skerray (Soviet Star)

Jane Chapple-Hyam

Simon & Jeanette Pierpoint & Paul Salisbury

PLACINGS: 0614/69240949171246- **RPR 115**

Starts	1st	2nd	3rd	4th	Win & Pl
41	6	5	4	6	£148,770
95	8/11 York	5¹/₂f Cls2 87-101 Hcap gd-sft			£19,407
89	7/11 Gdwd	5f Cls3 70-89 Hcap good			£9,704
92	12/10 Ling	6f Cls3 78-92 Hcap stand			£5,677
90	4/10 Wolv	6f Cls2 86-100 Hcap stand			£10,593
88	8/07 Bevl	5f Cls3 65-88 2yo Hcap gd-fm			£6,477
	6/07 Hayd	5f Cls5 Mdn 2yo gd-fm			£3,239

Produced by far a career-best when beaten just a short neck in Group 1 Prix de l'Abbaye at Longchamp; capable of winning Group races on that evidence but has to prove it wasn't a fluke and likely to be forced into better company as rated 19lb

higher than previous winning mark at York.

1194 Sepoy (Aus)

4 ch c Elusive Quality - Watchful (Danehill)

Peter Snowden (Aus)

Sheikh Mohammed

PLACINGS: 1/1112111111- **RPR 127+**

Starts	1st	2nd	3rd	4th	Win & Pl
11	10	1	-	-	£2,502,614
10/11	Flem	6f Gp1 3yo gd-sft			£197,712
10/11	Caul	5¹/₂f Gd2 Hcap gd-sft			£78,431
9/11	Moon	6f Gp1 soft			£199,346
9/11	Flem	6f Gp2 3yo gd-sft			£98,039
8/11	Caul	5¹/₂f List 3yo gd-sft			£39,542
4/11	Rose	6f Gp1 2yo gd-sft			£1,326,307
2/11	Caul	6f Gp1 2yo good			£401,961
2/11	Caul	5¹/₂f Gp3 2yo gd-sft			£49,510
1/11	Caul	5f List 2yo gd-sft			£39,216
9/10	Flem	5f List 2yo gd-sft			£33,333

Brilliant 6f performer for Sheikh Mohammed in Australia when winning multiple Group 1 contests and being crowned champion at two and three; due to move to Europe having stayed with current trainer for stint in Dubai; has Golden Jubilee Stakes at Royal Ascot as first major summer target.

1195 Shareta (Ire)

4 b f Sinndar - Shawara (Barathea)

Alain de Royer-Dupre (Fr)   H H Aga Khan

PLACINGS: 2/21711327-   **RPR 120**

Starts	1st	2nd	3rd	4th	Win & Pl
9	3	3	1	-	£905,717
	8/11	Deau	1m4¹/₂f Gp3 3yo good		£34,483
	7/11	Lonc	1m4f List 3yo gd-sft		£23,707
	5/11	Chan	1m2f 3yo good		£14,655

Impressive winner of Group 3 at Deauville in August and may have found very soft ground stretching stamina when third in Prix Vermeille; proved better than that when fine second in Arc at 66-1 (may have been slightly flattered by racing prominently) before never-nearer seventh in Japan Cup.

1196 Side Glance

5 br g Passing Glance - Averami (Averti)

Andrew Balding   Pearl Bloodstock Ltd

PLACINGS: 12/4651312/3113147-   **RPR 119**

Starts	1st	2nd	3rd	4th	Win & Pl
16	6	2	3	2	£199,566
	8/11	Sals	1m Cls1 Gp3 gd-fm		£28,355
	5/11	Wind	1m¹/₂f Cls1 List good		£17,031
	4/11	Asct	1m Cls1 List gd-fm		£17,031
96	8/10	Ches	7¹/₂f Cls2 89-103 Hcap gd-sft		£21,809
90	7/10	Asct	7f Cls2 80-103 3yo Hcap gd-fm		£31,155
	9/09	NmkR	6f Cls4 Auct Mdn 2yo good		£3,886

Much-improved miler in early part of last season, winning twice at Listed level and later adding Group 3 at Salisbury; just found out in better company, finishing third in Summer Mile and seventh in Queen Elizabeth II Stakes; should benefit from slight drop in grade.

1197 Sirius Prospect (USA)

4 b g Gone West - Stella Blue (Anabaa)

Dean Ivory   Miss N Yarrow

PLACINGS: 231/72101111

Starts	1st	2nd	3rd	4th	Win & Pl
11	6	2	1		£98,200

Made stunning progress in sprint handicaps last season, winning four of last five races in that grade despite going up 19lb before adding Listed race at Doncaster on final start; showed stunning turn of foot to land valuable Coral Sprint Trophy at York with lots in hand; already looks a Group 1 sprinter.

1198 Skilful

4 ch c Selkirk - Prowess (Peintre Celebre)

John Gosden   Mark Dixon & J L Rowsell

PLACINGS: 3/1212-   **RPR 111+**

Starts	1st	2nd	3rd	4th	Win & Pl
5	2	2	1	-	£23,004
93	9/11	Hayd	1m Cls2 86-98 Hcap gd-sft		£12,938
	5/11	Ling	1m Cls5 Mdn stand		£3,071

Galloped rivals into submission when wide-margin winner (despite being eased down) of Haydock handicap on penultimate start last season; looks Pattern class on that evidence and worth another chance after just unable to overcome drop to 7f in conditions race at Doncaster next time.

1199 Snow Fairy (Ire)

5 b m Intikhab - Woodland Dream (Charnwood Forest)

Ed Dunlop   Anamoine Limited

PLACINGS: 2439/1112411/422331-   **RPR 125+**

Starts	1st	2nd	3rd	4th	Win & Pl
19	7	4	4	3	£3,549,720
	11/11	Kyot	1m3f Gd1 firm		£741,617
	12/10	ShTn	1m2f Gp1 good		£906,921
	11/10	Kyot	1m3f Gd1 firm		£624,927
	7/10	Curr	1m4f Gp1 3yo gd-yld		£218,142
	6/10	Epsm	1m4f Cls1 Gp1 3yo good		£208,119
	5/10	Gdwd	1m2f Cls1 List 3yo good		£23,704
	7/09	Ling	6f Cls5 Mdn Auct 2yo stand		£2,388

Brilliant mare who burst on to the scene with four Group 1 victories in 2010; took time to find her feet last season but looked as good as ever when rubbing shoulders with leading colts, most notably when fast-finishing third in the Arc, before landing second win in Queen Elizabeth II Cup in Japan.

1200 So You Think (NZ)

6 b h High Chaparral - Triassic (Tights)

Aidan O'Brien (Ir)

Smith, Magnier, Tabor, Dato Tan & Tunku Yahaya

PLACINGS: 512/111113/11211426-   **RPR 129**

Starts	1st	2nd	3rd	4th	Win & Pl
20	12	4	1	1	£4,344,324
	9/11	Leop	1m2f Gp1 good		£374,569
	7/11	Sand	1m2f Cls1 Gp1 good		£226,840
	5/11	Curr	1m2¹/₂f Gp1 good		£112,241
	5/11	Curr	1m2f Gp3 gd-fm		£40,625
	10/10	Flem	1m2f Gp1 gd-sft		£334,722
	10/10	Moon	1m2f Gp1 good		£1,027,778
	10/10	Caul	1m2f Gp1 good		£135,000
	9/10	Caul	1m1f Gp1 good		£117,778
	8/10	Caul	7f Gp2 soft		£67,222
	10/09	Moon	1m2f Gp1 good		£898,058
	9/09	Rose	1m1f Gp3 3yo good		£79,757
	5/09	Rose	7f Hcap gd-sft		£8,519

Arrived from Australia with massive reputation last season and won three times at Group 1 level over 1m2f without quite fulfilling colossal expectations; stepped up to 1m4f to finish fourth in the Arc but trainer seems to prefer dropping to 1m; likely to win several more top races.

1201 Society Rock (Ire)

5 b h Rock Of Gibraltar - High Society (Key Of Luck)

James Fanshawe   Simon Gibson

PLACINGS: 5117/1227/0212600-   **RPR 119**

Starts	1st	2nd	3rd	4th	Win & Pl
15	4	4	-	-	£560,367
6/11	Asct	6f Cls1 Gp1 soft			£227,080
4/10	Asct	6f Cls1 List 3yo good			£22,708
9/09	NmkR	6f Cls2 2yo gd-fm			£135,425
8/09	Nott	6f Cls5 Mdn 2yo good			£3,724

High-class sprinter who will again have Royal Ascot as main aim having run best races for last two seasons at that meeting, winning Golden Jubilee Stakes last June; struggled to build on that last year but ran another fine race when second in Prix Maurice de Gheest.

1202 Sofast (Fr)

3 ch c Rock Of Gibraltar - Beautifix (Bering)

Freddy Head (Fr)   Wertheimer & Frere

PLACINGS: 1412-   **RPR 113**

Starts	1st	2nd	3rd	4th	Win & Pl
4	2	1	-	1	£135,857
9/11	Lonc	7f Gp3 2yo v soft			£39,310
8/11	Deau	6f 2yo good			£10,345

Slowly away when only fourth in the Prix Morny but put that behind him to take high rank among the French juveniles last season, winning Group 3 on very soft ground at Longchamp and proving equally effective in quicker conditions when just beaten by Dabirsim in Prix Jean-Luc Lagardere.

1203 Sole Power

5 b g Kyllachy - Demerger (Distant View)

Edward Lynam (Ir)   Mrs S Power

PLACINGS: 14/145651/031852039-   **RPR 120**

Starts	1st	2nd	3rd	4th	Win & Pl
21	4	2	4	2	£287,770
5/11	Hayd	5f Cls1 Gp2 gd-fm			£45,416
8/10	York	5f Cls1 Gp1 gd-fm			£136,248
4/10	Dund	5f stand			£10,075
11/09	Dund	5f Mdn 2yo stand			£9,057

Shock 100-1 winner of Nunthorpe Stakes in 2010 but proved that was no fluke with impressive win in Temple Stakes early last season; unlucky not to win again at top

level when fast-finishing third in Prix de l'Abbaye.

1204 Songcraft (Ire)

4 b g Singspiel - Baya (Nureyev)

Saeed Bin Suroor   Godolphin

PLACINGS: 11-11   **RPR 110**

Starts	1st	2nd	3rd	4th	Win & Pl
4	4	-	-	-	£134,538
110	2/12	Meyd	1m4f 100-113 Hcap good		£67,742
105	1/12	Meyd	1m2f 100-110 Hcap good		£46,452
	9/11	MsnL	1m1f 3yo soft		£10,000
	7/11	Claf	1m4f 3yo soft		£10,345

Won both starts for Andre Fabre last year without being seriously tested and maintained winning run at Meydan this spring following move to Godolphin; relished return to 1m4f when making it four from four in high-class handicap and looks a top middle-distance prospect.

1205 Spiritual Star (Ire)

3 b c Soviet Star - Million Spirits (Invincible Spirit)

Andrew Balding   Thurloe Thoroughbreds XXIX

PLACINGS: 317-   **RPR 106**

Starts	1st	2nd	3rd	4th	Win & Pl
3	1	-	1	-	£5,685
9/11	NmkR	7f Cls4 Mdn 2yo gd-fm			£5,175

Supplemented for Dewhurst Stakes after running away with Newmarket maiden by six lengths but faded into seventh having made the running; clearly well regarded and could prove better than bare form; likely to prove best on fast ground; due to leave for Hong Kong at end of July.

1206 Sri Putra

6 b h Oasis Dream - Wendylina (In The Wings)

Roger Varian   H R H Sultan Ahmad Shah

PLACINGS: 1157/1822280/233597-   **RPR 118**

Starts	1st	2nd	3rd	4th	Win & Pl
23	5	4	2	1	£464,812
	4/10	NmkR	1m1f Cls1 Gp3 gd-fm		£36,901
	8/09	Deau	1m2f Gp2 3yo good		£71,942
105	7/09	Asct	1m Cls2 82-105 3yo Hcap good		£28,040
	8/08	Sand	7f Cls1 Gp3 2yo good		£28,385
	6/08	Newb	6f Cls4 Mdn 2yo good		£5,828

Without a win since first start of 2010 but has run half of his races at Group 1 level since then and picked up good money last season when third in Eclipse and Prince of Wales's Stakes; below that form when dropped in grade, including when beaten at odds-on at Leicester.

1207 St Nicholas Abbey (Ire) *(below)*

5 b h Montjeu - Leaping Water (Sure Blade)

Aidan O'Brien (Ir)   D Smith, Mrs J Magnier & M Tabor

PLACINGS: 111/6/3113351-   RPR **124+**

Starts	1st	2nd	3rd	4th	Win & Pl
11	6	-	3	-	£1,655,787

11/11	Chur	1m4f Gd1 firm	£1,038,462
6/11	Epsm	1m4f Cls1 Gp1 good	£141,925
5/11	Ches	1m5½f Cls1 Gp3 gd-fm	£36,901
10/09	Donc	1m Cls1 Gp1 2yo gd-sft	£113,540
9/09	Curr	1m Gp2 2yo good	£72,573
8/09	Curr	1m Mdn 2yo sft-hvy	£11,740

Champion juvenile in 2009 who missed most of following season with string of niggling problems; bounced back to form superbly to win at Chester and Epsom last season, most notably in Coronation Cup, before frailties resurfaced; buoyed by use of Lasix to land Breeders' Cup Turf on final start.

1208 Starboard

3 b c Zamindar - Summer Shower (Sadler's Wells)

John Gosden   K Abdulla

PLACINGS: 61-   RPR **92+**

Starts	1st	2nd	3rd	4th	Win & Pl
2	1	-	-	-	£2,652

11/11	Rdcr	7f Cls5 Mdn 2yo good	£2,652

Disappointing favourite on Ascot debut but justified that market confidence when overcoming sluggish start to romp home by five lengths at Redcar on his second start at 1-2 with rivals well strung out; yet to run beyond 7f; could prove to be a high-class miler.

1209 Starscope

3 ch f Selkirk - Moon Goddess (Rainbow Quest)

John Gosden   Cheveley Park Stud

PLACINGS: 1-   RPR **87+**

Starts	1st	2nd	3rd	4th	Win & Pl
1	1	-	-	-	£4,398

10/11	NmkR	7f Cls4 Mdn 2yo good	£4,399

Sent off at 20-1 for her debut in a Newmarket maiden last October but belied those odds when showing a superb turn of foot to draw clear despite having dwelt at the start and raced greenly; likely to prove best at around 1m (out of a winning half-sister to Medicean); fascinating prospect.

1210 Strong Suit (USA)

4 ch c Rahy - Helwa (Silver Hawk)

Richard Hannon   Qatar Bloodstock Ltd

PLACINGS: 1132/613110-   RPR **126**

Starts	1st	2nd	3rd	4th	Win & Pl
10	5	1	2	-	£321,697

10/11	NmkR	7f Cls1 Gp2 good	£45,368
7/11	Gdwd	7f Cls1 Gp2 good	£79,394
6/11	Asct	7f Cls1 Gp3 3yo good	£39,739
6/10	Asct	6f Cls1 Gp2 2yo good	£56,770
5/10	Newb	6f Cls4 Mdn 2yo gd-fm	£4,209

Failed to build on Coventry Stakes win in 2010 until rejuvenated by breathing operation to win at Royal Ascot for second successive year; won twice more over 7f, including brilliant victory in Challenge Stakes; something to prove at 1m if asked to chase elusive Group 1.

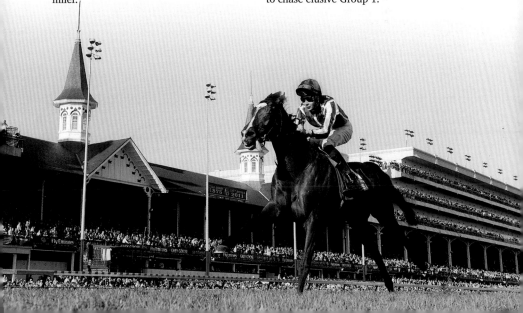

1211 Sunday Times

3 b f Holy Roman Emperor - Forever Times (So Factual)

Peter Chapple-Hyam   Allan Belshaw

PLACINGS: 41725-   **RPR** 110+

Starts	1st	2nd	3rd	4th	Win & Pl
5	1	1	-	1	£41,045
	8/11	Gdwd	6f Cls4 Mdn Auct 2yo good		£3,558

Fine second in Cheveley Park Stakes but ran well short of that form either side of that in Pattern company, struggling on bad ground at York and looking flat when disappointing fifth in Rockfel Stakes; something to prove but worth a chance to build on Cheveley Park run.

1212 Swedish Sailor

3 b c Monsun - Epitome (Nashwan)

Mahmood Al Zarooni   Godolphin

PLACINGS: 1-   **RPR** 84+

Starts	1st	2nd	3rd	4th	Win & Pl
1	1	-	-	-	£2,911
	10/11	Yarm	1m Cls5 Mdn 2yo soft		£2,911

Impressive when making a winning debut at Yarmouth last October, making most of the running and coming clear to beat smart newcomer Noble Mission by five lengths; seemed to relish the soft ground and should be suited by a stamina test; good middle-distance prospect.

1213 Sweet Lightning

7 b g Fantastic Light - Sweetness Herself (Unfuwain)

Michael Dods   Andrew Tinkler

PLACINGS: 66203/1259120/72471-   **RPR** 114

Starts	1st	2nd	3rd	4th	Win & Pl
28	5	6	3	4	£158,678
104	4/11	Donc	1m Cls2 93-110 Hcap good		£62,310
95	8/10	York	1m2¹/₂f Cls2 84-102 Hcap good		£12,952
90	5/10	Ches	1m2¹/₂f Cls2 86-100 Hcap good		£14,193
82	6/08	Ches	1m4¹/₂f Cls4 68-82 3yo Hcap good		£5,181
	4/08	Kemp	1m3f Cls6 Mdn 3-5yo stand		£2,590

Has done virtually all his racing over middle distances but produced clear career-best performance when dropped to 1m in Lincoln last season, benefiting from strong gallop to win well off mark of 104; missed rest of season but due to return to action in Dubai this spring.

1214 Takar (Ire)

3 b c Oratorio - Takarouna (Green Dancer)

John Oxx (Ir)   H H Aga Khan

PLACINGS: 41-   **RPR** 99+

Starts	1st	2nd	3rd	4th	Win & Pl
2	1	-	-	1	£10,629
	11/11	Leop	7f Mdn 2yo yield		£10,112

Won Leopardstown maiden by eight lengths last season over 7f having also travelled strongly before stopping quickly over 1m on his debut; well worth another crack at 1m and handled faster ground better than expected on final start; looks ready for Pattern company.

1215 Tales Of Grimm (USA)

3 b c Distorted Humor - Stupendous Miss (Dynaformer)

Sir Michael Stoute   Sir Robert Ogden

PLACINGS: 1-   **RPR** 88+

Starts	1st	2nd	3rd	4th	Win & Pl
1	1	-	-	-	£4,140
	8/11	Newb	7f Cls4 Mdn 2yo good		£4,140

320,000gns purchase who made strong impression on only start last season at Newbury, just touching off useful filly Firdaws despite being reported to be much less forward; well regarded at home and seems tough and genuine; likely to stay beyond 1m (dam won up to 1m2f).

1216 Tangerine Trees

7 b g Mind Games - Easy To Imagine (Cozzene)

Bryan Smart   Tangerine Trees Partnership

PLACINGS: 70330/1191411/10011-   **RPR** 116

Starts	1st	2nd	3rd	4th	Win & Pl
34	12	2	6	2	£251,675
	10/11	Lonc	5f Gp1 good		£147,776
	8/11	Bevl	5f Cls1 List gd-sft		£17,760
	4/11	NmkR	5f Cls1 Gp3 gd-fm		£28,385
	9/10	NmkR	5f Cls1 List soft		£19,870
	9/10	Bevl	5f Cls3 good		£6,231
77	6/10	Haml	5f Cls4 62-80 Hcap gd-fm		£6,476
74	4/10	Rdcr	5f Cls4 68-80 Hcap good		£4,209
69	4/10	Pont	5f Cls5 56-70 Hcap good		£2,590
67	7/09	Haml	5f Cls5 55-74 Hcap good		£4,533
65	6/09	Haml	5f Cls6 46-65 Hcap gd-fm		£2,388
63	6/09	Haml	5f Cls5 50-69 Hcap good		£3,238
	10/08	Wolv	6f Cls6 Auct Mdn 3yo std-fst		£3,071

Has a superb strike-rate for a sprinter and managed to break through at Group 1 level when landing Prix de l'Abbaye on final start, making all the running as main rivals stayed on too late; well suited by fast 5f but likely to find things a lot tougher under Group 1 penalty.

1217 Tazahum (USA)

4 b c Redoute's Choice - Huja (Alzao)

Sir Michael Stoute   Hamdan Al Maktoum

PLACINGS: 12/115424-   **RPR 116**

Starts		1st	2nd	3rd	4th	Win & Pl
8		3	2	-	2	£57,051
	5/11	Sand	1m Cls1 List 3yo gd-sft			£17,031
92	4/11	Sand	1m Cls2 83-96 3yo Hcap good			£11,029
	9/10	Kemp	7f Cls5 Mdn 2yo stand			£1,945

Slightly disappointing after winning first two starts last season, most notably pipping Fury in a Listed contest at Sandown; produced best subsequent run when chasing home Green Destiny over 1m1f in Group 3 at York; has shown best form on good to soft.

1218 Temple Meads (above)

4 ch c Avonbridge - Harryana (Efisio)

Ed McMahon   J C Fretwell

PLACINGS: 11418/

Starts		1st	2nd	3rd	4th	Win & Pl
5		3	-	-	1	£154,163
	9/10	Newb	6f Cls1 Gp2 2yo gd-fm			£37,468
	7/10	Newb	5f Cls2 2yo good			£98,480
	5/10	NmkR	5f Cls2 Mdn 2yo gd-sft			£9,714

Missed last season through injury but reported to be back in training this spring and looks a fascinating sprint prospect; had won three out of five starts as a juvenile in 2010, most notably in Mill Reef Stakes, and saddle slipped when eighth in Middle Park Stakes on final start.

1219 Tenth Star (Ire) *(above)*

3 b c Dansili - Alpha Lupi (Rahy)

Aidan O'Brien (Ir)

Niarchos Family, Mrs Magnier, Tabor & Smith

PLACINGS: 32132-					RPR **106**
Starts	1st	2nd	3rd	4th	Win & Pl
5	1	2	2	-	£49,629
6/11	Leop	7f List 2yo gd-fm			£21,013

Easily won a Listed race at Leopardstown before finishing a well-beaten third at 1-2 in the Tyros Stakes next time (only run on soft ground, with best runs both coming on good to firm); looked rusty after a long break but ran well when second in Royal Lodge Stakes over 1m.

1220 Testosterone (Ire)

4 b f Dansili - Epopee (Sadler's Wells)

Ed Dunlop

Ecurie La Boetie

PLACINGS: 3131120-					RPR **116**
Starts	1st	2nd	3rd	4th	Win & Pl
7	3	1	2	-	£199,879
6/11	StCl	1m4f Gp2 3yo gd-sft			£73,707
6/11	Chan	1m4f Gp3 3yo soft			£34,483
4/11	Lonc	1m3f 3yo good			£12,500

Changed hands for 1,200,000gns following fine season for Pascal Bary last year; showed progressive form to win pair of Group contests before producing best effort when second to Galikova in Prix Vermeille;

well below that form when disappointing in Arc; likely to be aimed at top middle-distance races.

1221 The Fugue

3 br f Dansili - Twyla Tharp (Sadler's Wells)

John Gosden

Lord Lloyd-Webber

PLACINGS: 1-					RPR **90+**
Starts	1st	2nd	3rd	4th	Win & Pl
1	1	-	-	-	£4,398
10/11	NmkR	7f Cls4 Mdn 2yo good			£4,399

Did remarkably well to post a winning debut at Newmarket last October, pulling away with useful runner-up (pair seven lengths clear) having got behind early; looked sure to benefit from outing and should improve over further (half-sister to 2m winner); potential Oaks filly.

1222 Thomas Chippendale (Ire)

3 b c Dansili - All My Loving (Sadler's Wells)

Sir Henry Cecil

Sir Robert Ogden

PLACINGS: 01-					RPR **88+**
Starts	1st	2nd	3rd	4th	Win & Pl
2	1	-	-	-	£4,010
10/11	Leic	1m½f Cls4 Mdn 2yo good			£4,011

375,000gns purchase who learned a lot from York debut and got things right at second attempt at Leicester when ridden with plenty of confidence and quickening up nicely under hands and heels; may well step up in trip (out of Oaks third) and could be a high-class colt.

1223 Tibet (Ire)

3 b c Dansili - Race For The Stars (Fusaichi Pegasus)
Aidan O'Brien (Ir)   Mrs John Magnier

PLACINGS: 16-				RPR **83**

Starts	1st	2nd	3rd	4th	Win & Pl
2	1	-	-	-	£6,206
	9/11	Gowr	1m Mdn 2yo good		£6,207

Bitterly disappointing when 7-4 favourite for Listed race at Leopardstown in November but had looked much better when just landing competitive maiden at Gowran Park on his debut (fourth reversed form later); may have found softer ground against him and may well bounce back.

1224 Timepiece

5 b m Zamindar - Clepsydra (Sadler's Wells)
Sir Henry Cecil   K Abdulla

PLACINGS: 211/428121/3411328-				RPR **116**

Starts	1st	2nd	3rd	4th	Win & Pl
16	6	4	2	2	£291,202
	7/11	NmkJ	1m Cls1 Gp1 good		£90,736
	6/11	Wwck	1m3f Cls1 List good		£17,031
	10/10	NmkR	1m2f Cls1 List gd-sft		£19,870
105	6/10	Asct	1m Cls1 List 93-107 3yo Hcap gd-fm		£28,385
	10/09	NmkR	1m Cls1 List 2yo good		£17,031
	10/09	Ling	1m Cls4 Mdn 2yo std-slw		£3,886

Has won over 1m3f but largely disappointed until tried over shorter trip last season, landing surprise win in Group 1 Falmouth Stakes over 1m; slightly flattered by bare form but still did well to finish third in Prix Rothschild and beaten by a short neck in Prix Jean Romanet over 1m2f.

1225 Times Up

6 b g Olden Times - Princess Genista (Ile De Bourbon)
John Dunlop   Mrs I H Stewart-Brown & M J Meacock

PLACINGS: 130/5144221/4112315-				RPR **116+**

Starts	1st	2nd	3rd	4th	Win & Pl
23	7	5	4	3	£195,746
	9/11	NmkR	2m Cls1 List gd-fm		£17,013
	5/11	York	1m6f Cls1 List good		£19,870
102	5/11	NmkR	1m4f Cls2 87-102 Hcap gd-fm		£24,924
97	11/10	Donc	1m4f Cls2 87-108 Hcap gd-sft		£62,310
89	7/10	NmkJ	1m4f Cls3 80-93 Hcap gd-fm		£9,714
84	8/09	NmkJ	1m4f Cls4 66-84 Hcap gd-fm		£5,181
	7/09	Pont	1m4f Cls5 Mdn gd-sft		£3,238

Won November Handicap in 2010 and

maintained progress early last season, easily winning at York on first run at Listed level; progress stalled on next two starts but relished step up to 2m when winning second Listed prize; raced too keenly in Long Distance Cup on final start.

1226 Titus Mills (Ire)

4 ch c Dubawi - Anayid (A.P. Indy)
Brian Meehan   Sangster Family

PLACINGS: 110/				

Starts	1st	2nd	3rd	4th	Win & Pl
3	2	-	-	-	£19,169
	9/10	Gdwd	7f Cls1 List 2yo good		£13,341
	7/10	Asct	7f Cls4 Mdn 2yo good		£5,828

Missed last season through injury but reported to be back in training this spring and remains a high-class prospect on juvenile form of 2010; won first two starts, including strong Listed race at Goodwood, before going wrong when sent off just 13-2 for Racing Post Trophy.

1227 Top Offer

3 b c Dansili - Zante (Zafonic)
Roger Charlton   K Abdulla

PLACINGS: 1-				RPR **92+**

Starts	1st	2nd	3rd	4th	Win & Pl
1	1	-	-	-	£4,140
	8/11	Newb	7f Cls4 Mdn 2yo good		£4,140

Leading 2,000 Guineas hope having won only start at Newbury last season, quickening up smartly and stretching well clear with the field spreadeagled; looked likely to improve for debut but missed late-season targets after a setback; has potential to become a top-class miler.

1228 Tough As Nails (Ire)

3 gr c Dark Angel - Soreze (Gallic League)
Michael Mulvany (Ir)   Laurence Mulvany

PLACINGS: 1d1223559-				RPR **111**

Starts	1st	2nd	3rd	4th	Win & Pl
8	1	3	1	-	£54,844
	4/11	Tipp	5f Mdn 2yo yld-sft		£7,733

Failed to follow up maiden win (had been disqualified at the Curragh prior to that) but ran several good races in top company, most notably when third in Phoenix Stakes; went off the boil later in season, though twice unsuited by step up to 7f; useful sprinting type.

1229 Treasure Beach

4 b c Galileo - Honorine (Mark Of Esteem)

Aidan O'Brien (Ir)　　　　D Smith, Mrs J Magnier & M Tabor

PLACINGS: 21123/1214103-　　　　**RPR 122**

Starts	1st	2nd	3rd	4th	Win & Pl
12	5	3	2	1	£1,245,009
	8/11	Arlt	1m2f Gd1 3yo yield		£149,231
	6/11	Curr	1m4f Gp1 3yo good		£625,000
	5/11	Ches	1m4¹/₂f Cls1 Gp3 3yo gd-fm		£28,385
84	8/10	Gway	7f 76-90 2yo Hcap gd-fm		£17,257
	8/10	Gowr	7f Mdn 2yo good		£9,465

Tough and consistent middle-distance performer last season, losing out close home in the Derby behind Pour Moi and proving that was no fluke with wins in Irish Derby and Secretariat Stakes; had limitations exposed in stronger Group 1 races and used as a pacemaker in the Arc.

1230 Trumpet Major (Ire)

3 b c Arakan - Ashford Cross (Cape Cross)

Richard Hannon　　　　John Manley

PLACINGS: 31021415-　　　　**RPR 114**

Starts	1st	2nd	3rd	4th	Win & Pl
8	3	1	1	1	£70,539
	9/11	Donc	7f Cls1 Gp2 2yo gd-fm		£42,533
	8/11	NmkJ	7f Cls2 2yo gd-fm		£7,763
	5/11	Gdwd	6f Cls4 Mdn 2yo gd-fm		£4,533

Showed patchy form during busy campaign last season but smart when getting his favoured good to firm ground, winning

Champagne Stakes at Doncaster; unlucky in Dewhurst Stakes on final start, staying on strongly into close fifth having suffered trouble in running; should continue to thrive.

1231 Twice Over *(above, left)*

7 b/br h Observatory - Double Crossed (Caerleon)

Sir Henry Cecil　　　　K Abdulla

PLACINGS: 1113/021231/1965110-　　　　**RPR 126**

Starts	1st	2nd	3rd	4th	Win & Pl
29	12	3	6	1	£2,424,143
	8/11	York	1m2¹/₂f Cls1 Gp1 gd-sft		£396,970
	7/11	York	1m2¹/₂f Cls1 Gp2 good		£56,710
	3/11	Meyd	1m2f Gp2 stand		£115,385
	10/10	NmkR	1m2f Cls1 Gp1 gd-sft		£213,739
	7/10	Sand	1m2f Cls1 Gp1 gd-fm		£283,850
	10/09	NmkR	1m2f Cls1 Gp1 good		£213,739
	9/09	Gdwd	1m2f Cls1 List good		£22,708
	9/09	Donc	1m2¹/₂f Cls2 3-5yo good		£15,578
	7/08	MsnL	1m2f Gp2 3yo good		£167,647
	4/08	NmkR	1m2f Cls1 Gp3 3yo good		£28,385
	11/07	NmkR	1m2f Cls2 2yo good		£9,348
	10/07	NmkR	1m Cls3 Mdn 2yo good		£6,477

High-class performer at 1m2f, winning four Group 1 races spread across last three seasons, though often gets found out in stronger races at top level; prefers tracks with long home straight, gaining both British wins at York last season while disappointing twice at Ascot (without a win in five attempts there).

1232 Twirl (Ire)

3 b f Galileo - Butterfly Cove (Storm Cat)

Aidan O'Brien (Ir)   Derrick Smith

PLACINGS: 31-   **RPR 94+**

Starts	1st	2nd	3rd	4th	Win & Pl
2	1	-	1	-	£11,137
	11/11	Leop	7f Mdn 2yo yield.................................£10,112		

Followed up promising debut third with impressive win at Leopardstown in November, breaking well from a poor draw and stretching six and a half lengths clear; faced only moderate opposition but exciting filly on pedigree (sister to multiple Group 1 winner Misty For Me).

1233 Up (Ire)

3 b f Galileo - Halland Park Lass (Spectrum)

Aidan O'Brien (Ir)   Derrick Smith

PLACINGS: 014-   **RPR 105**

Starts	1st	2nd	3rd	4th	Win & Pl
3	1	-	-	1	£46,194
	9/11	Dund	1m Mdn 2yo stand................................£7,733		

Justified connections' bold decision to go to Breeders' Cup when finishing fourth in Juvenile Fillies Turf, staying on well in final furlong having got too far back early; reported to have relished fast surface when winning maiden at Dundalk prior to that; should stay at least 1m2f.

1234 Vadamar (Fr)

4 b c Dalakhani - Vadawina (Unfuwain)

Alain de Royer-Dupre (Fr)   H H Aga Khan

PLACINGS: 61/137310-   **RPR 119**

Starts	1st	2nd	3rd	4th	Win & Pl
8	3	-	2	-	£126,164
10/11	Lonc	1m2f Gp2 good £63,879			
4/11	StCl	1m2½f List 3yo heavy £23,707			
11/10	MsnL	1m1f 2yo v soft £15,044			

Regarded as a Derby horse early last season but beaten at odds-on in trial at Saint-Cloud (won by Pour Moi) before finishing seventh at Epsom; returned from long break to finish third to Reliable Man in Prix Niel before winning Group 2; found good to firm ground too quick in Hong Kong.

1235 Vita Nova (Ire)

5 b m Galileo - Treca (Darshaan)

Sir Henry Cecil   H E Sheikh Sultan Bin Khalifa Al Nahyan

PLACINGS: 11/12229-   **RPR 119**

Starts		1st	2nd	3rd	4th	Win & Pl
7		3	3	-	-	£104,553
87	5/11	NmkR	1m2f Cls3 77-89 Hcap gd-fm £7,447			
80	8/10	Sals	1m4f Cls4 71-84 3yo Hcap soft £4,209			
	6/10	Kemp	1m4f Cls5 Mdn stand £2,590			

Desperately unlucky not to follow up wide-margin handicap win in a higher grade last season, most notably when saddle slipped in Lancashire Oaks; chased home Blue

Bunting in Yorkshire Oaks before disappointing at Ascot on Champions Day; looks capable of Group 1 win.

1236 Wading (Ire)

3 b f Montjeu - Cherry Hinton (Green Desert)

Aidan O'Brien (Ir)   Mrs John Magnier, M Tabor & D Smith

PLACINGS: 211-   **RPR 115+**

Starts	1st	2nd	3rd	4th	Win & Pl
3	2	1	-	-	£43,827
10/11	NmkR	7f Cls1 Gp2 2yo good			£34,026
9/11	Dund	7f Mdn 2yo stand			£7,733

Built on highly promising debut when landing Dundalk maiden and improved again with tremendous win in Rockfel Stakes at Newmarket; looks to have enough speed to take a hand in 1,000 Guineas but

promises to be even better over middle distances on pedigree; top-class prospect.

1237 Was (Ire)

3 b f Galileo - Alluring Park (Green Desert)

Aidan O'Brien (Ir)   Michael Tabor

PLACINGS: 1-   **RPR 91+**

Starts	1st	2nd	3rd	4th	Win & Pl
1	1	-	-	-	£10,112
8/11	Curr	1m Mdn 2yo good			£10,112

Bought for a whopping 1,200,000gns and confirmed status as a filly of immense potential when running away with a decent Curragh maiden on her only start, defying uneasiness in the market; expected to stay well by her trainer and could be a leading Oaks contender.

1238 Western Aristocrat (USA)

4 b/br c Mr Greeley - Aristocratic Lady (Kris S)

Jeremy Noseda   Vinery Stables

PLACINGS: 1/1337113-   **RPR 114**

Starts	1st	2nd	3rd	4th	Win & Pl
8	4	-	3	-	£142,855
10/11	Belm	1m1f Gd1 3yo Hcap firm			£96,154
9/11	Kemp	1m Cls4 stand			£4,075
5/11	Hayd	7f Cls3 79-88 3yo Hcap gd-fm			£8,419
10/10	NmkR	7f Cls4 Mdn 2yo gd-sft			£4,209

Stepped up sharply in class following handicap win on return last season, finishing third in pair of Group 3 races; found

more success when campaigned in America late last year, winning Grade 1 handicap before fine third in Hollywood Derby; may still be on the upgrade.

1239 Whiplash Willie

4 ch c Phoenix Reach - Santa Isobel (Nashwan)

Andrew Balding · J C & S R Hitchins

PLACINGS: 6413/27112- · RPR **110**

Starts		1st	2nd	3rd	4th	Win & Pl
9		3	2	1	1	£49,803
91	7/11	Gdwd	1m4f Cls2 77-100 3yo Hcap good			£24,900
79	6/11	Sals	1m4f Cls3 74-90 3yo Hcap soft			£7,771
	10/10	Ling	1m Cls6 Auct Mdn 2yo stand			£2,047

Progressive over middle distances and beyond last season and was an outside St Leger hope before injury setback; went up 18lb in handicap following wins at Salisbury and Goodwood but improved again when stepped up to 1m6f at York to finish second in Melrose Stakes.

1240 Wigmore Hall (Ire)

5 b g High Chaparral - Love And Laughter (Theatrical)

Michael Bell · M B Hawtin

PLACINGS: 5/122311225/1307419- · RPR **118**

Starts		1st	2nd	3rd	4th	Win & Pl
19		6	4	2	1	£860,050
	9/11	Wood	1m4f Gd1 firm			£192,308
	3/11	Meyd	1m1f Gp2 good			£96,154
	8/10	NmkJ	1m2f Cls3 2yo good			£8,723
101	7/10	York	1m2½f Cls2 90-105 Hcap gd-fm			£97,140
88	4/10	NmkR	1m2f Cls3 78-88 3yo Hcap gd-fm			£9,066
	9/09	NmkR	1m Cls4 Auct Mdn 2yo gd-fm			£3,886

Campaigned almost exclusively in top foreign races last season, making Group 1 breakthrough in Canada when stepped up to 1m4f; appeared to be found out by drop in trip and step up in class when ninth in Champion Stakes on final start.

1241 Wild Coco (Ger)

4 ch f Shirocco - Wild Side (Sternkoenig)

Sir Henry Cecil · Gestut Rottgen

PLACINGS: 21158- · RPR **114+**

Starts		1st	2nd	3rd	4th	Win & Pl
5		2	1	-	-	£27,259
	7/11	NmkJ	1m4f Cls1 List gd-sft			£22,684
	6/11	Hayd	1m4f Cls5 Mdn gd-sft			£2,267

Impressive when winning twice on good to soft last season, following maiden win with narrow defeat of Meeznah in Newmarket Listed race; below that level when beaten twice subsequently on quicker going; should progress.

1242 Wizz Kid (Ire)

4 b f Whipper - Lidanski (Soviet Star)

Robert Collet (Fr) · Mme Maeve Mahony

PLACINGS: 142/81552- · RPR **115**

Starts		1st	2nd	3rd	4th	Win & Pl
8		2	2	-	1	£201,809
	6/11	Chan	5f Gp2 soft			£63,879
	7/10	Deau	5f List 2yo gd-sft			£24,336

Beat Prohibit in Group 2 at Chantilly when dropped to 5f for first time since debut and ran well in defeat when second best of those drawn on wrong side in Nunthorpe and beating all bar Deacon Blues in Champions Sprint at Ascot.

1243 World Domination (USA) *(left)*

4 b c Empire Maker - Reams Of Verse (Nureyev)

Sir Henry Cecil · K Abdulla

PLACINGS: 140- · RPR **101**

Starts		1st	2nd	3rd	4th	Win & Pl
3		1	-	-	1	£13,235
	4/11	Newb	1m3f Cls4 Mdn 3yo gd-fm			£5,181

Subject of glowing gallops reports prior to

successful debut at Newbury last season but failed to live up to that promise when tame fourth to Carlton House in the Dante and last in King Edward VII Stakes; put away with view to coming back better this year; still a top prospect.

1244 Wrote (Ire)

3 b c High Chaparral - Desert Classic (Green Desert)
Aidan O'Brien (Ir)   Mrs John Magnier, M Tabor & D Smith
PLACINGS: 31131-   **RPR 115**

Starts	1st	2nd	3rd	4th	Win & Pl
5	3	-	2	-	£383,310
89	11/11	Chur	1m Gd1 2yo good		£346,154
	8/11	Gway	7f 75-89 2yo Hcap good		£16,810
	8/11	Cork	1m Mdn Auct 2yo gd-fm		£8,922

Earned step up to Pattern level with nursery win at Galway but still looked green when third in Royal Lodge Stakes at Newmarket, possibly struggling to cope with undulations; did much better when running away with Breeders' Cup Juvenile Turf; should cope with middle distances.

1245 Wrotham Heath

3 b c Dansili - Native Justice (Alleged)
Sir Henry Cecil   K Abdulla
PLACINGS: 71-   **RPR 92+**

Starts	1st	2nd	3rd	4th	Win & Pl
2	1	-	-	-	£3,234
	10/11	Nott	1m¹/₂f Cls5 Mdn 2yo gd-sft		£3,235

Bitterly disappointing on debut at Newmarket having been well touted beforehand but put that right next time at Nottingham when storming to a six-length win; looks a smart prospect and may well stay 1m4f; high knee action suggests he may prefer cut in the ground.

1246 Yellow Rosebud (Ire)

3 b f Jeremy - Nebraas (Green Desert)
Dermot Weld (Ir)   Dr R Lambe
PLACINGS: 124-   **RPR 105**

Starts	1st	2nd	3rd	4th	Win & Pl
3	1	1	-	1	£40,439
	6/11	Leop	7f Mdn 2yo good		£10,112

Ran a cracker when chasing home Maybe in Debutante Stakes at the Curragh, pipping subsequent Cheveley Park winner Lightening Pearl for second; disappointing fourth when stepped up to 1m in Prix Marcel Boussac at Longchamp; remains a potentially smart filly.

1247 York Glory (USA)

4 rg c Five Star Day - Minicolony (Pleasant Colony)
Kevin Ryan   Salman Rashed & Mohamed Khalifa
PLACINGS: 3212122115-   **RPR 106+**

Starts	1st	2nd	3rd	4th	Win & Pl
10	4	4	1	-	£26,311
88	8/11	York	5f Cls2 81-94 3yo Hcap good		£12,938
83	8/11	Thsk	5f Cls4 71-83 3yo Hcap gd-sft		£4,075
	6/11	Pont	6f Cls5 3yo gd-fm		£2,267
	5/11	Sthl	7f Cls6 Auct Mdn 3-4yo stand		£1,706

Made tremendous progress in handicap sprints last season, rising 23lb in handicap following maiden win at Southwell; did really well when landing big handicap at York and unlucky not to complete hat-trick having broken badly in Portland Handicap; has lots more to offer.

1248 Zantenda

3 b f Zamindar - Tender Morn (Dayjur)
Freddy Head (Fr)   Wertheimer & Frere
PLACINGS: 113-   **RPR 105+**

Starts	1st	2nd	3rd	4th	Win & Pl
3	1	-	1	-	£74,387
	9/11	Lonc	1m Gp3 2yo gd-sft		£34,483
	8/11	Deau	7¹/₂f 2yo soft		£10,345

Blotted her copybook when only third in Prix Marcel Boussac (raced much too keenly and looked unsuited by quicker surface); remains a top-class prospect on previous Group 3 win at Longchamp and trainer brought back Moonlight Cloud from poor effort in same race in 2010.

1249 Zip Top (Ire)

3 b c Smart Strike - Zofzig (Danzig)
Mahmood Al Zarooni   Sheikh Mohammed
PLACINGS: 1632-   **RPR 111**

Starts	1st	2nd	3rd	4th	Win & Pl
4	1	1	1	-	£63,650
	6/11	Leop	7f Mdn 2yo good		£10,112

Looked a good middle-distance prospect for Jim Bolger last season; not right when sixth in Anglesey Stakes but bounced back to finish good third in Somerville Tattersall Stakes (stayed on late over 7f) and proved well suited by step up to 1m when getting closest to brilliant winner Camelot in Racing Post Trophy.

Pen portraits written by Dylan Hill

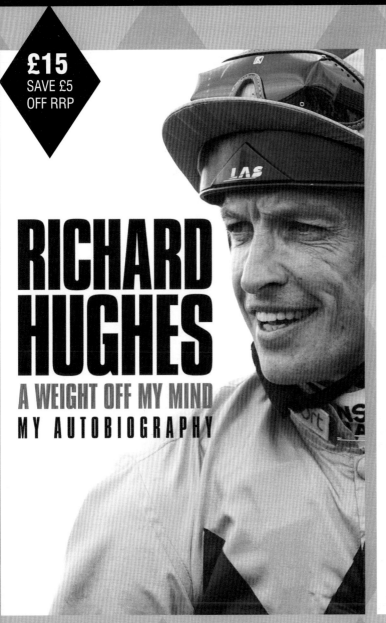

TEN TO FOLLOW HORSES LISTED BY TRAINER

Alan Bailey
1020 Barbican
Andrew Balding
1029 Bonfire
1062 Desert Law (Ire)
1124 Lay Time
1196 Side Glance
1205 Spiritual Star (Ire)
1239 Whiplash Willie
Mme C Barande-Barbe
1044 Cirrus Des Aigles (Fr)
David Barron
1107 Hitchens (Ire)
P Bary
1220 Testosterone (Ire)
J-M Beguigne
1128 Loi (Ire)
Michael Bell
1134 Margot Did (Ire)
1240 Wigmore Hall (Ire)
J S Bolger
1007 Alla Speranza
1160 Parish Hall (Ire)
1249 Zip Top (Ire)
Marco Botti
1028 Bohemian Melody
1083 Fanunalter
1116 Joshua Tree (Ire)
Henry Candy
1009 Amour Propre
Sir Henry Cecil
1042 Chachamaidee (Ire)
1091 Frankel
1115 Jet Away
1154 Noble Mission
1222 Thomas Chippendale (Ire)
1224 Timepiece
1231 Twice Over
1235 Vita Nova (Ire)
1241 Wild Coco (Ger)
1243 World Domination (USA)
1245 Wrotham Heath
Mick Channon
1189 Samitar

Jane Chapple-Hyam
1193 Secret Asset (Ire)
Peter Chapple-Hyam
1211 Sunday Times
Roger Charlton
1002 Al Kazeem
1021 Bated Breath
1045 Cityscape
1053 Cry Fury
1098 Genki (Ire)
1192 Sea Of Heartbreak (Ire)
1227 Top Offer
N Clement
1092 French Fifteen (Fr)
Robert Collet
1112 Immortal Verse (Ire)
1242 Wizz Kid (Ire)
Hugh Collingridge
1197 Sirius Prospect
Robert Cowell
1170 Prohibit
Clive Cox
1166 Poet
Luca Cumani
1120 Kirthill (Ire)
1171 Quest For Peace (Ire)
Tom Dascombe
1033 Brown Panther
A De Royer-Dupre
1179 Reliable Man
1195 Shareta (Ire)
1234 Vadamar (Fr)
M Delzangles
1068 Dunaden (Fr)
Michael Dods
1213 Sweet Lightning
Ed Dunlop
1034 Burwaaz
1152 Native Khan (Fr)
1175 Red Cadeaux
1199 Snow Fairy (Ire)
John Dunlop
1225 Times Up

Michael Easterby
1110 Hoof It
Tim Easterby
1101 Hamish McGonagall
David Elsworth
1106 Highland Castle
A Fabre
1022 Be Fabulous (Ger)
1031 Brigantin (USA)
1099 Golden Lilac (Ire)
1133 Mandaean
1138 Meandre (Fr)
Richard Fahey
1132 Majestic Myles (Ire)
James Fanshawe
1060 Deacon Blues
1201 Society Rock (Ire)
C Ferland
1054 Dabirsim (Fr)
Jeremy Gask
1139 Medicean Man
John Gosden
1013 Arctic Cosmos (USA)
1046 Colombian (Ire)
1071 Elusive Kate (USA)
1080 Fallen For You
1085 Fencing (USA)
1136 Masked Marvel
1151 Nathaniel (Ire)
1172 Questioning (Ire)
1198 Skilful
1208 Starboard
1209 Starscope
1221 The Fugue
William Haggas
1023 Beaten Up
1057 Dancing Rain (Ire)
1063 Diala (Ire)
1076 Entifaadha
1089 Firebeam
1095 Fury
1103 Harris Tweed
Richard Hannon
1024 Best Terms

1032 Bronterre
1041 Census (Ire)
1043 Chandlery (Ire)
1050 Coupe De Ville (Ire)
1051 Crius (Ire)
1067 Dubawi Gold
1102 Harbour Watch (Ire)
1118 King Torus (Ire)
1126 Libranno
1145 Monsieur Chevalier (Ire)
1210 Strong Suit (USA)
1230 Trumpet Major (Ire)
Jessica Harrington
1025 Bible Belt (Ire)
1065 Dragon Pulse (Ire)
1169 Princess Sinead (Ire)
1180 Remember Alexander
F Head
1096 Galikova (Fr)
1147 Moonlight Cloud
1202 Sofast (Fr)
1248 Zantenda
Charles Hills
1011 Angels Will Fall (Ire)
1017 Balty Boys (Ire)
1100 Gray Pearl
1162 Perennial
1173 Ransom Note
1177 Red Jazz (USA)
1178 Redwood
Mark Johnston
1047 Colour Vision (Fr)
1117 Jukebox Jury (Ire)
David Lanigan
1131 Main Sequence (USA)
E Lellouche
1165 Planteur (Ire)
Edward Lynam
1203 Sole Power
G M Lyons
1127 Lightening Pearl (Ire)
George Margarson
1174 Rebellious Guest

David Marnane
1155 Nocturnal Affair (Saf)
Alan McCabe
1039 Caspar Netscher
Ed McMahon
1014 Artistic Jewel (Ire)
1218 Temple Meads
Brian Meehan
1072 Elusivity (Ire)
1148 Most Improved (Ire)
1226 Titus Mills (Ire)
Peter G Moody
1026 Black Caviar (Aus)
Hughie Morrison
1048 Coquet
1161 Pastoral Player
Michael Mulvany
1228 Tough As Nails (Ire)
David Nicholls
1114 Inxile (Ire)
Jeremy Noseda
1104 Harvard N Yale (USA)
1163 Peter Martins (USA)
1238 Western Aristocrat (USA)
A P O'Brien
1012 Apollo (Ire)
1015 Astrology (Ire)
1016 Await The Dawn (USA)
1036 Camelot
1052 Crusade (USA)
1055 Daddy Long Legs (USA)
1059 David Livingston (Ire)
1079 Excelebration (Ire)
1081 Fame And Glory
1094 Furner's Green (Ire)
1109 Homecoming Queen (Ire)
1113 Imperial Monarch (Ire)
1121 Kissed (Ire)
1125 Learn (Ire)

1137 Maybe (Ire)
1141 Memphis Tennessee (Ire)
1153 Nephrite
1167 Power
1181 Reply (Ire)
1200 So You Think (NZ)
1207 St Nicholas Abbey (Ire)
1219 Tenth Star (Ire)
1223 Tibet (Ire)
1229 Treasure Beach
1232 Twirl (Ire)
1233 Up (Ire)
1236 Wading (Ire)
1237 Was (Ire)
1244 Wrote (Ire)
John M Oxx
1001 Akeed Mofeed
1004 Alanza (Ire)
1030 Born To Sea (Ire)
1035 Call To Battle (Ire)
1187 Saddler's Rock (Ire)
1214 Takar (Ire)
Kevin Prendergast
1122 La Collina (Ire)
P J Prendergast
1049 Coral Wave (Ire)
John Quinn
1176 Red Duke (Ire)
Jozef Roszival
1159 Overdose
J-C Rouget
1000 Abtaal (USA)
1019 Baraan (Fr)
Kevin Ryan
1018 Bapak Chinta (USA)
1027 Bogart
1135 Masamah (Ire)
1158 Our Jonathan
1247 York Glory (USA)

P Schiergen
1058 Danedream (Ger)
David Simcock
1111 I'm A Dreamer (Ire)
Bryan Smart
1216 Tangerine Trees
Peter Snowden
1105 Helmet (Aus)
1194 Sepoy (Aus)
Sir Michael Stoute
1037 Carlton House (USA)
1086 Fiorente (Ire)
1191 Sea Moon
1215 Tales Of Grimm (USA)
1217 Tazahum (USA)
Saeed Bin Suroor
1006 Alkimos (Ire)
1061 Delegator
1108 Holberg (UAE)
1129 Lost In The Moment (Ire)
1143 Modun (Ire)
1183 Rio De La Plata (USA)
1186 Saamidd
1204 Songcraft (Ire)
James Toller
1188 Saigon
Marcus Tregoning
1040 Cavaleiro (Ire)
J Van Handenhove
1008 American Devil (Fr)
Roger Varian
1003 Alainmaar (Fr)
1005 Aljamaaheer (Ire)
1070 Ektihaam (Ire)
1073 Elzaam (Aus)
1077 Eton Forever (Ire)
1084 Farraaj (Ire)
1087 Firdaws (USA)
1149 Nahrain

1206 Sri Putra
Edward Vaughan
1056 Dance And Dance (Ire)
David Wachman
1088 Fire Lily (Ire)
1182 Requinto (Ire)
Chris Wall
1168 Premio Loco (USA)
1185 Royal Rock
Dermot Weld
1010 Anam Allta (Ire)
1074 Emulous
1082 Famous Name
1184 Rite Of Passage
1190 Sapphire (Ire)
1246 Yellow Rosebud (Ire)
Stuart Williams
1078 Eton Rifles (Ire)
Mahmood Al Zarooni
1038 Casamento (Ire)
1064 Discourse (USA)
1066 Dubai Prince (Ire)
1069 Ecliptic (USA)
1075 Encke (USA)
1090 Fox Hunt (Ire)
1093 French Navy
1097 Gamilati
1119 Kinglet (USA)
1123 Lacily (USA)
1130 Lyric Of Light
1140 Meeznah (USA)
1142 Mighty Ambition (USA)
1144 Mojave (Ire)
1146 Monterosso
1150 Naqshabban (USA)
1156 Ocean War
1157 Opinion Poll (Ire)
1164 Pimpernel (Ire)
1212 Swedish Sailor

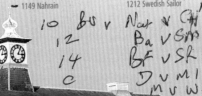

INDEX OF HORSES

David Marnane
1155 Nocturnal Affair (Saf)
Alan McCabe
1039 Caspar Netscher
Ed McMahon
1014 Artistic Jewel (Ire)
1218 Temple Meads
Brian Meehan
1072 Elusivity (Ire)
1148 Most Improved (Ire)
1226 Titus Mills (Ire)
Peter G Moody
1026 Black Caviar (Aus)
Hughie Morrison
1048 Coquet
1161 Pastoral Player
Michael Mulvany
1228 Tough As Nails (Ire)
David Nicholls
1114 Inxile (Ire)
Jeremy Noseda
1104 Harvard N Yale (USA)
1163 Peter Martins (USA)
1238 Western Aristocrat (USA)
A P O'Brien
1012 Apollo (Ire)
1015 Astrology (Ire)
1016 Await The Dawn (USA)
1036 Camelot
1052 Crusade (USA)
1055 Daddy Long Legs (USA)
1059 David Livingston (Ire)
1079 Excelebration (Ire)
1081 Fame And Glory
1094 Furner's Green (Ire)
1109 Homecoming Queen (Ire)
1113 Imperial Monarch (Ire)
1121 Kissed (Ire)
1125 Learn (Ire)

1137 Maybe (Ire)
1141 Memphis Tennessee (Ire)
1153 Nephrite
1167 Power
1181 Reply (Ire)
1200 So You Think (NZ)
1207 St Nicholas Abbey (Ire)
1219 Tenth Star (Ire)
1223 Tibet (Ire)
1229 Treasure Beach
1232 Twirl (Ire)
1233 Up (Ire)
1236 Wading (Ire)
1237 Was (Ire)
1244 Wrote (Ire)
John M Oxx
1001 Akeed Mofeed
1004 Alanza (Ire)
1030 Born To Sea (Ire)
1035 Call To Battle (Ire)
1187 Saddler's Rock (Ire)
1214 Takar (Ire)
Kevin Prendergast
1122 La Collina (Ire)
P J Prendergast
1049 Coral Wave (Ire)
John Quinn
1176 Red Duke (USA)
Jozef Roszival
1159 Overdose
J-C Rouget
1000 Abtaal (USA)
1019 Baraan (Fr)
Kevin Ryan
1018 Bapak Chinta (USA)
1027 Bogart
1135 Masamah (Ire)
1158 Our Jonathan
1247 York Glory (USA)

P Schiergen
1058 Danedream (Ger)
David Simcock
1111 I'm A Dreamer (Ire)
Bryan Smart
1216 Tangerine Trees
Peter Snowden
1105 Helmet (Aus)
1194 Sepoy (Aus)
Sir Michael Stoute
1037 Carlton House (USA)
1086 Fiorente (Ire)
1191 Sea Moon
1215 Tales Of Grimm (USA)
1217 Tazahum (USA)
Saeed Bin Suroor
1006 Alkimos (Ire)
1061 Delegator
1108 Holberg (UAE)
1129 Lost In The Moment (Ire)
1143 Modun (Ire)
1183 Rio De La Plata (USA)
1186 Saamidd
1204 Songcraft (Ire)
James Toller
1188 Saigon
Marcus Tregoning
1040 Cavaleiro (Ire)
J Van Handenhove
1008 American Devil (Fr)
Roger Varian
1003 Alainmaar (Fr)
1005 Aljamaaheer (Ire)
1070 Ektihaam (Ire)
1073 Elzaam (Aus)
1077 Eton Forever (Ire)
1084 Farraaj (Ire)
1087 Firdaws (USA)
1149 Nahrain

1206 Sri Putra
Edward Vaughan
1056 Dance And Dance (Ire)
David Wachman
1088 Fire Lily (Ire)
1182 Requinto (Ire)
Chris Wall
1168 Premio Loco (USA)
1185 Royal Rock
Dermot Weld
1010 Anam Allta (Ire)
1074 Emulous
1082 Famous Name
1184 Rite Of Passage
1190 Sapphire (Ire)
1246 Yellow Rosebud (Ire)
Stuart Williams
1078 Eton Rifles (Ire)
Mahmood Al Zarooni
1038 Casamento (Ire)
1064 Discourse (USA)
1066 Dubai Prince (Ire)
1069 Ecliptic (USA)
1075 Encke (USA)
1090 Fox Hunt (Ire)
1093 French Navy
1097 Gamilati
1119 Kinglet (USA)
1123 Lacily (USA)
1130 Lyric Of Light
1140 Meeznah (USA)
1142 Mighty Ambition (USA)
1144 Mojave (USA)
1146 Monterosso
1150 Naqshabban (USA)
1156 Ocean War
1157 Opinion Poll (Ire)
1164 Pimpernel (Ire)
1212 Swedish Sailor

TOP TRAINERS: 2011

Trainer	WINS-RUNS	%WINS	2nd	3rd	4th	WIN £	TOTAL £	£1 STKE
Richard Hannon	159-1109	14	158	123	130	£2,114,304	£3,485,327	-59.93
Aidan P O'Brien	16-81	20	10	10	10	£1,408,506	£2,894,457	+6.42
Sir Henry Cecil	51-249	20	37	29	32	£2,084,319	£2,730,438	-58.67
John Gosden	76-452	17	59	71	53	£1,769,799	£2,442,259	-41.45
Mahmood Al Zarooni	73-346	21	46	43	38	£1,444,072	£1,829,899	+154.38
Richard Fahey	118-983	12	109	91	116	£889,061	£1,516,925	-250.14
Sir Michael Stoute	47-330	14	55	44	36	£555,181	£1,501,267	-121.43
Mark Johnston	125-1050	12	114	108	93	£804,054	£1,365,628	-244.45
Kevin Ryan	88-604	15	74	58	48	£884,799	£1,198,285	-5.09
William Haggas	69-357	19	60	49	34	£814,920	£1,167,428	-62.19
Mick Channon	79-682	12	78	95	77	£576,213	£1,037,688	-131.08
Andrew Balding	54-427	13	54	47	43	£584,739	£915,584	-30.59
Tim Easterby	80-860	9	85	94	92	£456,688	£849,414	-113.14
Saeed Bin Suroor	43-320	13	48	37	32	£419,046	£824,714	-100.31
Andre Fabre	1-3	33	1	1	0	£709,625	£749,733	+2.00
Mme C B-Barbe	1-1	100	0	0	0	£737,230	£737,230	+12.00
David Simcock	30-258	12	29	30	32	£527,397	£737,227	-72.21
Roger Charlton	41-201	20	28	19	25	£280,752	£705,629	+31.86
Brian Meehan	53-455	12	40	38	45	£339,698	£693,814	-90.24
Roger Varian	48-234	21	33	22	29	£373,949	£680,728	+67.54
Luca Cumani	43-274	16	43	30	20	£351,466	£661,670	-70.68
James Fanshawe	18-131	14	26	12	12	£556,997	£630,392	+104.00
Ed Dunlop	27-262	10	32	27	32	£150,276	£570,770	-119.01
David Nicholls	61-727	8	61	65	53	£302,012	£565,745	-193.05
Michael Bell	35-253	14	30	26	21	£358,330	£547,719	-67.58
Marco Botti	19-129	15	19	16	18	£207,369	£542,514	-12.00
Barry Hills	41-302	14	43	36	25	£228,273	£539,153	-79.38
Hughie Morrison	36-238	15	22	21	22	£426,656	£534,729	+27.30
Clive Cox	37-311	12	28	48	34	£252,897	£501,284	-71.63
David O'Meara	40-368	11	43	43	43	£282,569	£455,066	-127.33
John Dunlop	44-289	15	29	26	37	£313,853	£433,927	-18.01
Tom Dascombe	30-318	9	34	30	32	£178,210	£398,359	-86.34
David Barron	35-317	11	36	35	36	£187,301	£394,082	-84.88
Charles Hills	15-132	11	19	17	14	£153,549	£375,249	-23.20
Bryan Smart	43-321	13	32	32	35	£212,736	£364,263	+25.18
Jeremy Noseda	38-175	22	15	20	19	£223,727	£349,175	+6.76
David Elsworth	22-163	13	16	20	15	£238,585	£347,530	+16.54
Mick Easterby	31-357	9	29	32	34	£228,789	£315,411	-64.00
Robert Collet	1-4	25	1	1	0	£141,925	£310,678	+5.00

Figures for March 30 - November 5, 2011

Jockey	WINS-RUNS	%WINS	2nd	3rd	4th	WIN £	TOTAL £	£1 STKE
Paul Hanagan	142-986	14	142	111	101	£818,651	£1,435,862	-281.87
Silv. De Sousa	127-816	16	113	86	77	£664,431	£1,108,923	-121.63
Kieren Fallon	114-709	16	84	86	66	£938,214	£1,755,060	-107.51
Richard Hughes	108-619	17	90	72	60	£1,701,036	£2,566,848	+8.18
Jamie Spencer	82-500	16	58	64	49	£1,023,722	£1,700,340	-65.74
Ryan Moore	80-451	18	69	47	52	£992,673	£2,539,101	-143.33
William Buick	78-495	16	59	61	53	£1,767,211	£2,409,187	-57.33
Tom Queally	75-569	13	53	46	55	£1,815,648	£2,481,508	-149.04
Frankie Dettori	68-342	20	52	37	36	£1,671,431	£2,209,779	+5.20
Tom Eaves	65-722	9	70	68	76	£263,481	£447,785	-178.11
Robert Winston	62-484	13	43	65	47	£344,194	£506,598	+43.04
Phillip Makin	60-550	11	49	51	46	£556,757	£744,229	-180.27
Neil Callan	57-528	11	62	66	60	£494,746	£901,643	-118.45
P J McDonald	53-499	11	54	47	59	£178,863	£278,253	-81.65
Frederik Tylicki	51-483	11	46	47	67	£255,535	£372,112	-40.13
Dane O'Neill	51-476	11	64	65	57	£249,115	£503,428	-136.56
Jimmy Fortune	50-465	11	56	40	44	£546,480	£894,813	-55.96
David Allan	49-488	10	52	61	54	£281,027	£530,942	-126.39
Richard Hills	49-337	15	53	43	37	£298,693	£812,358	-143.79
Jim Crowley	48-455	11	44	46	50	£366,039	£615,294	-109.85
Graham Gibbons	48-439	11	55	51	34	£243,337	£406,741	-30.99
Hayley Turner	48-303	16	26	32	34	£684,257	£803,870	+19.19
Cathy Gannon	46-513	9	67	61	53	£139,305	£292,887	-192.01
Ted Durcan	46-376	12	32	42	40	£336,518	£534,722	-59.44
Adam Kirby	46-371	12	38	45	33	£278,621	£512,146	+0.33
Joe Fanning	46-308	15	28	29	32	£262,560	£376,660	+34.11
Seb Sanders	42-366	11	47	44	41	£211,387	£376,785	-107.04
Eddie Ahern	42-364	12	38	46	29	£497,928	£699,494	-67.80
Daniel Tudhope	42-358	12	40	42	42	£286,812	£463,847	-47.25
David Probert	41-359	11	34	30	42	£308,356	£473,317	-79.01
Martin Dwyer	40-376	11	34	34	38	£282,261	£486,995	-95.72
Kieran O'Neill	40-303	13	32	38	40	£131,560	£225,097	+0.63
Pat Dobbs	39-268	15	30	26	35	£221,039	£319,603	-20.34
James Sullivan	38-500	8	47	39	44	£175,948	£259,883	-178.79
Harry Bentley	37-298	12	36	33	34	£180,984	£259,924	+12.10
James Doyle	37-295	13	23	28	32	£115,078	£169,353	+23.63
Martin Harley	36-301	12	38	38	33	£106,121	£192,049	-53.04
Steve Drowne	34-333	10	37	26	37	£235,270	£558,778	-38.28
Fergus Sweeney	33-354	9	39	41	28	£133,864	£195,359	+123.79
George Baker	33-312	11	33	29	35	£268,986	£488,017	+15.44
Richard Kingscote	33-287	11	32	30	27	£187,439	£278,944	-51.97
Luke Morris	32-507	6	54	65	56	£152,551	£335,163	-280.80
Adrian Nicholls	32-328	10	30	33	29	£160,223	£285,884	-73.40
Lee Newman	32-282	11	25	21	30	£118,169	£178,883	-47.38
Ian Mongan	32-274	12	34	32	28	£507,868	£703,479	-43.43

Figures for March 30 - November 5, 2011

INDEX OF HORSES

INDEX OF HORSES

totepool.com

fancy a placepot at the parade ring?

place your favourite totepool bets on the move with our new mobile service!

 text **TOTE** to **89660**